The Lie Effect:

An

Overcomer's

Journal

Collene James

Ashley Fugleberg	Nancy Bowser
Matthew Bailey	Andrea Fugleberg
Shawn Carter	Vicki Joy Anderson

Contact us at: LieEffectProject@gmail.com or www.LieEffectProject.com

*Yet in Your manifold mercies
You did not forsake them in the
wilderness.
The pillar of the cloud did not depart
from them by day,
To lead them on the road;
Nor the pillar of fire by night,
To show them light,
And the way they should go.
You also gave Your good Spirit to
instruct them,
And did not withhold Your manna from
their mouth,
And gave them water for their thirst.*

(Nehemiah 9:19-20)

And the LORD went before them by day in a pillar of cloud to lead the way, and by night in a pillar of fire to give them light, so as to go by day and night.

(Exodus 13:21)

Then the LORD will create above every dwelling place of Mount Zion, and above her assemblies, a cloud and smoke by day and the shining of a flaming fire by night. For over all the glory there will be a covering. And there will be a tabernacle for shade in the daytime from the heat, for a place of refuge, and for a shelter from storm and rain.

(Isaiah 4:5-6)

The Spirit of the Lord shall rest upon Him,
The Spirit of wisdom and understanding,
The Spirit of counsel and might,
The Spirit of knowledge and of the fear of the Lord.

(Isaiah 11:2)

Table of Contents

11

Shepherd Me
Collene James
Monument Valley, Arizona
(For the Overcomers: John 16:33   Hebrews 12:1-2   Revelation 3)

Forward

Nearly four years ago, Tom Dunn, leader of Through the Black, invited me to mentor a woman who volunteered with his ministry. In my head, I envisioned the mentorship including phone calls, a few Zoom meetings, and possibly an in-person meeting – all of which were manageable in an already full schedule. With little hesitation but much enthusiasm, I responded with a resounding "Yes."

My desire to honor Tom's request stemmed from our mutual involvement with the now late Russ Dizdar's Shatter the Darkness Core Team. As fellow warriors in Christ, friendship and loyalty formed throughout those years, in the adventures, and watching the hand of God Almighty move in the lives of those shattered by humanity influenced and directed by evil. After a sincere "Thank you," Tom stated this woman would be soon arriving at my home to stay for a couple of weeks. I heard Tom chuckling as he clicked off the call.

Collene did, indeed, arrive in her motorhome affectionally known as "Tammy Tioga," along with her spunky pups, Moses and Miriam. What I discovered was a woman passionately pursuing the heart of the Father for those in deep suffering and pain. We spent days and evenings in ministry together – a picnic for the homeless; prayer targeting as we walked the neighborhood; listening to and praying with individuals on the streets whom most would rather walk by; and precious times helping an individual encounter the tenderness and healing from Jesus the Christ on deep levels. The hours of discussion centering on the desire of God to set the captives free, no matter the depth of the fractures, allowed Holy Spirit to forge a friendship on which I value and rely to this day. We have rejoiced along the peaceful waters of life but also in the fury of the storms meant to destroy.

"The Lie Effect: An Overcomer's Journal" honors the treasure of creative expression placed within each of us by Creator. Poetry. Painting. Drawing. Song. No matter the avenue of communication, each effectively expresses the struggles and the victories in our life journeys. The power lays not in the talent but in the extraordinary transparency with which the story is communicated. Secrecy, isolation, and worthlessness crumble when faced with a mustard seed of faith – and courage.

Romans 8:26 reads, ***"Likewise, the Spirit helps us in our weaknesses, for we do not know what to pray for as we ought, but the Spirit Himself intercedes for us with groanings too deep for words."*** Holy Spirit moves on our behalf. He draws and invites each of us to ***"stand still and see the***

salvation of the Lord, which He shall show to you today." (Exodus 14:13)
The written word, painting, or drawing may be the means of showing Him the condition of the heart even before the prayers spill forth from our lips. Art is one way to invite the Redeemer to exchange the heaviness which we carry with His yoke which is light. Holy Spirit will delicately and accurately draw from the whole essence of your being – mind, spirit, and body- every stronghold of bondage as an offering to the Lord to redeem, forgive, heal, and free.

Today, this invitation of exchange stands for you. Not from me, but the One who desires to reveal the fullness of His glory within your life.

Sherry Clausen,

Reap The Harvest, Shatter Ops, Counselor

As The Deer
Psalm 42
Collene James

*Dedicated to the overcomers before us,
and those that will follow. May you receive the rewards
offered to all those who persevere.*

Lamentations 3

I am the man who has seen affliction by the rod of His wrath.

He has led me and made me walk in darkness and not in light. Surely, He has turned His hand against me, time and time again throughout the day.

He has aged my flesh and my skin and broken my bones. He has besieged me and surrounded me with bitterness and woe.

He has set me in dark places, like the dead of long ago.

He has hedged me in so that I cannot get out; He has made my chain heavy. Even when I cry and shout, He shuts out my prayer.

He has blocked my ways with hewn stone; He has made my paths crooked.

He has been to me a bear lying in wait, like a lion in ambush. He has turned aside my ways and torn me in pieces; He has made me desolate.

He has bent His bow and set me up as a target for the arrow. He has caused the arrows of His quiver to pierce my loins.

I have become the ridicule of all my people— their taunting song all the day.

He has filled me with bitterness, He has made me drink wormwood. He has also broken my teeth with gravel and covered me with ashes.

You have moved my soul far from peace; I have forgotten prosperity and I said, "My strength and my hope have perished from the Lord."

Remember my affliction and roaming, The wormwood and the gall. My soul still remembers and sinks within me.

This I recall to my mind; therefore, I have hope.

Through the Lord's mercies we are not consumed, because His compassions fail not. They are new every morning; great is Your faithfulness.

"The Lord is my portion," says my soul, "Therefore I hope in Him!" The Lord is good to those who wait for Him, to the soul who seeks Him.

It is good that one should hope and wait quietly for the salvation of the Lord.

It is good for a man to bear the yoke in his youth. Let him sit alone and keep silent because God has laid it on him.

Let him put his mouth in the dust— there may yet be hope. Let him give his cheek to the one who strikes him and be full of reproach.

For the Lord will not cast off forever.

Though He causes grief, yet He will show compassion according to the multitude of His mercies.

For He does not afflict willingly, nor grieve the children of men.

To crush under one's feet all the prisoners of the earth, to turn aside the justice due a man before the face of the Most High or subvert a man in his cause— the Lord does not approve.

Who is he who speaks, and it comes to pass, when the Lord has not commanded it?

Is it not from the mouth of the Most High that woe and well-being proceed?

Why should a living man complain, a man for the punishment of his sins?

Let us search out and examine our ways and turn back to the Lord; let us lift our hearts and hands to God in heaven.

We have transgressed and rebelled; You have not pardoned. You have covered Yourself with anger and pursued us; You have slain and not pitied.

You have covered Yourself with a cloud, that prayer should not pass through. You have made us an offscouring and refuse In the midst of the peoples.

All our enemies have opened their mouths against us. Fear and a snare have come upon us, desolation and destruction.

My eyes overflow with rivers of water for the destruction of the daughter of my people.

My eyes flow and do not cease, without interruption, till the Lord from heaven looks down and sees.

My eyes bring suffering to my soul because of all the daughters of my city.

My enemies without cause hunted me down like a bird. They silenced my life in the pit and threw stones at me.

The waters flowed over my head; I said, "I am cut off!"

I called on Your name, O Lord, from the lowest pit.

You have heard my voice: "Do not hide Your ear from my sighing, from my cry for help."

You drew near on the day I called on You and said, "Do not fear!"

O Lord, You have pleaded the case for my soul; You have redeemed my life.

O Lord, You have seen how I am wronged; judge my case.

You have seen all their vengeance, all their schemes against me.

You have heard their reproach, O Lord, all their schemes against me,

The lips of my enemies and their whispering against me all the day.

Look at their sitting down and their rising up; I am their taunting song.

Repay them, O Lord, according to the work of their hands. Give them a veiled heart; Your curse be upon them!

In Your anger, pursue and destroy them from under the heavens of the Lord.

Jeremiah the Prophet

Oasis
Collene James
Tampa, FL

Preface

The *Lie Effect Project* is a "Spirit and Truth" endeavor. **John 4:23** tells us that ***"true worshipers will worship the Father in the Spirit and in truth, for they are the kind of worshipers the Father seeks."*** Some of us will naturally be drawn to the solid "truth," aspects of Yahweh, while others of us will be more interested in experiencing the "Spirit's" move in our lives. However, scripture makes it clear that one without the other will leave us unbalanced and in danger. Truth without Spirit becomes an academic study that does not have the power to change a life- or worse, an abusive religious weapon that crushes wounded souls. Spirit without truth leaves us vulnerable to deceiving spiritual experiences that are intended to entrap us and lead us to destruction. Along with the truth laid out in *"The Lie Effect: Overcoming Soul Abduction," "The Lie Effect: An Overcomer's Journal"* is intended to be a depiction of our spiritual-application process; it's our testimony of spiritual, emotional, and even physical healing according to the truth of scripture, which always reveals the character of Yahweh. The head knowledge needs to be experienced by the heart and the heart understanding needs to be grounded in truth.

Matthew 6:33 reminds us to ***"seek first the kingdom of God and His righteousness, and all these things will be added to you."*** The ***"all these things"*** statement includes matters of daily need, healing, wisdom, deliverance- anything that causes anxieties in us. What we have learned is that the key to overcoming is not approaching God as a vending machine for these issues to be met in the light of how we see them, but rather to seek relationship and understanding of Yahweh Himself, and to pursue righteousness according to His perspective of righteous living, thinking, and doing. Healing, deliverance, and a peaceful mindset and countenance are the side effects of that endeavor.

We do hope that you find within this *Lie Effect Project that* "Why?" is not an illegal question to ask in Yahweh's court; nor should a survivor of the effects of deception be shamed for asking it. The only tragedy in asking the deeper questions would be in the premature giving up on finding Yahweh's answers- or rejecting them once you have...

This book can be used as a stand-alone tool or as a companion resource to *"The Lie Effect: Overcoming Soul Abduction A Survivor's Handbook"* by Collene James and Nancy Bowser.

Contributor Intros

Collene James currently lives in Westminster, Colorado with her husband Jeremy. A cosmetologist for 25 years by profession, she has left the salon to serve full-time in ministry- discipling survivors of occult crimes, organized abuse, complex trauma, and deep religious discouragement in the Word of God. Collene is also the host of The Reclamation Project on Through the Black's YouTube channel, a weekly discussion aimed at reclaiming all that the enemy of God has stolen from His body of true believers. Collene is co-author of *"The Lie Effect: Overcoming Soul Abduction, A Survivor's Handbook"* and has also published *"The One Year Chronological Bible Reading Plan,"* a booklet designed to help readers study the entire Bible in a year, in its chronological context. Collene's experience with journalling as a way to document the various stages of her healing from her own life's traumatic events, has given her insight into just how patient, gentle, and intentional the healing work of the Spirit of Yahweh is. She has been so blessed by the contributions of Nancy, Ashley, Andrea, Matthew, Vicki Joy, and Shawn. While written years and hundreds of miles apart, each piece fits together as though they came directly from a project planning meeting! Praise God for what He has done in each of His servants! Collene is pleased to have also included in this project a couple of representations of her earthly father, Larry G. Sears. Larry's faith walk has dramatically impacted Collene, both in his life and in his death.

Nancy Bowser and her husband, Jim, have been happily married for forty-one years. They live in the foothills of the California Sierra Nevada Mountains, and their two sons and families live close by. Nancy enjoys spending time with their five grandchildren. She also enjoys writing and has written seven and a half books. As a Satanic Ritual Abuse overcomer, she has been able to share the process of healing and deliverance with other women. Nancy loves to watch Jesus Christ bring healing to the broken-hearted, set the captive free, comfort those who mourn, turn ashes into beauty, and exchange a spirit of heaviness for a garment of praise. All glory to God! Nancy is co-author of *"The Lie Effect: Overcoming Soul Abduction, A Survivor's Handbook."* Links to Nancy's other books and her most recent blog writings are at: www.buriedtreasureunlimited.wordpress.com

Ashley Fugleberg resides with her family in an undisclosed location deep within the mysterious Ozarks of Missouri. An oldest by birth, a professional by education and training, and an artist by design, Ashley has always been an observant person. Throughout her life, poetry, drama, music, and writing have been her means of experiencing (or in the case of writing, expressing) the observations she makes of herself, other people, and the worlds we all exist in. Ashley's writing, and in the pages of this book, poetry, reflect said introspection and self-reflection, her observation of social complexities, and her sense of accountability -both personally and corporately to the Most High Elohim. When asked who she is, Ashley will tell you she is one who has been bought and paid for: reclaimed by the Blood of the Lamb, Jesus the Messiah-Yeshua Ha Mashiach, who is both fully God and fully flesh, Son of the Most High Elohim: the God of Abraham, Isaac, and Jacob, the God of the Bible, Creator of the Universe, YHVH. When asked why she writes, she will tell you its deepest purpose is to convey the existence of the One who has saved her, to communicate this back to herself and to communicate this to others -all to allow a brief look into what a life with the Most High can look like with its struggles and its blessings - and the beauty and richness both can bring.

Vicki Joy Anderson is a researcher, speaker, poet, and author of 8 books. Vicki Joy delves into the taboo topics typically swept beneath the carpet by leadership in the modern Church. Issues such as sleep paralysis, new age deceptions, same sex attraction and the LGBTQ agenda, and much more. Vicki Joy graduated from University of Northwestern in St. Paul, MN with a bachelor's in English with a Writing Emphasis and a Major in Bible. Vicki Joy currently writes for RealDarkNews.com and L. A. Marzulli's Politics, Prophecy & the Supernatural; and co-hosts the YouTube shows Through the Black and Audiotopsy with Tom Dunn. More information about Vicki Joy's work can be found at www.vickijoyanderson.com

Andrea Fugleberg was raised with her three sisters in Central Minnesota, where drawing became her passion even prior to kindergarten. Throughout school, while Andrea sometimes struggled with reading, she could identify with the story through the artwork of a children's book. Once Andrea developed the ability to read and comprehend a book, she also developed the skill to be able to describe on paper through her own artwork, what elements of a story she was connecting with. Depicting her own life or another person's story through images has helped her articulate the details of what has caught her attention for as long as she can remember. In adulthood, Andrea finds her art to be very personal, healing, and a favorite vehicle to express herself emotionally and spiritually. People are her favorite artistic subject because, as creations of God, we are made in His image. To be able to display a person in a specific way or emotion is exceedingly healing and rewarding both for herself and for those she represents in her work.

Matthew Bailey and his wife Racheal are currently raising their daughter, Marcella, in Mason, West Virginia. Matthew, a stay-at-home father, is dedicated to providing full-time parental guidance, especially in his daughter's formative years. In the evenings and on the weekends, Matthew can be found doing street ministry in his own community as well as others, as the Spirit of God leads. Open air preaching, private conversations, and personal prayer, while proclaiming a "you matter" message, is his heart's call. Matthew's early poetry was a way to cope with pain and to find healing and to get to know himself. Now it has become a tool to inspire thought and conversation about eternal matters. Matthew realizes that the pain of his past is now to be used to encourage and help others who are currently in similar situations. Poetry writing as well as drawing help keep him on track to remind him why he does what he does for the Kingdom of Righteousness.

Shawn Carter pastors a weekly congregation in Meadows of Dan, Virginia. He and his wife, Carrie, have raised a daughter and a son and now enjoy serving the Lord in their community. In addition to the pastoral duties of his local congregation, Shawn provides weekly content regarding spiritual warfare, the paranormal and the occult for Through the Black on YouTube. Shawn also hosts his own YouTube channel called Unveiling the Paranormal. Shawn's entire adult life has been devoted particularly to helping those desiring to come out of ritual life, the occult, gang life and all forms of bondage through discipleship in repentance, renunciation and walking in the new covenant of the Messiah. Shawn especially wants to share with our readers the healing power of talking to God through everyday conversation, rather than recited, formal, rhetoric prayers.

Sometimes, Baking Doesn't Turn Out,

and there's more to a story.
There's always more and usually it's not anything
you thought or wondered.
It'll slap you right in the face
if you're not careful –
if you're not painfully, delicately
aware there is more to what you see,
more to the thought of now –
the idea presenting itself as truth.
Because most of the time
it won't be what you think:
it won't actually be the country
whose colors you think you see flying,
it won't be the cake whose fragrance
you think you smell baking.
Some stories are better than you think –
are truer, prettier, and more tangible than
a thought you can muster could create.
But others are less than,
are narrower still, and uglier more.
So know that story – the story you're listening to,
the story you want to explore –
there might be, just might be, more to it than you see,
because there's always more and usually it's not anything
you thought or wondered.
There's more to that story:
there's more to you and more to me and
sometimes, just sometimes, baking doesn't turn out.

Ashley Fugleberg

I Am Done

Heavenly Father,

You have the power to change things in an instant, yet I can't see You working at all. I would just like to see some slight movement of Your hand in this situation.

Lord, help me to not get upset at You in this long battle. I am frustrated, mad, and tired- yet I know, deep down, You are with me and that You are working in this.

Please help me to keep moving forward with no frustration towards You or others. When I say I am done with You or I am done with this situation, please refocus my soul upon Your face. Don't let me quit before I'm complete.

I ask You, Yahushua, to forgive my dissatisfaction and my ugly thoughts. Lord, even if I don't see Your hand moving, I know You are with me and the plans You have will be done.

In Jesus name, I ask these things.

Amen

"And let us not be weary in well-doing: for in due season we shall reap, if we faint not." (Galatians 6:9)

"Cast thy burden upon the Lord, and He shall sustain thee: He shall never suffer the righteous to be moved." (Psalm 55:22)

Shawn Carter

Fall
Collene James

Solitude

November 14th 2011

"I am the raindrop falling down, always longing for the deeper ground. I am the broken, breaking seas. Even my blood finds ways to bleed…. I am the one that you left behind, I am the dried-up doubting eyes, looking for the well that won't run dry…running hard for the infinite, with the tears of saints and hypocrites. I am restless… (But now) I can hear you breathing, feel you leading, more than just a feeling."

I first heard this song "Restless" by a group called Switchfoot a few weeks ago. *"Even my blood finds ways to bleed,"* could not more accurately describe the internal emotions of the last two years. However, that was sooo last season!

I have been trapped in an internal, bitterly cold winter. I did do some writing in my journal over the last 24 months, but those entries are too raw to share. Really, they're too raw for me to even re-read. In fact, I destroyed most of the ugly things I wrote then…

Let's just suffice it to say: Spiritually and emotionally I was a burn patient in need of a good dead flesh scraping. Someday, maybe I'll tell you all about it, but not today.

All of these thoughts of the burning and the scraping, brings me to today… the changing of spiritual and emotional seasons- spring for me, fall for the outside world.

Today was the windiest day. I hate the wind. It is unsettling; It shatters the peace. That shattered peace isn't ideal, especially because today is also Day One of a challenge I am participating in.

The challenge: "spend at least five minutes a day in solitude, reflecting on creation and journaling my thoughts."

Then, the challenge continues: "do something radical- something that reinforces what you're learning about yourself."

This blog journal is my "radical act"- allowing myself to be known and understood, risking being misunderstood.

If you know me well, or at all, you know I am not a loner. I never have been. I am not at all comfortable with stillness or silence. My mind moves fast and relentlessly. I have been accused of over-analyzing everything which makes being alone with my thoughts nothing short of torturous most days- especially recently.

So, here it is, week two of the class, day one of the challenge:

Even though it's a windy day, I'm choosing to spend Day One's Silence-in Creation Challenge outside on a picnic table at Riverfront Park. The leaves are gone from the trees, except the most stubborn few. How are they hanging on with such a vicious act of gusting wind being perpetrated against them? To me they look unprotected by their own trees, and by the trees next to them. At first, I'm thinking that they are the survivors, the stronger ones. However, the longer I watch them cling, I begin to wonder, "what's the worst that could happen if they just let go and gave in to the wind?"

They would fall, but not hard. They would float gently to the ground or maybe be whipped along chaotically for a bit until they eventually, softly, reached their destination. Don't they understand they have a purpose both in the tree and on the ground? I can see that even for a tree, the seasons all have their importance. The leaves have importance to the entire ecosystem in every season, not just in their freshest bloom. Why then, do some hold on to their completed past with such determination and resistance to the future?

I am unprotected. I feel as though I have always been. This is one of my "internal narratives" working its way to the surface of my thoughts, demanding to be heard. I haven't taken the time to tell you that the homework for week one was to identify our internal narratives and measure them up with the truth of God's Word. I may come back to this one of these days too. I'll suffice it to say, the things I have learned to think and believe about myself at a subconscious level are shocking.

As I sit here in the wind, I realize that I don't trust the winds of change. I cling desperately, strongly, stubbornly, to what I used to know- even after the season has ended- even if it no longer serves me, nourishes me. Somehow, I have believed that maybe I'll be the one and only leaf that doesn't float gently on the wind. Maybe I'll plummet like a leaf made of iron. The thought of allowing myself to experience more chaos by letting go is nerve wracking. Yet, I already know I have no control in this change of season in my life.

"...I can hear you breathing, I can feel you leading, more than just a feeling," the lyrics return to my thoughts. God is in this wind, in this chaos. He will gently, eventually, bring each leaf to its resting place, for His perfect use in

the next season. The strong leaves, the stubborn ones, will need a little more force than the others, but they will be held with just the same gentleness on the wind.

"Who is this? Even the wind and the waves obey him!" (Mark 4:41b)

Prove Me
Collene James
Crete, Greece

Mountain
Andrea Fugleberg

Just Bricks

Come love.
Drop that bag of bricks
crippling your knees.
Hold My Hand instead.
I'm leading you to a mountain.
A mountain of bricks.
If you ask, I'll show you
how to but whisper
a mustard seed
and the mountain quivers.
Let your bricks crumble
because bricks are just bricks
but I AM the Rock.
Hold My Hand and
climb this mountain
you were made
to walk upon.

Ashley Fugleberg

Old White Church

"Amazing Grace" fills my ears,
With every verse, I draw nearer.
For this grace that I don't know,
Sung off key, it's still beautiful.

Though I cry and I feel old,
Give me peace and mend my soul.

Old white church,
Little stream,
Swinging bridge,
Great big dream.

Little church,
Beneath the hill,
Standing strong,
Doing His will.

Yes, I was raised,
Love and faith,
What ever happened to amazing grace?

Although it's been many days,
I need to go back...
Bible raised and Jesus praised,
I am blessed to know this place.

Now I am grown,
Family of my own,
They grow too fast,
And the looking glass...

There I stand,
In front of the mirror-
Looking back at what I fear

Because I am lost,
I've lost my way.
Back to Christ,
I must find and stay.

Through that,
Little church,
Beneath the hill,

Standing strong,
Doing His will.

Old white church,
Little stream,
Swing bridge-
You know what I mean.

Matthew Bailey

Country Church
Larry G. Sears
Posthumously Contributed

On Healing:

Do you see them

(the scars)?

Arms, a light dusting

of striped skin.

Lines that paint.

There, a faintly etched chest

points a path to nothing.

A rivet splits forehead,

hairline to brow.

Back, invisible but marked,

a mapped spine.

Cheeks almost spared but there,

on each side, framing a mouth

that can't tell a story stolen.

No words

(just scars).

Do you see me?

Ashley Fugleberg

The Shy Little Kitten

Said the homeless little kitten sitting by the side of the road:

Prrrrr…..
I'm just a shy little kitten
Hungry and afraid.
Won't someone take me home and feed me?
What could one little kitten hurt?

Said the woman passing by:

Ohhh!
What a cute little kitten,
Hungry and afraid.
I think I'll take him home and feed him.
What could one little kitten hurt?

Prrrr…..Grrrrrrr….
Time goes by,
I hide in the dark.
She seems not to see
How big I'm beginning to be.

GRRRRR….
My appetite grows stronger.
I'm waiting for the day….
It won't be long now
And I'll have to seek more prey.

Nancy Bowser

How Does the Saying Go,

wild hearts can't
be broken?
Well, I say broken hearts
can't be wild.
They don't shift from
running to open sprint,
ripping through grass
as if it's nothing
but the sound of
cheering on:
faster, faster,
fly over that hill
and then on.
Broken hearts aren't
wildly, deliciously,
unpredictable
as they snort,
stomp the ground,
nervously circling a
new something,
new someone –
maybe foe, maybe
friend, maybe the One
that will take care of them
the rest of their days.
Broken hearts aren't
wild, you see,
but hobbled.
Turn them loose.
Marvel at the glory
when once again
the hills – they are painted
with their abandon.

Abandon: ə-băn′dən

transitive verb

1a: to give up to the control or influence of another person or agent

(he abandoned the old man)

b: to give up with the intent of never again claiming

a right or interest in abandoned property

(he abandoned the old man)

2: to withdraw from –

often in the face of danger or encroachment – to abandon ship

(he abandoned the old man)

3: to withdraw protection, support, or help from

(he abandoned the old man)

4: to give (oneself) over unrestrainedly

(he abandoned the old man)

5a: to cease from maintaining, practicing, or using

(he abandoned the old man)

b: to cease intending or attempting to perform

(he abandoned the old man)

Ashley Fugleberg

Long Live the King

November 16th 2011

I am not a girly-girl. I can pull off a feminine look, but I am generally a low-maintenance woman. Except that I love what I do for a living, I am nothing like the stereotypical salon girl; maybe this fact is a result of the environment of my upbringing. With a 'tomboy' for a mom, a 'manly-man' father, five brothers, and two much-younger sisters, there weren't a lot of dolls and dresses around for my younger years. I remember hours upon hours spent building roads with our Tonka trucks for our Matchbox cars, weekends trash-talking opponents during football and baseball games with the brothers, playing "night games" (our version of military-style searches of the "enemy") with the neighbors, and shooting gophers in the field next door with a 0.22 rifle on the weekends. I find it hard to remember a single time I dressed up as a princess, imagined a some-day wedding, or had a tea party...

I know I raised more than one set of eyebrows when I announced during my freshman year of high school, that I wanted to go to cosmetology school. Why? I still can't pinpoint all that it was that was so deeply appealing, but I do remember the day I decided. My mom, who is uneducated in the field, had always cut our hair. The week before school started that year, my maternal grandmother visited and put her foot down regarding the home-style back-to-school haircut plans. The girls were going to a real salon and Grandma would pay.

The haircut itself was horrible. My mom could have done better with her eyes shut. I spent the remainder of that awful first year of high school hating my curls and wishing I had a hat. I do, however, remember in detail the smells, my first ever shampoo in that fantastic sink, the upbeat music, the sound of the shears next to my neck as my long hair hit the floor, the stacks and stacks of photographed style possibilities in the enormous style books... I was hooked. THIS is what I wanted to do!

Anyway, I digress. The challenge today is the same: "solitude in nature for at least five minutes, journaling about our thoughts." I am sitting outside my salon between appointments. Not the most picturesque location, nor the most peaceful. People are repairing the portion of our building that burned last month. WOW!! I am thankful to still have a place to work!

(Week 2 Day 3)

It's COLD today! Although we've had snow already this season, there is not snow on the ground anymore in town. The sun is bright; bright enough that I braved the 34° F jacketless, just to feel the contrast of the cold air and the hot sun. The wind is gentle, swirling the leaves at our door. When the drilling and hammering stop, I can hear birds. They seem happy- excited even. In my head is a song, as usual. I imagine the birds know it, or one like it.

"But I know the King of All Creation reigns completely
Over every moment great and small
Long live the One who gives us
Life and peace and hope for tomorrow ...

All I have is Yours - Long live the King."
(Lyrics for "Long Live the King" by Aaron Shust)

I remember yesterday's exercise. My thoughts of the deeply loving Father turn into Him being King. Does that somehow make me a princess? I'm wearing green today, so naturally I see myself as Shrek's woman, Fiona. I feel a little ogre-esque most days.

Princesses are so undeserving! All they did to get the title was be born, and they really had very little control over that. Mercy is receiving what we don't deserve and didn't earn. The King of Kings mercifully adopted me, a tomboy villainous monster, an ogre, to represent His Kingdom as His daughter. Unfathomable. But I think I like it.

Mist
Collene James
Mason County, Washington

Praying For You

When my heart is breaking,
When my feet are aching.
I don't even know if I am making
Any difference now?

I wonder how
This is going to be okay someday.

Cuz you know you matter,
You have met Creator.
Doesn't seem to make sense to all the haters.
But you can't quit now,

You go on somehow.
It all be worth it; won't it later?

Do the times get rough?
All the gold is rust.
I don't know if I'm going to be tough enough.
But I have to try;

I will succeed.
Dear Lord, I follow where You lead.

If you ask me now, if it all was worth it,
I would have to say- you know I don't really deserve it.
I chose to quit. I chose to give up;
I was on the ledge then I chose to jump.

But a helping hand
Reached out and then,
I learned what it means to actually be a man,

I can't tell you why
I didn't die.
But I know what I'm doing here, and this is why.

You matter and I love you;
I don't want you to go through the things I went through.
The trials tribulations are a must;
Got to find that way just to have enough.

Daily bread to fill your gut,
All the riches in the world- just ain't enough.

When I feel that thirst, I start to cry.
When I think that He chose this guy.
That is me. That is who,
And it's all because of you.

Dear God, You know I matter.
I am here Lord. You fill the platter.
My cup is overflowing. I know it's true.

And I've got to spread the message to
All the people in the world-
They need to know of Salvation and the Word.

So, I walk the streets.
I hold my sign.
I tell people about my Lord. He is so divine.
I can't give up, no longer my choice,
I just tell people about how I rejoice.

Cuz you know, you matter
And I know it's true.
I'm never giving up on you.
Although I can't see
You anytime soon,
I know you matter and I'm praying for you.

Praying for you...

Matthew Bailey

You've Called

YHVH,
oh YHVH,
oh my YHVH.
You've called me to meet You –
meet You here my Adoni,
my Elohim,
my Most High.
You've called me.
You've called me here
and I'm here
reaching
to the sky.
YHVH, YHVH, YHVH.
Your name is brightness in
the breath of the Ruach
that wraps – keeps me –
in Your Way.
I reach to the sky
and fall at Your feet
my Adoni, my Elohim, my Most High.
You've called me there –
meet with me here.
Create in me the clean heart
You desire
and the right spirit
through the Ruach's fire.

Ashley Fugleberg

November 17th 2011

It's not all fun and games. This week has been exhausting. Today I have remnants of thoughts from the last week and a half mingling with the internal narratives of the last three decades. For an over-thinker like me, it's over-load.

If there are readers of this blog, there are at least three categories of you:
a) the ones that knew me when...
b) the ones that are confused and had no idea that I was even divorced, much less back in Montana...
c) those that know me well today.

It's a little overwhelming to realize that I have no control over WHO reads this. These two years have been excruciating in terms of relationship loss. I shudder a little to imagine my heart so open, in the hands of "the enemy." But, whatev. They've had their fun, and allegedly I'm better for it. Maybe one day I can genuinely thank them. Today is not that day.

If you've known me for a long time, you know how connected to the church community I have always been. You may have known me in the context of Mexican missions. Some of you have taught me in a class of some kind. Others have heard me sing week after week on the church praise team. A select few of you have been in Bible studies I have led- on marriage. (The irony is not lost on me, trust me.) A precious group of you have met with me in a small group setting- for years, dissecting sermons and discussing their life applications...

There's another group of you that know me recently. You know how angry I have been at Christians and God and "churchiness." This maddening facade, the stained-glass masquerade- fake, fake, fake. I loathe the churchy phrases. I have absolutely NO tolerance any longer for theological debate and ideology. You have probably heard me use astounding language to express my distaste. You are the group of people that are most amazed by entries this week in my blog.

To the very small handful of you that knew me when, knew me last year, and have stuck with me so far this week:

Why?!

I am amazed by your mercy and compassion and empathy and LOVE. So here it is:

(Week 2 Day 4)
The internal narrative I fear the most is circling my heart and head relentlessly today. "I am not worth fighting for. Pursuing. Winning." This is not something I made up on my own, ladies and gentlemen. It comes from months, no- years, of proof. I have not been worth it, to the ones I have given myself to the most. Without going into a personalized list of names (what good would that do you anyway?), I see faces of no less than 10 people I genuinely loved who have been stripped from my life very recently. We could go through that list together and come up with excuses for each one, but would it help? I can tell you, no; I've already tried.

So, last week's exercise was to replace the false narratives with truth. This one is tough for me. I don't have a lot of experience being pursued. This will have to be narrative replacement exercise done strictly by faith that His Word is truth.

Psalm 136 has 26 verses. All of them end with ***"His steadfast love endures forever."*** For today's challenge I went to Riverfront Park again. This time I went to the river side to watch the water move. I took note of a few things:

There is a gorgeous green color in the water. Parts of the river that got caught up on the bank and slowed down have slime and muck and trash collected in it. The water is low this time of year, exposing lots of rocky gravel bars. The edges of the river where it slows have started to freeze. There is an amazing light show on the water as the sun dances its way to noon. There is an elderly man with a walking stick muttering to his golden ranch dog as they walk the path. He is careful to avoid looking at me, which is satisfying, since I'm in my solitude.

There are three things I notice, really notice.

a) The choppy waves made by the wind on the upstream portion of the river are relentless, steadfast.
b) There is a full-sized cottonwood tree washed up on a gravel bar. It is soft and worn, like driftwood, shaped by the power of the water.
c) Downstream the water is meandering, slowly, calmly.

There is no chaos. The river is moving powerfully, relentlessly. Softening and shaping and moving all that it encounters. Steadily pursuing the ocean, with confidence.

I am craving this kind of pursuit, by the Creator who knew today how to reveal it. Am I experiencing it? Possibly. I feel like I am being shaped, softened, moved. I am not in control. I am fearful. I am excited.

Lighthouse
Andrea Fugleberg

Deep Calling Deep

November 15ᵗʰ 2011

(Week 2 Day 2)
I woke up wishing for today's exercise to be carried out in Alaska. Maybe at Beluga Point, somewhere in Seward- ooooh, or Kenai on the point! Ocean water fascinates me, scares me- no terrifies me. I love the beach, but even now as I write, I am catching my breath a little as I recall my first whale-watching boat tour of Prince William Sound.

"How deep the Father's love for us, how vast beyond all measure...," Stuart Townsend's lyrics permeate my thoughts.

In my time in Alaska, I took three wildlife viewing tours out of Seward and a halibut charter out of Homer. All were incredible, with scenery and wildlife you couldn't make up. Stunning. Majestic. Birds, grey whales, breaching orcas, otters, bears, sheep, calving glaciers, you name it, I saw it!

If I kept my eyes fixed on the horizon or kept my mind dwelling on the attributes of the water's surface, I was fine. However, whenever I allowed my thoughts to drift to attributes of the depths beneath me, it would cause me to panic a little, to even stop breathing for a second.

Avoider. Runner. What I can't grasp, understand, manage, or master, it seems I've spent a lifetime fleeing.

So, today, since I was unable to catch a flight to Anchorage before my 11:00 client, I headed to the city's sandstone feature called "The Rims" for today's challenge. The city is hazy this morning. There are clouds. The sun is out and even seems bright on the grass and weeds near me, but the city looks grey, cold, dead. The mountains towards Columbus are getting snow and look miserable.

This pullout that I am parked in is the same one I chose to flee to the night before my divorce was filed. I think I was parked here for nearly 4 hours that night. The first couple of those hours I was on the phone begging, pushing, pleading, crying, fighting what was coming... listening for the words that I needed to hear to be able to stop the horrid process, and that after 2 hours, were never spoken.

That night, after the pleading call, I hung up and called my daddy. He was in Phoenix having dinner with friends, but he got up from the table and went out to be alone. For me. For nearly an hour.

44

I have never learned to truly rely on my parents. Obviously as a child I did for food, shelter, education... but emotionally somehow, I figured that I would be an unnecessary burden or worse, a disappointment. Many, many things I should have shared with them, but the more I kept from them, the harder it was to tell them anything at all. On June 22, 2010, the night before filing for divorce, I had nowhere else to turn so my poor daddy got, uh, relied on...

Dad is strong. He has incredible character; really, he's like no other man I've known. He has always been hard on us to do the right thing. I have not very often seen his gracious side. In the 17 months since that night, I have finally caught a bit of understanding of what a father's grace, love and protection are supposed to feel like. Oh, I wish I had not waited 33 years to test that.

My view of God, His role as Father, and the depth of His love for me have been so warped. I can recite His Word, but I haven't experientially KNOWN a single drop of it personally. I've become a master runaway, tester, avoider, doubter, pusher.

Today I am sitting here thinking of real love. I don't "get it" any more than I did yesterday, but I know I would like nothing more than to stand on the edge of the "boat," contemplate the attributes of it and, eventually, dive into the vast-beyond-all-measure depths of it. Abba, help me learn to stop running away from Your love in a panic...

Deep Dive
Collene James
St. Petersburg, FL

Black Cats, Ladders & Broken Mirrors

November 18th 2011

"Superstition." It's the word that's been floating around my mind since Wednesday. I don't consider myself to be superstitious in the slightest. Black cats, ladders and broken mirrors mean nothing to me. I don't follow horoscopes or have any interest in "the year of the...," whatever-it-is. In fact, those things pretty much never cross my mind.

It was suggested to me Wednesday that those of us who see God as always being either a "punishing" or a "blessing" kind of God- depending on our behavior- are exercising a form of superstition. So now we bump up against, perhaps, my most crippling internal narrative:

"God loves me when I'm good but is angry and holds back from me when I'm bad."

Because of my church background, I know in a recited-memory-verse kind of way, that this narrative doesn't match up exactly with what the Bible says about God through Jesus and His teachings. But as of today, simply memorizing these verses has done nothing to change my internal beliefs or my daily thought operation.

"He makes the sun rise on the evil and the good and sends rain on the righteous and the unrighteous." (Matthew 5:45)

This makes sense to me in broad terms like with natural disaster, but somehow, as it pertains to personal application, it hasn't meshed for me...

I am a rule follower. Growing up, the most rebellious thing I knowingly did was paint my nails, with my best friend T.J., in the "No Trespassing" labeled abandoned cabin near our houses. Both the trespassing and the nail painting were naughty! Dad, for some reason, hated nail polish, and the cabin was falling and completely unstable. I still have no idea why we didn't get crushed on a windy day next to that antique potbellied stove.

I followed the 'rules' when it came to school, dating, even marriage. I had a mental list of 'dos' and 'don'ts,' and I checked every single box. I assumed I was in the clear. I was wrong. Devastatingly wrong. Doing the "right thing" didn't save me and in some ways, God didn't bless me for being "good." Obviously, I am not asserting that I have lived my whole life without blessings. Three major ones in the form of offspring come to mind! But in specific ways, I feel let down by God and I worked hard to do it "His way."

Superstition. Rabbit's foot. Maybe I have turned "His way" into something it was never meant to be. This week I am starting to see things a little differently...

(Week 2 Day 5)
The time-in-creation part of my assignment today is going to have to be carried out on my back step, for time's sake.

This summer I bought each of the kids a small cactus to care for. They had a fruit fly infestation, so I set them outside in the cool weather to kill the flies. The back step is where they are in quarantine. I will confess that I don't remember which belongs to who or even what their child-given names are, but that doesn't matter for our purposes today.

All of them are spiky for protection. The one on the left is soft to the touch. If you don't brush your fingers upwards, you can even pet it. The one on the right is not soft enough to pet but is not off-putting either. Clearly the cactus in the center has an axe to grind. Maybe the little guy is fearful. He must be expecting the worst.

I'm thinking about bitterness and the power unbridled anger has in a person. I've met a few people like that center cactus. I'm guessing that most of us are more like the one on the right. Guarded, a little sharp at times, but not altogether off-putting. What would it be like to live life like the soft one? Approachable, gentle, but still with the ability to protect the heart of myself. With all of my disillusions, hurt, anger and lost hopes, God help me be like that little guy.

Heart of Stone
Collene James

47

Shadows

November 19th 2011

(Week 2 Day 6)

I am not a quitter. This is the reason you're reading this today. I've lived a lifetime of thinking this week. I'm hoping, as you may be too, to have a few lighter days ahead. I won't say that these two weeks haven't been productive, however.

Our second snow of the season fell last night. This could be the lasting kind. It's not deep, but it's bitter cold. Today is a gorgeous clear day, as are all the coldest days during the winter in the North. As I write, the 111-year tradition of the MSU Bobcats vs. the U of M Grizzlies football bloodbath is taking place at MSU in Bozeman. As of this date, the majority of those games have been won by U of M, so odds are the Griz will be victorious again. In fact, they're up in the third quarter right now. The TVs, radios, internet and every corner bar or casino in the state are tuned in and inundated with trash-talk between fans. I don't have a preferred team on these match-up days; I have strong emotional connections to both schools. I love Montana. I love Montanans.

My house is cozy today. The kids are generally friendly, helpful, happy... The pot roast I made yesterday has been turned into a stew and is simmering on the stove with a fresh loaf of French bread ready and waiting. Things feel perfect. Except...

Lurking beneath the surface of my mind there are shadows. I left the house in the middle of the third quarter, told the kids I have my "homework" to do, and drove. I'm searching for a quiet place to put these shadowy, restless thoughts on paper. Driving through the deserted streets of my frozen neighborhood, I am amazed at how I'm noticing shadows everywhere. The trees, power lines, cars, houses, dogs- all casting shadows across my path.

I make my way to Pioneer Park. I notice the abandoned bleachers of Daylis Stadium. There are still balloons- Helena High Capital's colors- attached to a section. Helena High beat Billings West High in the State AA Championship last night. Funny how empty it seems now.

I drive past the tennis courts and park next to the frisbee golf course section of the park on 3rd. There are footprints meandering all over the rolling hills. Abandoned picnic tables and grills stand out against the snow. A lone person, a mailman, is trudging through the snow on the sidewalk. Here again, shadows layer themselves across the snow.

Last night after my day five posting I felt like it should be "Friday" for me. I shouldn't have homework on the weekend, right? I started getting restless. I know that this work to be done in my heart and head is not a 9-5, Monday through Friday deal. Now I really have the urge to flee.

"Shutdown Collene, you've been too open, too exposed. Board up the windows, hibernate in your bed, fly South for the winter, rocket ship to the moon, take it all back. RUN AWAY." My thoughts overwhelm my emotions.

After what I just went through for 24 1/2 months, wasn't this just the most foolish thing I could have done? I just KNOW more heartache is right around the corner and now look at me; I'm wider open, more unprotected than ever before.

I have amazing friends who have discernment as well as the ability to absolutely make me laugh- at myself! So, last night I was talked down from the "ledge," reminded why I'm here, and assured of the true narratives to replace the screwed-up ones. I'm not coming this far to turn and run. I'm not quitting. In terms of battle- there's no sitting down for me on the battlefield. My choices are wave the white flag or win the war and get home. So, I'm fighting on.

As I'm looking at this park I'm flooded with memories. "Blink, Collene." For some reason I'm getting watery. Right there is the place I sat with my mom and children this summer at The Symphony in the Park. I've been here 9 years, and this was a first for me. I'm thankful I just DID it, finally!

Just over the hill, my sister, Deborah, got married on the grass near the sidewalk a year ago. That feels like a lifetime ago. Okay, tears are pressing in. "Blink faster." The playground... I wonder how many hours I spent there? They have since taken down the merry-go-round and the metal ladder climby thing. I took pictures of my children in that place every year, including the times we came down for a visit from Alaska, sometimes, with the other side's cousins... The toddler wading pool- my first pregnant-with-Isaac picture was taken in that pool, with baby Nathan sitting on my hip.

There is the tree I sat under, exhausted, struggling inside, losing hope, pregnant again- this time with a girl- watching the boys run. My littlest sister, Susan, was living with me then. She was fabulous, helping me with the boys.

Just west of that tree and the playground is the creek. That thing is magnetic to little boys. Ducks, sticks, frisbees, bare feet, leaves. You name it, we either put it in, dug it out, or tried to catch it for hours!

On the other side of the park is where my photographer brother, John, took our pictures for last year's Christmas card. (Don't expect one this year, by-the-way; I'm not doing that now...) The raw, beautiful, excruciating memories are flooding in now; these are just a few...

Shadows and light... Deep sadness mixed with bright hope, mixed with fear, mixed with nostalgia, mixed with exhaustion, mixed with joy. All mixed with a medley of whole and broken love. I am looking forward to the Son shining bright enough to cause these shadows to flee.

Hope That Does Not Disappoint
Collene James
Yellowstone County, MT

Fight of Faith

O, the highs and the lows,
this febrile fight of faith bestows!
How they blow,
help us grow,
until the Savior's strivings, our souls know.

Blindfolded doubt: grabble, grope;
blow back and forth like a Hangman's rope.
Hope! Hot hellish hoax,
chills and chokes,
stirs and stokes
flames of freedom into yielding yokes.

Parched spirits drained and dry;
dehydrated – slaked from asking, "Why?"
My tired heart tries,
it decries
all the lies,
but my ears hear only lullabies.

O, the highs and the lows,
this febrile fight of faith bestows!
It ebbs and flows
it sows,
then grows
from stuttering speech to precious prose.

Vicky Joy Anderson

What's Smaller Than a Mustard Seed?

November 20ᵗʰ 2011

I made it! A whole week of the crazy that is in me, publicly pouring out! I know I'm a bit of a mess, but I feel like I'm being swept clean as we "speak." Today is Sunday. I went to church three weeks in a row. That's kind of a big deal these days. Not that I got a gold sticker or anything, but it's evidence of me beginning some healing- which is more than a little encouraging. We were given a quote that I must share with you. Jerry Sittser, who apparently suffered incredible loss, wrote *"A Grace Disguised."* The book, which I have not read and cannot vouch for, is on the topic of grief and loss. He wrote:

"...depth of sorrow is a sign of a healthy soul...it is not something to escape, but to embrace... sorrow is noble and gracious. It enlarges the soul until the soul is capable of mourning and rejoicing simultaneously, of feeling the world's pain and hoping for the world's healing at the same time. However painful, sorrow is good for the soul."

The fact is this: If you live, you will grieve.

While I do not intend to minimize my situation, or anyone else's, I will say that I am acutely aware of experiences survived by many of you, that are much more deeply devastating than anything I have experienced this far in my life. I've been thinking about some of these scenarios over the week. These thoughts have brought me to today's exercise:

(Week 2 Day 7)

After bringing the kids to their dad, I decided to head out of town. I took Rimrock Road to the west. Out past Yellowstone Country Club, past the Iron Wood subdivision, to the end of the gravel road just before the curve.

I chased the sunset to get here. Tonight, it is not extremely vivid. Pastel blues and greys melt into soft oranges and yellows. Swirled in the mix, behind the whirlpool of clouds there is a bright pink, where the sun is still glowing. Here where I parked, tufts of golden grasses stand above the drifted snow. The sage brush has, with the help of the wind, shaken the snow completely off. In the farmer's field, plow lines show their ruts through the thin layer of crusted snow. I got out of my car to take a few pictures in each direction.

The day was warm, but now with the sun all the way down, the chill has set in again. I return to my heater, turn the phone off and sit...

There they are again. Those two words I have been watching chase each other around my mind for nearly two months: FAITH and TRUST.

"Do you ever wonder if God is still in control?" I asked a friend a few weeks ago.

"He is always in control, it's up to you to trust Him" was the reply.

"Well, what if I can't anymore?" I asked.

"You can, you just have to get past yourself first," he said.

Okay, I want that. How am I getting in my own way? I've been struggling with this question since that night. My limited understanding of my circumstances as they pertain to me right NOW, gets in my way. My short-sighted, what feels most comfortable, allergy to the seasons of change in my life, gets in my way. (Yes, this is why "Seasonal Allergy" is the name of my blog journal.) My quick-to-flee reflexes get in my way. My perfectionism and pride and daydream fantasies get in my way. My microscopic, essentially invisible, smaller than a mustard seed faith, gets in the way.

Trust is a screwy thing for me. I started out trusting everyone. I was taught that a person's word, their integrity, is all they have. I assumed everyone knew that- along with the understanding that it's kinda bad to kill people. It turns out not everyone sees life that way. So, I recently have swung in the opposite direction. Trust no one. Everyone is lying and will use me. Everyone has an "angle" to play. Have I mentioned I tend to operate in absolutes?

It's time to grow-up, to wise-up. It's time to start finding my way down the center, walking by faith, with discernment. In this process I am hoping to figure out how to stay open, but not give myself wholeheartedly to everyone- to watch trust being earned.

It seems extremely ridiculous to even say it, but it's true: The God of the universe, Creator of everything, Knitter of me, Painter of tonight's sunset, Sculptor of The Rims next to me, is earning my trust. I've been sensing Him for months now, even in my anger, being faithful. He's meeting my most desperate internal needs, without my asking or deserving. Now He is softly, persistently, firmly drawing me back into the comfort of His arms. Hmmmm, I think I see now that the condemnation I experienced from His people is not actually coming from Him.

P.S. I just peeked at next week's lesson. Guess what the chapter is called? "God Is Trustworthy." Coincidence? I think not! Oh, and guess what else? The "soul training" exercise? "Count Your Blessings"- Irony, with it being Thanksgiving week? Hmmmm...could be a good week.

Faith
Matthew Bailey

November 21st 2011

For some reason tonight I am unable to refine my journal entry for today enough to make it public. My head is wandering around this incredible task I've been handed called mothering. Specifically, mothering men. I'm feeling pretty darn inadequate, having never been a man myself. I have a pretty clear understanding of the kind of men I want to raise: adventurers, honest, protectors, humble, courageous, peacemakers, strong leaders, unafraid of the right kinds of battles, able and willing to exercise self-control...

This culture offers so few examples of that man. I have never heard of one single little boy that ever looked to his mother to figure out how to be a man, yet I know my role is important. Anywho.... I guess I'll let these thoughts steep and proceed with the challenge:

(Week 3 Day 1)
This week's challenge is to come up with at least 100 things I consider to be a blessing in my life. It is truly coincidental that this chapter fell on Thanksgiving week. In no particular order or ranking, here's my start as they come to me:

1. Coffee- a drink of necessity and nostalgia. I love the depth of the flavor, variety of beans and roasts and the comfort of the fragrance. I love that "going to get coffee" with someone leads to friendships, intimacy through conversation, acceptance.

2. My House- the circumstances of purchasing this house, in this location, at the exact right time, involving just the right people, could not have been more perfectly orchestrated.

3. My Salon- I say "my," but let's be clear: Marilyn is the best owner in the history of salons, it has been a complete blessing to rent a spot from her! I am doing what I am passionate about, surrounded by the perfect mesh of gracious personalities. These women are like big sisters to me- providing a protective, creative, welcoming atmosphere.

4. A Generous Stranger- the $1000 gift of cash, tucked in a bag of clothes for my kids last year, when I didn't have two quarters to my name. I am still humbled and blessed today for that.

5. The Generosity of Friends- countless lunches, coffees, furniture, kitchen gadgets, a tank of gas, rent money, birthday gifts for the kids, soft shoulders for crying, warm homes- with Super Mario Brother's and Wii Golf/Bowling- for weekend escapes, work appropriate clothes- in my size, strong muscles for moving my whole house, and then again and again... The list continues. I am incredibly, magnificently blessed.

6. Tulips- the signal of spring. The most graceful flower, yet strong enough to force through the cold ground and withstand the inevitable spring snow.

7. Scars- a sure sign that healing has taken place.

8. Music- for when my own words fail.

9. Water in Nature- all forms fascinate me; today I'm thinking waterfalls.

10. Perfume- for making an ordinary tomboy feel like a lady.

11. Obedient, Respectful Children- who struggle at home at times, but live what they're taught when I'm not around.

12. Second Chances- and thirds.

13. Comfortable Silences- because we "get" each other.

14. Montana's Big Sky- because it really is bigger here.

15. Travel- the soothing for the soul of a wanderer.

16. Sunrises- it's not up yet this morning, but yesterday it was bright enough to bathe my whole bed in pink.

17. Sunsets- offer closure, the promise of a do-over or the perfect wrap on a great day.

18. Thunderstorms- a powerful cleansing of the earth, with a light show to boot!

19. Family-By-Choice- amazing people who have invited me into their own family lives to share holidays when my own family is too far away. All of you bless me more than you know.

20. Puzzles- because they bring people together.

21. Charles, Gary, Daniel, John, Brian- whether they are twenty months older, fifteen years younger, or somewhere in between- they are protective and understanding and just plain comfortable to hang out with. Brothers are the best.

22. Hair Color- because I'm not old enough to have my arctic blonde show yet.

23. Anesthesia- because my last two surgeries may have sucked without.

24. Four Wheel Drive- takes me more places I want to go.

25. D and J- all nieces and nephews are blessings, but these are preemie miracle blessings.

26. Shoes- not just shoes, pretty shoes. Somehow, they make the hard stuff easier to walk through.

27. Lamp- "I love lamp. I love carpet?" Okay, I'm kidding, I started to feel a little goofy. But seriously, what would we do without a little light in the darkness?

28. Fantastic Neighbors- that cul-de-sac in Anchorage was packed full of them and this block appears to be too!

29. Friends Who Paint- Britt and Jessi N., you rock. They even do the cutting-in ladies and gentlemen.

30. Buckets of Paint- a cheap way to make a dingy old house feel fresh.

31. Nathan- responsible, thoughtful, gracious, intelligent, hardworking, protective, creative, excellent at fishing and baking and not afraid to be himself.

32. Isaac- witty, intelligent, deep-thinking, adventurous, charming, even tempered, sensitive, strong, with a keen sense of right and wrong.

33. Hannah- generous, affectionate, sweet, peacemaking, funny, gorgeous inside and out, obedient, strongly individual, assures me she's never going to hate me! (Do you think I should get that on paper before jr. high?)

Happy Thanksgiving my friends. I'll keep trudging (in pretty shoes) along this process, "off" days or not.

Thawing
Collene James

57

Slumber Party

November 25th 2011

I don't like being told how or when to do what. I think that's why I generally resist the "spirit" of most holidays. I think things get blown so out of proportion and un-simplified by our culture. That being said, I really enjoyed this week's assignment- even if it fell during the same week that everyone else in America was thinking the same thing.

The kids and I spent the last two days with a close friend of mine. We did the math last night. As of 2011, this girl and I have been friends for 22 years. Of course, being barely 22 ourselves.... (Yeah, whatever, I already admitted to the arctic blonde...) Needless to say, we've been through some stuff together. Real deep grief stuff.

I have no idea when our first slumber party was, I assume it was soon after the start of 7th grade. Early on conversations were typical and girly. There was lots of giggling, a few tears now and then, more energy than I can fathom anymore! We discussed a boy or two, parents, siblings, first kisses, jr. high "dances" (if we can call that dancing), movies, music, trips, dreams.... Over the years things got more complex. Some things I'm not prepared to share publicly, but she was there, and then for her, I was there. Always.

The last two nights, as we talked, and giggled the hours away, we reflected on some of the stuff we went through together. I can say beyond a shadow of a doubt, that it was the heartbreak, trauma, and the tragedies that have shaped us into the individuals we are. They have been the same tools that have given us the respect, trust and admiration we have now for each other as friends. As a result, the sweet times are that much sweeter.

As we lay in bed this morning, hoping to squeeze out another 15 minutes of rest (while sick kids took turns hugging the toilet, mind you), we talked about this blog. My friend- who knew me when, knew me last year, and sticks in it with me so far this week- reminded me of who I am. So, today, because it has always been "our number," I'm adding to my Blessed List 21 things for you Jess:

1. I Have Not Always Been A Runner- this is a temporary, coping thing. I am blessed because at the end of this, I get me back. A deeper, richer, more firmly planted, me. Thank you for the reminder of the steadfast, immovable girl you knew then...

2. Cruise Control- helps me restrain myself. That is a good thing!

3. Sweet Tea- with not too much, not too little, just enough real sugar.

4. Grief- only because it has made me deeper, wiser, stronger, sweeter.

5. Tears- for the power wash that they are.

6. Mirrors- because they don't lie. The naked eye compensates, over-corrects, deceives... mirrors are important in my job, because they show the truth of every line and angle. They are important figuratively in my life because they show the truth of every choice, reflex, and direction.

7. Golden Grass- the reflection of the sun on the blades catches my breath.

8. Clouds- the constant shifting of shapes and colors, never bore, never disappoint.

9. Gum- the mint kinds specifically.

10. Second Generation Sleepovers- what a blessing to see our six kids building forts with the couches and giggling themselves to sleep 22 years later.

11. God's Perfect Timing- the way He moves people, places, and things in and out of our lives is astounding to me.

12. Baby's Greasy Handprint- that I just couldn't wash off my oven before I sold my first house. Sorry, whoever bought that. He left one on my heart too.

13. Jeans That Fit Just Right- need I explain? The day after Thanksgiving, especially!

14. Surrogate Aunts- the handful of you girls who treat my kids like they're of your own blood. You bless me.

15. The $20 In My Pocket After the Wash- doesn't get much better!

16. Laying on The Floor in a Sunspot- warm, secure- reminds me of being a child.

17. Mountains- snowcapped or otherwise. The view means I'm home.

18. Sharpies- every color, every point size.

19. The Dishwasher- because I recently ran a household without.

20. Maggie & Joe- the Jack Russell Terriers I call mine; loyal, always.

21. Communication in A Glance- because I am known by someone.

Bright Spots
Collene James
Crystal Mill Road- Crystal, CO

Crowd Noise and Blessings

November 26th 2011

Thanksgiving and football go together. Ever since I can remember there was at least one game being monitored while the fragrance of a roasting turkey spread through the house. Every year Mom and Dad would go hunting early on Thanksgiving morning. About the time I reached 12 or 13 Mom trusted my kitchen skills enough to extend their time away and I would start the meal myself. By age 15, I was doing the entire thing on my own. As vital to the holiday as turkey, hunting and thankfulness, was the noise of the football crowd, my yelling brothers, and the sound of a good tackle.

My first Thanksgiving away from my family was not much different as far as football was concerned. In fact, if we were at my in-laws', the men/boys were usually tossing a ball around in the yard or street, while the girls made dinner- the game on TV keeping us company inside.

When I started hosting the holiday at our home in Alaska, we usually invited a few guys without family to visit. You got it- the games were always on.

This was my first noticeably football-less Thanksgiving. On the actual day, it was not a big deal. I hardly noticed the lack of crowd noise with all of the kid noise in the house. However, the girls and I did check the scores on my phone now and then- mainly because we had unanimously decided Green Bay and Dallas needed to lose.

So yesterday, as the dust settled from my trip and I tried to find something to do now that the kids were back at their dad's, the college games called to me. Isn't it weird to be a girl, sitting alone- the nearest family boys being at least 5 miles away- flipping back and forth between games? Probably, so I'm probably not going to risk explaining to you my love of naps plus NASCAR!

Today, in lieu of football, I worked a short day at the salon. Then I had lunch with the girls. Then more great conversation with a valuable friend. I am tired. My mental gymnast has pulled a muscle, so I will spare you from the subsequent processing and continue my Blessed List. Yesterday's 21 things, added to the 33 before, brings me to:

55. Stretching- lift your tight aching arms above your head and streeeeeetch- or press your toes up on the wall and stretch your calf muscles.... hold it.... oh, that hurts! But now, that's done, doesn't it feel good to stretch? Now take yourself out of the comfort zone and blog, or contact someone you've been afraid you've hurt, or _____; you fill in the blank. What stretches you? Oh, it hurts a bit. Now that it's done, it's feeling pretty good to stretch.

56. Recipes- make me feel like a whiz in the kitchen. Someone else's vision on my table is very satisfying when put together by me.

57. Pictures- tell the truth in an artistic way. I love photographers, the ones who consider themselves to be "real photographers" and those who don't. You all bless me with your point of view.

58. New Socks- If I had a trillion dollars, I'd wear new socks every day and buy some for you too.

59. Grace- a blessing, unearned, undeserved, beautiful, and rich.

60. Lilacs- the purple ones especially. I love how they stink up a whole neighborhood! I love that my new house has them. I love the memories they give me.

61. My Old Horse Charlie- a million years ago he was the vehicle I accessed to go fast, get away, think, and process.

62. Crosses- used to mark the memory of someone important. Used to pay the price by Someone vital.

63. Spontaneity- because it makes the day worth seeing through.

64. Jewelry- the special pieces- a reminder of a loved one or an important event. The inherited pieces, the going away gift from a friend, the birthstone of a child, the gift from a brother the year he fought cancer, the gift from another brother deployed half a world away, the plastic "diamond" my kids gave me to remind me that I'm loved...

65. Architecture- artistic, functional lines.

66. Childlike Faith- pure, simple, trusting.

67. Pockets- a fabulous addition to every clothing item. Okay, well almost every, I just remembered the shoes with the zippered pockets we all used to have. Those shouldn't come back. Ever.

68. Naps- Mom, you were right when I was four. I remember the adamant fit I threw when you told me that someday I would love the opportunity to take a nap. "I will NEVER want a nap," I had said then. Write it down: Mom knew better!

69. Newborn Snuggles- what's not to love? They smell so good, feel so warm and squishy. They grunt and sigh and depend on you wholly!

70. Nail Polish- because it dresses up a tomboy's appearance quickly.

71. People- everyone has a story. Everyone is valid.

72. Contacts- because wearing my glasses somehow makes me feel disconnected from the people around me.

73. Laughter- because it's contagious.

74. Lunch with The Girls- blesses me, just because I have "girls."

75. Fire- the sounds, colors, power, warmth, and smell. Amazing.

Delicate Strength
Collene James

Shake It Off
Collene James
Milwaukee Zoo- Milwaukee, WI

Blessings, Bears, Beets, Battlestar Galactica...

November 27th 2011

Today is the final day of the Blessings week. The challenge was to try to come up with at least 100 over the course of the last 7 days. I got to 100, then blew past- and not just because I counted the silly ones too! Today, even after I stopped writing them down, my thoughts kept circling the unwritten, obscure blessings in my quick-as-a-vapor life. At one point I was reminded of an illustration told by George Buttrick:

"A lecturer to a group of businessmen displayed a sheet of white paper on which was one blot. He asked what they saw. All answered, 'a blot'. The test was unfair, it invited the wrong answer. Nevertheless, there is an ingratitude to human nature by which we notice the black disfigurement and forget the wide-spread mercy. We need to deliberately call to mind the joys of our journey. Perhaps we should try to write down the blessings of one day. We might begin; we could never end. There are not pens or paper enough in all the world. The attempt would remind us of our 'vast treasure of content.'"

This has been a bit of a tough weekend for me. My heart has been rescued by this exercise more than once. Last night I re-read my blog entries over the last two weeks. It feels good to see progress "on paper." I have a feeling that I will need to refer to these days from time to time...

76. Phone Calls- shorten the miles, ease the missing.

77. Mercy- undeserved compassion.

78. Peace- the absence of debate, turmoil, war.

79. Barns- old, rickety, a place of refuge, the smell of animals and dust and hay, the loft to play in, the scurrying mice, the smell of old leather and grain...

80. Tire Swings- the rush of wind, feeling of suspension just before the return swing, the creaking of the rope around the tree.

81. NASCAR- the soothing, comforting sound of tires on pavement, the excitement and pride of watching an uncle race, the love of cars and speed and engine noise.

82. Blue Eyes- six specific ones that look at me with trust and love and hope and admiration, whether I've earned it or not.

83. Purple- because I can make it work on me

84. Straightening Irons- because I remember the days without them, and my hair has only gotten curlier over the years.

85. Volleyball- the only sport I was (mildly) able to do! The blessing is in the team.

86. Making S'mores- the campfire, friends, chill of the evening and melty mallows and chocolate do not have to be explained.

87. Dark Chocolate- but only the smooth stuff.

88. Northern Lights- especially watching them next to me out of a plane window! Spectacular!

89. Fragrance of Rain- fresh and clean.

90. Stranger's Smile- brings me out of myself, reminds me that people matter.

91. Friend's Smile- knowing encouragement.

92. Baby Smiles- eager, excited, pure.

93. Lip Gloss- especially in the dry Montana winter!

94. Fragrance of Leather- deep and rich and nostalgic.

95. Dimples- not sure why, but they bless me. What a gift that my daughter got a set!

96. Holding Hands- with a parent, friend, child, lover.

97. Memory- the ability to hang on to life's experiences, the good and the bad, and to retain the growth that comes from them.

98. Salmon Fishing- makes trout fishing extremely uninteresting. Sorry guys.

99. The 20 Mile River- some of my best Alaska memories took place on that river- with old friends, family, strangers that became friends...

100. Back Rubs- safe human touch, relief of stress, rare and relaxing.

101. Redwoods- if you don't understand, I'll just have to take you there...

@whocldgvahOOt

Cold, Tired, Tangled-
Wilderness Walking
Collene James

Family

(Ephesians 3:14-21)

Chorus 1

```
Am7              Bm7/A              Am7
  Every family in heaven and on earth
Am7                       Bm7
  Has been named by the Father, God.
Am7                  Bm7           Am7    Bm7
  He's got a plan and a purpose   for every family.
Am7            Bm7                        Am7  Bm7
  For this reason I bow my knees and pray for you.
```

Verse 1

```
C                 G      D      C
  According to the riches of His glory.
C                                  G                  D      C
  May you be strengthened with might through God's Spirit in you.
C                  G          D            C
  That Christ Jesus may dwell in your hearts through faith.
            G
Through faith.
```

Chorus 2

```
Am7              Bm7/A        Am7
  Every family is joined by God
Am7                    Bm7
  To live in love and unity.
Am7                  Bm7               Am7    Bm7
  He's got a plan and a purpose   for every family
Am7            Bm7                        Am7  Bm7
  For this reason I bow my knees and pray for you.
```

Verse 2

```
C                      G        D            C
  That you'd be rooted and grounded in God's love for you.
                                G              D
  With the power to know what is the breadth and the length and the
  C                       G
Height and the depth of His love for you.
```

Verse 3

C   G   D   C
  May you know the love of Christ which goes past all knowledge;
C   G   D
  That you may be filled with all the fullness of God
     C   G
  To overflowing, Overflowing.

Repeat Chorus 1

C   G   D   C
  Now to Him who by His power is working in you;
C   G   D   C
  He can do far more than you even ask or think.
C   G   C   Am7   G
  Be the glory forever, To all generations (3X) Amen.

A Song of Nancy Bowser

Not Alone
Collene James

Halcyon

Let down thy wings, fluttering bird;
lay aside your want and will.
Sweet chords of faith can be heard
    as they vibrate -- sing!
While the voice of doubt -- muttering,
    when told to be still.

Tie down thy pinions, restless bird;
why be so eager to fly?
For the snake, he has deterred
    to his dominion,
countless ones who would have preferred
    rest in branches high.

Lie down thy head, O, wearied bird;
meet with shelter in thy nest.
Take flight in storm? How absurd
    to rush on ahead
into thunderclouds, undeterred,
    raging east to west.

Lay down thy feathers, anxious bird,
against thy quieted breast.
Take heart! Do not be demurred -
    wait out dark weather!
The songs that come from hope deferred
    glorify Him best.

Vicki Joy Anderson

Out

C   Dm7
Out of the cloud came Your GLORY

C   Dm7
Out of the womb came HOPE

C   Dm7
Out of the BLOOD came Your Cleansing

C   Dm7
Out of the tomb came LIFE

C   F
Who controls the winds of time?

C   F
Who opens doors and leads the blind?

C   F
Who heals the sick and brings forth life?

C   Dm7   C   Dm7
JESUS JESUS JESUS JESUS   Your Name is LOVE… JESUS

We know Your Name, Jesus;   We praise Your Name, Jesus;   We love Your Name, Jesus

C   Dm
Out of YOUR SPIRIT comes POWER

C   Dm7
Out of YOUR WORDS come AUTHORITY

C   Dm7
Out of the darkness comes Your LIGHT

C   Dm7
Out of YOUR LIFE comes LOVE

A Song of Nancy Bowser

The Waterfall

November 30th 2011

Tonight, I am sitting in my quiet house reflecting on the emotions of the last week and a half. I am listening to the winds of change outside my window as they bring in, presumably, the first real winter storm of 2011-2012.

I should probably admit that since my internal season has been entering a new spring, I had a bit of an internal "spring snow" of my own last week. For some reason I clung a bit again to the familiar icy winter I was just starting to come out of. I ran around the garden of my heart and pulled and kicked each little delicate flower of hope that had started blooming.... I'm not sure what to do about that, so I'll tell you what else is on my mind:

Waterfalls have been crossing my mind off and on over the last several days. There are no substantial ones close enough to town for me to spend the afternoon watching, so I'm going back in my memory a few weeks- to our visit to the Yellowstone Falls.

Today I re-read my Steadfast Pursuit blog. I needed to be reminded that along with this powerful shaping will come the smoothing. I imagined that the fallen cottonwood tree fell up-river near the falls in Yellowstone. (Although it's highly unlikely that a whole cottonwood tree would have washed all the way to Billings without getting caught on a sand bar or bridge, just go with me on this...) I was feeling pretty good, floating along on the river, when last week, during Blessings Week none-the-less, I whoooooooshed over the waterfall. The pressure of the water forced me under at the base of the cliff and held me down there for a bit. I spent the next several days struggling to make sense of it, gasping for breath, trying to right myself. Not sure if I was seeing the river bottom or sky. In some ways I was completely taken off guard by the thoughts I was being confronted with. Some of these I had put aside years ago...

If you've been following any of this thread, you know that I am working through a set of challenges with a few friends. This week's challenge is: "Read/recite *Psalm 23* twice a day, memorize it if possible- until it feels like breathing to you, think of these words throughout each day."

Okay, I'm not going to soften this for you, because my internal response was a little... uh, raw. My reaction was anger with complete irritation. I was not just mildly ticked. If there is one thing that has felt like pouring acid on a burn patient over the last year or two (more really, but who's really keeping track?) it's the churchy, "Chritianese," cliche garbage people say when they have never lived through anything more inconvenient than not having a Starbucks close to their office. Why, when I've had so much progress and hope, would I be thrown a bumper sticker phrase to marinate on? Where's the deep stuff of Job or some crazy obscure place in Zephaniah? Okay, so now that I've offended half of you, here's what's happened this week, so far:

I'm a rule follower, so I had my fit, then followed the rules. In case you're not familiar with the chapter here it is:

"A Psalm of David. The Lord is my shepherd; I shall not want. He makes me lie down in green pastures. He leads me beside still waters. He restores my soul. He leads me in paths of righteousness for His name's sake. Even though I walk through the valley of the shadow of death, I will fear no evil, for You are with me; Your rod and Your staff, they comfort me. You prepare a table before me in the presence of my enemies; You anoint my head with oil; my cup overflows. Surely goodness and mercy shall follow me all of my days and I shall dwell in the house of the Lord forever."

On day one of this week, I wrote in my journal before I did the reading/reciting thing. Yeah, I've tried, there's really no way for me to clean my thoughts up to make them public. It's not that they're evil or awful really, just really intense. I feel a real sense of responsibility to respect, even in some ways, protect, the people I have been hurt by. There will just be some experiences, both recent and ancient history, that I will not be specific about on here for that reason alone.

That night I finally got around to reading the verses, mentally checked the box for the day, turned out the light and closed my eyes. *"Restores My Soul,"* kept drifting through my mind quietly. Then with more persistence. What? How? It's crushed, tattered- no, fed through a commercial sized meat grinder. Hmmmm? What's that? I knew I needed to turn the light on and look it up to get it right: *"...but we have this treasure in jars of clay, to show that the surpassing power belongs to God and not to us. We are afflicted in every way, but not crushed; perplexed, but not driven to despair; persecuted, but not abandoned, struck down, but not destroyed..."*

By now, if you knew me then, you'd know that I'm slightly musically bent and that both *Psalm 23* and *2 Corinthians 4:7-9* have several songs based on them. So, as you can imagine, the light stayed on. With the songs pouring through my head. Words were flying from my pen into my journal. Tears streamed. Raw, gut-wrenching hurt being expressed. It felt good to get it all out, so after a while, I laid back down. Lights out. Eyes closed...

"He leads me beside still waters and makes me lie down in green pastures" is the echo I heard. Okay. My eyes opened again. I wondered, "So why is my mind not still? Why am I not resting on green pastures?" I told you last week that my mental gymnast pulled a muscle and now it's clear that this wrestling with stuff is not producing anything. "HOW do I do this?" My mind screamed... ***"Be still and know that I am God,"*** His words whispered.

The light came on again; I retrieved my journal. This time, less upset, more intentional, I wrote down the most secret fears and desires and griefs- some that I have been unwilling to openly admit to anyone. Six pages later, I put the light out- eyes closed; sleep on its way...

Or not.

Yesterday's sermon title popped into my mind. "The Impossible Is What God Does Best." Really? Somehow the six pages I just wrote seem beyond impossible, but I was now completely exhausted. I slept.

Tuesday, I woke up to numbness. Not restless, wrestling, racing thoughts, hurt, fear, hope. Nothing. Just numb. The word "restoration" floated and flickered throughout my morning; I pushed it away. I didn't even care. I checked the box of reading/reciting. I tried to be productive around the house. I was completely ineffective. The hats I've been wearing all these years and months have started to fall off. I'm not even sure I like hats. I certainly wouldn't have chosen some of them. I wouldn't have even been caught dead shopping in the aisle of a few of them. I have no choice, so I will wear hats, and do it as well as I can, for as long as I need to.

I am numb.

Tuesday wore on. Numbness started to turn into pain. I drifted in and out of pain, tears were strangely falling- disconnected from emotion. When I had my hysterectomy, my wake up from surgery was like this. I would start to gain consciousness and tears would flow, uninhibited. My sweet nurse, a big Southern lady named Debbie, told me to go back to sleep. Every time I woke up crying, she would assure me I was okay and tell me to go back to sleep. Eventually on that day, I woke up completely; there were no tears.

As I have been re-reading my stuff since Monday, I cannot believe it's only Wednesday. This morning I woke up completely. There were no tears. I'm not numb. I even laughed a lot today. This idea of Him restoring my soul is not so inconceivable right now. As far as I can tell nothing on my six pages of fears, desires and griefs has been addressed specifically and the delicate little flowers I kicked and picked are still lying around the ground of my heart, but today I can be still and know that He is God.

Cleanse Me
Collene James
Natural Falls State Park- Colcord, OK

Joy For the Moment

December 7th, 2011

Having made it through the waterfall and near drowning last week, I have begun week five of my little journey of challenges. I'll be honest here:

I'm feeling pretty good these days, floating in peaceful waters! I find myself unsure of how to function this way. Yes. That is dysfunctional!

I had so many days in a row of actual lightheartedness, I began to instinctively throw up walls of protection again. I didn't see it myself. Thank God for a good friend, again. She gently- or was it boldly, directly, firmly- gave me the verbal spanking I needed. She's right: I'm used to living in the future- always prepping for disaster, forgetting to be thankful for right now, not able to trust the joy or excitement I feel, even about silly stuff, constantly waiting for the bottom to fall out.

Why?

I had recent examples of why this "prepping" makes sense, but I had no idea when or why I started living this way. I didn't really have the energy to care at the time, but I figured that this would be the process of the week.

The morning started out with the word "TRUST" once again making the rounds of my thoughts. The phrases *"afflicted in every way, but not crushed," "perplexed, but not driven to despair," "persecuted, but not abandoned," "struck down, but not destroyed"* were also again making the rounds...

This brought me to this evening. I was minding my own business- making deposits in different accounts, doing (yet again) tire maintenance, paying a bill or two, returning calls, when it hit me: It has been 19 years this Christmas, since I sustained my first major internal injury. This thought was so loud in my head, I actually said, "God WHY?" out loud in my car.

The "why" I had never investigated at the time. In fact, I spent the next five years pretending the incident never even happened. It seemed so much less complicated that way. When finally, I was forced to confront the situation, I deflected. There were other people who needed support and I was apparently supposed to be the strong one.

Over the years I have not been afraid of the facts of that night. I am never specific, but I don't have to be. I told my story a time or two, when I felt like it would benefit someone. Then there were the times I told my story to the ones I trusted most. I was hoping to be known, understood, fully accepted by them. Instead, I was accused, verbally shot at, emotionally struck down, rejected, unprotected. With that kind of price tag, I felt it was much easier to shove the hurt a little deeper, pull up my bootstraps and keep marching as though it didn't matter...

In many ways I feel like the woman I became, does not know, never met, that 15-year-old girl. I can recite her history, but I generally do not allow myself to feel her insecurity, fear, anger, or pain. Instinctively I have trained myself to anticipate, distrust, doubt, fear, and push back, before I ever feel that unprotected again.

The cool thing about tonight is that I don't hurt as I'm writing this. I also don't feel numb. I feel peace. I know that I can trust that this will be healed from the inside out. The "why" doesn't really matter. Those that I trusted, who took the shots at me, don't matter much anymore- have lost their power over me. I will one day, very soon, be functioning completely in the here and now with joy for the moment.

I will not be crushed. I will not despair. I will not be forsaken. I will not be destroyed.

Veiled Hope
Collene James

77

That Four Letter Word

December 8th 2011

"Perseverance" was the roaming word of the day, in my mind. Earlier in the week I tried to sit down and start the week's challenge. Once again, I REALLY didn't like what the guy wanted me to do. I checked the box of "doing something" and chose a different set of verses to use for the exercise. But... over the last four days I have been haunted by what I was supposed to do:

"Using *1 Corinthians 13:4-8*, spend some time slowly reading (multiple times, mind you) each phrase. Write down words or phrases that stand out to you. Repeat them, pray about them, think about other verses that come to mind while you're reading them...."

Yep, that's me rolling my eyes, squirming, being extremely evasive. You know, I've given this stuff more than a month. I'm good. I've learned a lot about myself. I'm fairly happy, well-adjusted. I can coast this week. I'm busy, have a lot on my mind, I'll get back on task next week... Besides, it's not like I did NOTHING this week, I just used a different verse.

So, "perseverance" is again the word I'm fighting against tonight. "Remember? Just this week, I told you I am trustworthy Collene," I hear in my head.

"But God, it's another bumper-sticker, poster phrase. Worse- it's the WEDDING one. I cannot do this...."

"Persevere, Collene."

So, I obeyed.

Here it is, in case you're the only person on the planet that doesn't know it:

"Love is patient, love is kind. It does not envy, it does not boast, it is not proud. It is not rude, it is not self-seeking, it is not easily angered, it keeps no record of wrongs. Love does not delight in evil but rejoices with the truth. It always protects, always trusts, always hopes, always perseveres. Love never fails..."

My stomach is in knots. I'm sad and mad and... REALLY mad. I probably won't be having another wedding, ever, but if I do, this will not be what is read in it. Mark my words.

Now here's where this blog gets a little dicey for me. I wrestle with the fact that I have no idea who actually reads this, if anyone. I also have no idea how my processing of these things impacts the reader. I have no desire to hurt or disrespect anyone. I do, however, feel like it's necessary to be genuine- otherwise what's the point?

My marriage- in fact none of my romantic relationships, resembled this definition of love. In addition, the relationships with some extended family members and church friends failed big in the same way. I recognize that people aren't perfect. In fact, I've done my best as a wife, in-law, mother, daughter, sister, friend, to resemble those love qualities to the best of my ability- and have still fallen way short at times. Whatever, some of that's over forever; why does it still matter? My disillusionment, however, is holding steady.

Okay, tonight I did what I was supposed to. While I was thinking about the phrases that stuck out to me and the "what's the point" thoughts, I remembered a conversation I had with my good friend just this September.

She said, "Collene, if a good looking, respectful, incredible guy did come along and try to love you, you would find a way to reject, sabotage, and push him away."

I looked at her like she was crazy. "Why would I do that? Nonsense."

She persisted, "you are unwilling to accept it from anyone as it is, including from God- and His love is perfect."

THEN, ladies and gentlemen, she gave me recent examples!

Well now, I'm not sure why I keep her around anymore... except that I love mirrors. I love directness, honesty... and, because she really does "get" me, and I don't want to be this way anymore. She really was loving me that morning with her statements.

At the end of the exercise the guy had us go back through and, because **"God is Love"** according to **1 John 4**, put the word "God" in the place of "Love"... *"God is patient, God is kind. He does not envy; He does not boast. God is not proud, God is not rude, God is not self-seeking, God is not easily angered, God keeps no record of wrongs, God does not delight in evil, but rejoices with truth. God always protects, trusts, hopes, perseveres, God never fails."*

This is going to take some practice, but tonight I know I need to start accepting His perfect, patient, protective, pursuing, honest, enduring, L-O-V-E. Then, maybe- just maybe- if eventually, some sort of godly "Prince Charming" shows up, I might just be ready to let him l-o-v-e me too...

Tiger Lilly
Andrea Fugleberg

Waiting for Rain

December 28th 2011
I'm being pursued!!!

He called me, out of the blue, a few weeks ago, on a "down" day none-the-less. The first time I saw him was two summers ago, at a day camp for the kids. He recognized me from years ago- before I was married. We caught up briefly, he invited me to chat "anytime." I ran into him again at a sandwich shop a few months later. Again, an invitation to call him, anytime. Over the next year I heard from friends that know him that he'd been asking about me, again encouraging them to have me call. So, I finally did. We met to talk for a couple of hours in his office. I was a mess that day, but left feeling encouraged and exhausted. The invitation to call anytime was again extended. I've seen him often over the course of the last six or seven months. He's a busy guy. I assumed the "anytime" invitation is just something people in his position say, possibly even with sincerity, but really don't have time to follow through with. Besides, I don't NEED anyone.

So, now in this call a few weeks ago... He was direct- "Collene, if you're not going to take me seriously and set up a time to see me, I'm coming to you. When can you cut my hair?"

I laughed him off. I know he has a hair girl already. I told him, "Alright, I'll come in again- after the Christmas rush?" I know he's busy and so am I.

Nope. He wants to see me, now.

We set it up for the next day. The conversation, in my itty-bitty salon, was deep, loving, encouraging. I am amazed and the depth of grace and love I feel coming from this guy. It, quite honestly, confuses me.

I spent the next few days re-reading this blog, moving backwards in time. It's funny to me that one day's thoughts seem to prepare me for the next day. The common threads start to emerge.

That's when it hit me: God has been pursuing be through this man. For the first time in my life, even being born into and growing up in the church, I have a pastor! A shepherd, in the true sense of the word.

I didn't see him again for nearly two weeks. When I did, he came to me for a huge, emotional even, hug. He looked me in the eye and said directly: "Collene, I loved our time the other day. I feel God has given me a special heart for you for a couple of years. You are beautiful inside and out... precious. I love you. It is my mission to tell you what I see in you every time I see you until you believe it. If I have such a heart for you, imagine God's love for you." He went on, but I honestly can't remember everything he said- it was just too much to absorb.

Dear Reader, this is not easy stuff for me to hear.

Why?

I have no idea. It goes against the narratives I've nursed for decades, I guess. I suppose I'm okay with the pastor's mission, but quite honestly, my instinct is to run. I hope I don't because it's exactly what I want...

Over Christmas, the salon was closed, so I went to Mom and Dad's. Since Thursday afternoon, I logged 2,444.4 miles on my brand-new tires. There is nothing like the hum of my tires on a road, the flash of changing scenery, chasing the sun from rise to set, iPod on shuffle, and the crossing of state lines. My mind moves fast, so it makes sense to me that sitting still has never worked for me when it comes to processing thoughts. Road trips, however, work wonders on my mind and heart. This break is just what I needed...

On this particular trip I solved the world's problems, then went to work on my own. My mind again hovered on the familiar two topics: Pursuit and Perseverance. While in Arizona, I was reminded of a movie quote, although I cannot remember which movie anymore:

"Two farmers need rain. Both pray for it, but only one prepares his field for the rain. Which one has more faith?"

I spent three remarkably peaceful days with the family, got some much-craved brother time, hugged on a niece, saw again the breathtaking beauty of the Grand Canyon, and headed home with three VERY happy kids...

Then a friend called me somewhere around Salt Lake City on my drive home. She said she had been thinking of me and needed to read me this from *James 1* (how she knew perseverance was the theme of the trip, I don't know):

"Consider it pure joy, my brothers, whenever you face trials of many kinds, because you know that the testing of your faith develops perseverance. Perseverance must finish its work so that you may be mature and complete, not lacking anything. If any of you lacks wisdom, he should ask

God, who gives generously to all without finding fault, and it will be given to him. But when he asks, he must believe and not doubt, because he who doubts is like a wave of the sea, blown and tossed by the wind. That man should not think he will receive anything from the Lord; he is a double-minded man, unstable in all he does."

This morning I woke up, in my own bed finally, after restless dreams. Worry, fear, stress- the theme of the night. My mind immediately went to the dysfunctional secret place in my heart- that I've only shared with one other. The place that is comfortable only because it's familiar yet has nothing of life or hope for me. In the shower I heard in my head:

"As a dog returns to its vomit, so a fool repeats his folly." (Proverbs 26:11)

The day was dark, gloomy, cloudy. Will I learn? Will I change? Will I get this far only to forget what God is teaching me? Will I have to repeat the pain?

I refuse to. I will not settle in. I will finish, with patience/perseverance, the race that is set before me- looking to Jesus, the author and finisher of my faith...

With all this driving and thinking and solving, I know what I want. I know what I'm praying for. Now, it's time to finish preparing my field for the rain.

Wilted
Collene James

New Mercies For Today, Hope for Tomorrow

December 31st 2011

Well now, it seems to be a fertile week for processing... er, I mean, preparing my field. This is GREAT news for me, because some stuff is getting worked out inside me and I think an internal summer is right around the corner. On the other hand, it's not great news for those around me because my over-worked, teeny brain is starting to smell like burned rubber.

More good news for me: I tested my new pastor today. He's a champ, and completely, willingly, took me on when I called in tears. Some guy huh?! Whew! As is becoming somewhat the usual thing on this blog journal, I'm not going to share the nitty gritty details for the whole world to sift through, but the guy is wise. And gracious. And patient. And right.

In a nutshell, the narrative I'm processing this week has to do with fear. I've actually been a bit panicky for a couple of weeks, off and on, over a few different topics. Today all the topics collided in a masterful display of fireworks, crashing gongs, and tears. Okay the tears were actual, the fireworks and gongs were internal. Thank God that I got stood up today for a color during this time, so I had time to leave work to fall apart privately.

I am afraid that God is going to MAKE me do something I cannot, do not want to, will not allow myself to do. On the other hand, I am afraid that God will not allow "summer" in my life until I "obey." Furthermore, this week happens to be the week that the "super-Christians," who apparently have a red phone direct to God (one that, mind you, I was not issued) are assisting Him with getting me saved again. (Or something like that- my words and assessment of their actions, not theirs)

Please understand as you read this, that I am doing my level best to not sound mean, sarcastic, angry, or disrespectful... I'm feeling a little tender and mashed today and I really am doing my best. Anywho... the good pastor assured me that no one is qualified to speak for God about specific circumstances in my personal life and make conjectures as to what He has planned specifically for me in my near future. That's cool, because I assured the sweet pastor that I spent years OUT of church because of this very thing and am still feeling a bit flighty as to the whole situation. I don't want a God that is that small. I want the BIG version I was promised in Sunday School a million years ago.

Even though I didn't write at all Thursday, the theme washing through my head was **"the mercies of the Lord are new every morning."** It was a cute little phrase that lingered, brought to mind a couple of songs from forever ago, and made me smile. Thursday was a great day, for the most part. I was able to keep the fearful thoughts at bay all day. Today... I woke up- nope, I really didn't sleep. Really, I just gave up and got up, feeling absolutely trashed in every way. Eventually, at the very end of the longest day ever recorded, I was compelled to research this "new mercy" thing... I finally found it in Lamentations of all places. (YES!! This is not a bumper sticker to me, so I am fully embracing it!)

Lamentations 3:19-25

I remember my affliction and my wandering,
the bitterness and the gall.
I well remember them,
and my soul is downcast within me.
Yet this I call to mind
and therefore I have hope:
Because of the LORD's great love we are not consumed,
for His compassions never fail.
They are new every morning;
great is Your faithfulness.
I say to myself, "The LORD is my portion;
therefore I will wait for Him."
The LORD is good to those whose hope is in Him,
to the one who seeks Him.

Okie Doke. That's good enough for me tonight. My fears have been put to rest. I will wait and see. He will be good to me, because I have hope in Him and am seeking His plan- not a uber-super-exuberant Christian's plan for me. And also, you saw it right? It says it right there: *"because of His great love for me I won't be consumed."* That's cool. I'm tired.

Goodnight.

85

Fabric of Man
Collene James

"As a father has compassion on his children, so the Lord has compassion on those who fear Him; for He knows how we are formed, He remembers that we are dust."
(Psalm 103:13-14)

Dust Frames
Collene James
Arches National Park, UT

Martyr

O Father, in the throes of grief,
is it wrong to long for relief?

Every trial sent from above,
do we ignore its horror and learn to love?

Do you expect us to applaud
every bruise you choose to maraud?

When the enemy throws us in the dirt
do we try not to cry, or admit that it hurt?

In anguish, is our only choice
to celebrate our fate and rejoice?

From all comforts, must we abstain;
and sing to the sting that caused our pain?

And even if mercies are new tomorrow,
must we laugh on the path that leads to sorrow?

O Father, in the throes of grief,
is it wrong to long for relief?

Vicki Joy Anderson

Gentle

Have you ever thought of what you will be remembered for?

Or who, if anyone, will remember you at all?

I have thought about this an oddly large number of times in my life. From a pretty young age I have often wondered what people will say about me when it's all over.

My goal up until this time was to be remembered for being kind, or loving, or giving. That is no longer my goal.

Please do not believe that I now feel these traits are not great or describe a man who lived a life not worth having. In fact, I do- in a way- think many will remember me that way as well.

Kindness is very important and a powerful likeness to possess, but it doesn't always describe me.

Sometimes on occasion, I would not describe my daily actions, words, or even thoughts, as kind. I do strive to be kind and polite to all, but I think I want to be known as a greater man than just "kind."

Some would argue that certain things are kind, while others would say they are not. One parent spanks a child, and the child turns out great; another parent uses time-outs only, and the child also turns out great. The latter of the two parents might think the first parent isn't kind. The first parent thinks he's kind and is doing what a parent should do if they love their child. Are both right? Are either wrong?

Which brings me to my next point:

Loving.

I again strive greatly to be as loving as possible to all; however, just like with operating in kindness, I fall short often- especially when past personal experience and emotions get involved. I say things and do things that even I don't consider loving. Some of my most loving moments and actions are seen as the exact opposite to those receiving it.

In trying to love, I've been accused of being hateful and awful and selfish.

Speaking of selfishness, what about being a giving person? I give where I can and often where I really can't. Sometimes I'm taken advantage of, and it causes trust issues for me.

I do give what I have to offer for the good of another, although it means some believe I'm selfish and am trying to gain something for myself in these actions. I believe my time and friendship is a value to give; others would not agree.

Here's the truth about all this- the question about how I want to be remembered:

People will remember me as they choose to, based on their own perspective and closeness to my life.

I can't control what others say about me or choose to believe about me.

I would hope those closest to me would remember me as the man I am trying to be.

I hope my loved ones, and those who hate me as well, remember me as-

Gentle.

In everything I am, and all I do, I think gentleness is the cornerstone of my personality.

When I love, I am gentle,

When I am angry, I am gentle- I don't hit people or cause violence even at my greatest enraged fury.

I give this world what I am-

I am gentle.

When I leave this earth, I pray my daughter remembers me as gentle. I pray that more than all other things, she understands the beauty and importance of gentleness. I pray she lives a peaceful and gentle life to the best of her ability and loves and fears God with all her might.

I pray that when she is married and has a family that her children remember their gentle old grandpa. I pray the gentle fragrance of tobacco wafting from an old corn cob pipe brings a smile to their hearts- years after I'm gone.

I pray because of my example my daughter will not settle for a husband lest he be a gentleman- and a gentle man- himself.

As far as the rest of the world goes, remember me as you wish, if you wish. For those close to me, the ones who truly know me and love me, they will remember me as gentle.

Matthew Bailey

Soft
Collene James

Pathway
Andrea Fugleberg

Walking the Line
Andrea Fugleberg

The Walk

Mile by inch and day by year,
I walk a little taller now.

If I start to slump, the weight on my aching back might break me.
Yet, I know I can't just break.

No, not yet. I won't fail. No, not yet.

I have gained many enemies in a very short amount of time,
They come with slander and use of force.

They work together, often unknowingly, in an effort to kill me.

They need me to sit down and shut up.
Yet, they can't break me. No. Yet; they will fail. Not yet. No, not yet.

The more I travel this spiritual path, standing completely still, the more people drop out of the race. The more good men I see fall, the more hearts collapse in front of me- Some fall on the path with me-- I help them up and we work together on this terribly difficult and beautiful journey.

Some stumble and fall off the path, yet they were so close to the way! I reach for them and some reach back. We go on together...

Most wander so far from the road that when their heart gives out, I can't find a way to help them.

If I try, they hate me. They blame me for their fall and run farther away.

Sometimes I have considered going after them, but I can't. I won't fail because of them; I won't break because of them.

The path is so difficult, it's bumpy and full of ruts and hills. The path is winding.

My hope is that some way down the road in a big bend of the path, I will see them there, sitting on the path. They will be exhausted and weak, but they will be back on the path.

I will be stronger then. I will help them. We will walk this narrow street hand in hand.

Until then, I walk mile by inch and day by year.

Until then I will be hated by most

Until then I will be loved by a few- a very special and wonderful few.

Until then I will stay on the path.

Until then I'll walk tall and humble.

Praise God for the journey.

A Freestyle Song by Matthew Bailey

Take Heart

January 30th 2012

This week is dumb. Actually, soothing and stabbing is a better way to describe it. This is the week two years ago that my marital unraveling became public. On this day in 2010 I signed a 6-month lease on my apartment and started the awful task of separating nearly 14 years of life together. Superbowl Sunday 2010 was moving day. Most of the memories of the week are horrible to reflect on, but today I vividly remember that, somehow, I still had hope.

Also, this week in 2011, I went in front of the judge with the stack of thoughtfully, tearfully, lovingly, (expensively) crafted details of what life is supposed to look like, legally speaking, for us from now on. She signed them with barely a glance, hardly a question- ending 4 days, 4 months shy of 14 years of my life and identity. I was the first case that day. There would be no way to over-exaggerate the sadness of that morning. I went directly to work following court. I had a brand-new client, I needed to be professional, creative, witty, charming. There would be time for tears later. My first client that day was a godsend. Another example of a gracious, protective Father- who has been moving people in and out of my life, just in time, with just the right words. And I had hope.

This week in 2012 began with another end. This time, soothing, stabbing, awful, okay. I'm not ready to shout out loud, but maybe I can find the strength to whisper the words of the song in my head all day:

"So, take heart
Let His love lead us through the night
Hold on to hope
And take courage again
In death by love
The fallen world was overcome
He wears the scars of our freedom
In His Name
All our fears are swept away
He never fails

All our failure
And all our fear
God our love
He has overcome

All our heartache
And all our pain
God our healer
He has overcome."

(Lyrics for "Take Heart" by Joel Huston)

I'll get through this week just like I did last year, the year before, next year, one step in faith at a time. I haven't been consumed by this refining fire yet. God's love has not failed, has not given up, has not run out on me!

I still have hope.

"Finally, brothers, whatever is true, whatever things are noble, whatever is just, whatever is pure, whatever is lovely, whatever is commendable, if there is any virtue or anything praiseworthy, think about these things." (Philippians 4:8)

Broken
Collene James

I Feel Pain

I feel pain, but I see purpose.
I get tired yet I know it's worth it.
You asked me where I'm going, but I don't know yet.
I feel pain but I see purpose.

Not knowing where, it's just a gift.
I find my strength when I have to lift.
The weight of the world sits on my shoulders.
Mustard seed faith can move those boulders.

Sometimes I bleed, sometimes I hurt.
Dust to dust is dirt to dirt.
My soul longs now for an answer to why.
Sometimes I hurt, sometimes I cry.

Is victory as sweet if you've never been defeated?
Could the war have been won if you've never once retreated?
To fight the good fight, you take some hits.
To win the good fight, you never quit.

The enemy comes in many different ways,
He strikes at my heart he stabs with his blade,
Yet I stand strong with the One who is ALL!
Wearing His armor, I shall not fall.

A faithful and humble and lowly servant,
I've been given His grace though I don't deserve it,
I will do His will and I will follow Him through,
For He saved me, and He did not have to.

I feel pain, but I see purpose.
I get tired, yet I know it's worth it.
You asked me where I'm going, and I don't know yet.
I feel pain but I see purpose.

Matthew Bailey

Freedom Has a Feeling

February 5th 2012

Vacation started for me three days ago. About four hours before I had to be up to catch my flight, I received an email from an old 'friend.' For the last few days, my mind has not completely slipped into vacation mode as I have thought about how I would respond, if I cared to...

The email was long and stuffed full of "loving" (his words) condemnation, mostly regarding my divorce, from a man who considers himself to be a follower of Christ. The email was riddled with accusations, ignorance and arrogance, his words were intended to fearfully force me into humility, repentance, submission... The list is fascinating, and goes on and on... My initial response was shock and that familiar ole' emotional friend, Discouragement.

Then I reread it and couldn't help but laugh! I'm soooo thankful. I cannot believe that in three short months, these areas of my mind and heart have been changed and healed so completely. This life I am discovering is what freedom feels like!!! If I had gotten such an email in October, I think it would have completely devastated me. Now, I am very grateful to have gotten a glimpse back into the prison I just came out of. What a contrast to the grace, mercy, love, forgiveness, and peace I found in Jesus, once I stopped looking to 'His people' to tell me who He is and started asking Him, Himself.

So, I'm not going to waste my breath or your time with this guy's words, but I will share with you what I have learned in 90 days or so:

1. I am not expected to clean myself up for God. He does that, slowly, subtly, gracefully. I don't desire to be "clean" naturally. It's easier not to, let's be honest. He chose me, reached out to me, pursued me, won me- all while I was in this messy, broken place. His work is being done as an undercurrent, behind the scenes. I feel it. It's not me. I like it.

2. God does not expect me to do anything while withholding His love, until I complete the task. His love is constant. He wants what's best for me- according to His understanding, not mine. His best is not "back there" in my past, but up ahead- following His leading.

3. I am going to keep messing up. That's the fact of the matter. I will continue to desire to mess up less, probably, but I will keep being blind or stubborn or lazy or... human. I will use this fact as motivation to NEVER,

NEVER, EVER think of myself as God's little gate keeping, pit bull. I will, however, keep an answer ready, for the hope I have in Him- if you should ask.

I have no idea how my 'friend' can say "it is clear (I) have never..." when we haven't even spoken in years. That's okay. I know what's clear. I know where I stand. I know who I am. I know where I'm going... and I know Who's holding my hand.

Feels
Collene James
Beartooth Pass, Montana

The Nothing Season

February 25th 2012

"Pen sure" is the term the kids and I use when we do crosswords together. Now the words have been crisscrossing my mind over the last two weeks regarding a couple of situations. The best part about having a blog journal for me, is that it forces me to be "pen sure!" (I'll pause while you thank the good Lord that I'm not writing out EVERYTHING I think or feel...)

This morning, I'm pen sure, finally... As usual, before I write, there's a theme or a word that rolls around my head and heart. "Wait" continues to be the persistent nagging of the voice in my head. I hate that word. I'm not a "wait" kind of person. Thankfully, this heart dialysis I'm undergoing is gentle and the concepts are persistently, lovingly, continuing to be presented until they change me!

The old me was an impatient doer. If someone, anyone, needed it: I did it, found it, gave it, chased it... If I needed it- well now, that's just weakness, so never mind... I was not choosy about who I allowed in. My motto was "the more the merrier" and I would absolutely never ask for anything from anyone. (Yeah, I know, pride, pride, pride- I get it, now!) As you can imagine, the emotional, spiritual, and physical nutrients were completely depleted from the soil of my being.

So now, this process of restoration is well underway.

My writing, so far, has centered on the emotional and spiritual remodel. In this blog I've shared very little about the physical aspects of my "undoing." While the physical things I dealt with changed me forever in some ways, I have not written about it because, mostly, I'm feeling whole again. The processing of those things has already been done in my head; I think. Maybe one day it'll come up, but not today.

So now, I've been trying to come up with a way to describe this "wait" sense I have internally. The concept is applying to everything, as I think and process and mull and rethink and over-think the experiences I have had, both emotionally and spiritually in the last month. I've struggled with "wait," not because I'm feeling impatient, or desperate, or lonely or needy or unhealthy- but because it's exactly the opposite! I feel GREAT! I'm settled, sure, peaceful, relaxed, happy. I am starting to feel energy in just about every way again. Isn't it time to use it? Shouldn't I be putting myself back in the game?

Coach says, "no."

A friend used the word "fallow" the other day. It's too perfect! This is it. "Wait" makes sense with this word.

fal·low
adjective   /ˈfalō/
(of farmland) Plowed and harrowed but left unsown for a season in order to restore its fertility as part of a crop rotation or to avoid surplus production

Inactive

(of a sow) Not pregnant

verb   /ˈfalō/

Leave (land) fallow

I chose to give you both the adjective and verb versions of the word since I recognize that with a verb, I actually have the choice! I like a little control, let's be honest...

As I researched "fallow," I realized that this spring-headed-towards-summer season of my heart that I've been writing about, anticipating, participating in- is exactly when the Farmer would "fallow" me. Cool. My heart, which has never been at rest, is about to get more nutrients. Oh, and I'm not a sow, but I'm not pregnant either, so I left that part in there.

Ducky
Andrea Fugleberg

All I Need is a Cape and a Sidekick

February 27th 2012

I had one once- A sidekick that is, I still have a cape or two- even if they are just for cutting your hair. We'll call her Marie. I lost her before my divorce, which sucks because that's one super-hero kind of mission I could have used a sidekick like her for...

A few months ago, a friend and I were talking about relationships and the process of letting people 'in' to the deepest places of ourselves- exposing vulnerabilities, trusting completely. As we were talking, I realized that every now and then, you meet someone that you don't actually have to 'let' in. Somehow, there's an effortless connection that can't be explained. There's understanding and knowledge that comes without experience. I suppose this is where the term "soul mate" comes from. Marie was that kind of sidekick to me, so you'll understand when I tell you that this story is the deepest, most troublesome one I have yet to tell. In fact, I promised to never allow myself to lose someone like that again and just to be sure- I promised myself I wouldn't allow that kind of connection with anyone again either. (Silly me, I had forgotten that I didn't intentionally 'let' her in.)

I met Marie when I was 5. She was younger- kind of a crybaby actually. I didn't mind her in the beginning. Then it turns out, she was ALWAYS around. She really irritated me after a while, but I still sort of cared about other people making her cry. It annoyed me that she looked up to me so much. I obviously didn't have stuff figured out and I felt a lot of pressure to not mess up, in her eyes. Sometimes I would rescue her from her annoying (her words) little sister and take her to a fancy restaurant for dinner- especially for her birthday. I taught her about cloth napkins, boys, annoying little sisters (I have two to draw on for intel), the importance of listening to her parents, and other important information...

I moved away from that town the summer before she started high school. Then her parents moved her family 3,000 miles away. That was a rough year for her, so we talked a lot. That's the year I met the guy I married; she came back to be a part of my wedding.

Eventually, she moved back to Montana and lived with us to get a fresh start for herself. Over the years we did everything together. I was the cautious balance to her free-spirited nature.

I left her in Montana when we moved to Alaska, but not a single day went by that we didn't talk. Eventually, I'm not sure when, she stopped being

103

younger than me. She had life experience that I did not have. She had insight into people because of her experiences. She was deep, in many ways- wise, funny, fun, smart, incredibly generous, spontaneous, compassionate...

This story is the hardest to tell because I don't understand it. She's gone. It makes no sense why she chose to walk away. I cannot seem to completely process the grief. It's different than any other. It is the knife that turns every day in my heart. Sometimes, with something as simple as a glance at the clock, I nearly drown in a wave of heartache. I miss Marie.

All I can possibly get out of this story is this:

We all have a choice, every day. Sometimes we make the wrong choice. Sometimes those choices destroy the people that love us. That is all.

Sidekick
Collene James
Milwaukee Zoo- Milwaukee, WI

Summer
Collene James

Twin's World

There is a quiet world within my soul.
None can see it,
Most don't try.
None can hear
The silent cry.
Jesus knocks,
But does not pry.
He waits patiently
For the reply.

Scattered pieces lay within,
Remains of past abuse
And sin.
Years of pain
Lodged deep within.
I'll trust You, Jesus.
You must win.

There is a quiet world within my soul.
None can feel the peace
I know.
Jesus heals
Where none can go.
My heart is full
And joy can flow,
Here within the quiet world
Of my touched soul.

Nancy Bowser

Living the Good Life?

March 3rd 2012

"Duplicity." It's the word that won't escape me this week. As I put my key in the lock of my back door, during that silent moment between songs on my iPhone, as I shampoo the soggy color out of my client's hair... the word weaves its way through my week. I don't know why it's there. I haven't heard it used in a sentence in years, but now the voice in my mind has started providing them for me...

Here it is, so you don't have to look it up:

du·plic·i·ty (d-pls-t, dy-)
n. pl. du·plic·i·ties
1.a. Deliberate deceptiveness in behavior or speech.
  b. An instance of deliberate deceptiveness; double-dealing.
2. The quality or state of being twofold or double.

It's the word that describes what doesn't work in so many areas of my life lately. Really the second definition is the one I'm dealing with in my mind mostly- "deliberate deceptiveness" is too strong for most of my thoughts...

In the beginning of the week, the voice in my mind used the word to describe my romantic relationships. (My fallow heart was still kicking out, pulling up, the remaining weeds that had tried to stick around.)

"They wanted this but also, that... they were duplicitous."

I kept thinking.

"That can't work."

Then as the thoughts evolved, they got more personal.

"You say this, but sometimes do that Collene."

Ugh! Right to the core... but, it got me thinking. I am sick to death of being stuck somewhere in the middle of who I want to be and who I actually am.

Soooooo, timing being what it is in this process I'm in, the second part in the set of challenges I'm working through started this week. I should also add that I wasn't planning to actually DO my bookwork this week. I was busy and exhausted and furthermore, some health challenges sort of hit me like a brick this week...

Today, as often happens, my mind drifted to a few conversations I had with my friend Patricia Brown a few years back... They stick with me, mostly because they were deathbed conversations. Those conversations aren't about the weather, usually. She was a laugher. Before I met her, she had survived brain cancer. She seemed to be in the clear, health-wise, for a long time. She was vibrant, spunky, gorgeous, witty, wise, intelligent, grounded, humble.

The day she told us that there was another brain tumor, I remember thinking:

"Well good, another surgery, and life goes on. She's strong, healthy- a survivor."

It didn't turn out to be so simple. The tumor was located in a place that made surgery impossible. Oh, and it was the fastest growing kind.

It was confusing, because that diagnosis, and the resulting prognosis, didn't fit with her attitude. She was downright joyful. Excited even. Her words? "Oh, good! I get to see Dr. So-and-So at the treatment center again. I love him, and his staff..."

Ladies and gentlemen, we are not talking about a delusional woman. I told you she's intelligent, grounded...

As it turns out, Patricia was accepted into a research treatment program at UCLA. Every other week she and her husband would fly to L.A., from Anchorage, for exhausting, painful, slim-hope treatments.

Her outlook? "Well obviously, there's someone in L.A., or at an airport between here and there, that needs me to tell them about Jesus' love, grace, mercy, redemption power..."

I know that if you are not one of the extremely blessed humans that got to call this woman a friend, you cannot fathom the attitude I am trying to describe. I wouldn't believe it myself, if I hadn't seen it.

Oh, there were hard days... She had a few wigs; this is what she and I spent the most time laughing about. I was her wig tucker/straightener/fashion consultant in public. Not that she needed it, FASHIONABLE she was!

No woman wants to lose her hair. That was hard. It was hard when the tumor started pressing, causing facial disfigurement and partial paralysis. It was hard when she had to ask me, after checking her wig, if she was drooling. It was also hard that we, her friends, had to drive her everywhere during her husband's "slope weeks"- while he worked hundreds of miles away. It was hard for her, when she was no longer able to eat her meals alone and she had to rely on us to take turns feeding and medicating her.

We, of course, were completely blessed to be allowed to serve her this way.

It was hard when she no longer could master the stairs to her bedroom, and she had to have a hospital bed moved into her living room. It was hard when her family decided to call hospice... Still, until the very last day of her life, we visited. We laughed. We sang her favorite songs to her. We loved her. Even more remarkably, she loved us. She ever encouraged, taught, smiled, thanked, praised... Why???? Because, as she would say, "God is SOOOO faithful to me. He loves me."

She wasn't dying from cancer. She was LIVING with cancer. That woman lived until her last breath.

C.S. Lewis said, *"God cannot give us happiness and peace apart from Himself, because it is not there. There is no such thing."* James Bryan Smith said, *"God is not being stingy and withholding joy apart from (my) obedience; there simply is no joy apart from a life with and for God."* Patricia would have wholeheartedly agreed with both.

So then, if that is how to live, and die, with such grace and peace and JOY... I want it.

Duplicity.

It can't work.

So why do I still faithlessly, untrustingly, continually try it?

Make Me Like You

INTRO: Cm7 Bm7 Am7 Fm7

Cm7
I'll bow before Your Throne of Grace
   Bm7   Am7
I'll seek Your mercy and Your Face, Jesus.
                     Bm7   Cm7
I want to be like You, Jesus.   Make me like You.

Cm7
I give You my heart
 Fm7
I give You my mind
G6/C   Fm7   G6/C   Fm7
I give You my soul, spirit, body, my life... Lord Jesus.

      Cm7   Bm7
You're loving & kind, faithful & true.
    Am7   Bm7   Cm7
You're holy & righteous, please make me like You, Jesus.
                 Bm7   Cm7
I want to be like You, Jesus.   Make me like You.

I've heard it said that:

Cm7   Fm7
One must die that one can live
   G6/C   Fm7   G6/C   Fm7
And so You died that I could live, Live in You Jesus
   G6/C   Fm7   G6/C   Fm7
And now I'll die so You can live in me...Jesus

         C   C2   C   Fm7   C   C2   F2
Your Kingdom come on earth as it is in Heaven. Jesus.
   C   C2   Fm7   C C2 C F2
Your will be done on earth as it is in Heaven.

  Cm7   Bm7
I'll embrace Your love; Surrender to You

Am7   Bm7   Cm7
Fulfill my destiny; Draw close to You, Jesus

Bm7	Cm7

I want to be like You, Jesus.   Make me like You.

Cm7   Fm7   G6/C   Fm7
I've set my heart on You, Jesus; For You've, You've set Yours on me.
   G6/C   Fm7
You set me apart. In You I am free.
 G6/C   Fm7   G6/C   Fm7
I <u>be</u>long to You, You've given me keys. Lord Jesus.

Cm7   G6/C
Make me like You.

A Song of Nancy Bowser

Rooted
Collene James
Yellowstone County, MT

Psalm 88

Luc Bat

Never-ceasing anguish;
pain and sorrow languish. My soul
shrieks loudly, and my whole
life draws near to Sheol. The dead
are my allies. My bed
is made of darkness. Dread covers
me like a shroud—hovers
like jealousy when lovers spar.

Your wrath, it burns to char,
leaving a grotesque scar behind.
I can no longer find
friends whose hearts once entwined as one,
who once loved, but now shun—
they turn around and run in fear.

Every day, I draw near
and pray that you will hear my cries.
But once a sinner dies,
can one departed rise to praise
like in his former days?
Can deaf ears hear the phrase: "I save;
I raise life from the grave!"
And can mere darkness stave what's bright,
or the grip of death smite
his will? In morning light I cry,
"Lord, do not let me die!
Do not let my soul fly away!
Do not hide when I pray!"

From my very first day, the pale
rider's hooves did assail,
melting armor and mail to dross,
attempting to emboss
an emblem of my loss and shame.

Not even Death can tame
your wrath once its hot flame ignites!
Once the tempest incites
wild waters and excites the sea
with waves surround me.
You caused my friends to flee, to leave;
my soul, left to bereave,
but will gladly receive—anguish.

Vicki Joy Anderson

Repenting for Willful Sin

Father in Heaven, Judge overall- my Judge- I give my all to You. Humbly I ask for Your forgiveness for all my wrong doings. I have purposely and knowingly done deeds that I knew were wrong and I ask now for forgiveness of _____ (offending deeds, actions, or thoughts). In humility, I ask you for forgiveness for wanting to do _____ (deeds, actions, or thoughts.)

Jesus, please help me to deal with the lust and desire to participate in these deeds, actions, and thoughts. Please give me the right desires, deeds, actions, or thoughts, so that I might walk right before You. I need Your help changing my life. Thank You for hearing and acting upon my requests. I love You and I want to learn to obey all that You have said.

"Keep back thy servant also from presumptuous sins; let them not have dominion over me: then shall I be upright, and I shall be innocent from the great transgression." (Psalm 19:13)

"Repent ye therefore, and be converted, that your sins may be blotted out, when the times of refreshing shall come from the presence of the Lord;" (Acts 3:19)

Shawn Carter

Pray
Collene James
Pray, MT

Tough Man Surrenders

*This prayer was shared with me by a Navy Seal, who had come to me for some pastoral counseling. In our first moments together the combat veteran asked me, "Can I be real with God in prayer, because I have a lot of hard questions for Him? I don't want to be killed by God for disrespect, but I have a few things I need to say to Him." I told Him the following, "God knows your heart and He knows your pain. In **1 Peter 5:7** it tells us to 'cast our cares upon Him for He cares for us.'"*

Then I told the soldier to cast all his anger, pain, and cares unto God. He then proceeded to walk about 50 yards away from me, into the field, and started yelling. I saw the tough man rant and rave for about twenty minutes, then he fell to his knees, and his face hit the ground. He did not tell me all that he prayed, but here is what he did share:

God, I have hated You, I have talked bad about You. You left me in pain. Why did You take my son? Why have You not killed me?

The things You know I have done to anger You, yet I am still here.
How can I love You?

Please let my son know I love him. Why God the pain, I wanted to see my son grow up? (Silence for minutes)

Pastor said You gave Your Son. I would never give my son. (More silence)

I have stood in the darkness with no fear, yet I know I can't meet You, God, like this. If You're real I will be crushed.

Forgive me, for I have hated You. I don't know how to be good, so I surrender my soul now, save me from the hell in my heart.

"For with the heart man believeth unto righteousness; and with the mouth confession is made unto salvation. For the scripture saith, whosoever believeth on Him shall not be ashamed. For there is no difference between the Jew and the Greek: for the same Lord over all is rich unto all that call upon Him. For whosoever shall call upon the name of the Lord shall be saved." (Romans 10:10-13)

Shawn Carter

When Sleep Beats Me Up, I Obey

March 5th 2012

It was another one of those sleeps today, the kind that leaves me feeling less rested than when I laid down. It was worse than restlessness... This was the kind of vivid sleep battle that left me with my heart racing, body sweating, gut wrenching, soul crushed- with deep unexplainable sadness, emotional/spiritual turmoil. Not a nightmare, really. Not a dream either... and I had only had my eyes closed for 20 minutes.

The person in my sleep is not someone with whom I'm in contact anymore, which makes it all the more unsettling. The fact is this friend has been the subject of three others like it in the last several weeks. So, since I don't know what else to do to get my mind and heart to rest, I prayed again for my friend. Now I'll write:

"What is it you want?"

The question has haunted me for years. The friend in my dream today was wrestling with it too... I know what I don't want, but up to now, I have been unable to put into words what I DO want. I'm guessing that my inability to do so is somehow linked directly to pride (the bad kind). If you know anything about me, you know that I'm not weak minded. I'm not afraid to make a decision. I'm not afraid to "do." I just don't know how to ask for things I want or need.

Okay, so what I didn't tell you yesterday is that my week's challenge was to write a letter that starts like this:

"Dear God, the life I most want for myself is..."

Yeah, I wrote it. I feel a little silly (pride again?) sharing it, but you people are starting to know me as well as I do by now anyway...

Dear God,

The life I want most for myself is... to be a stable, capable mother. I want to be deeply connected with all three of my kids- for life. I want to be able to teach them the tools for honest living in this mad world. I want to be better at providing for them financially, emotionally, spiritually.

I want graciousness and love to be my instinct. I want to be humble enough to accept love and help. I want to live honestly and without duplicity. I want to live like my friend Patricia- with thanksgiving on my tongue. I want to be wise- discerning of character and situations. I want to be faithful, a servant. I want to sing again.

I want to have relationships started, mended, restored, reshaped, made stronger...

I want to continue to enjoy my job- being with people all day, encouraging them through words, touch, and beauty; being encouraged by them.

(I also want pretty shoes that I can stand in all day, maybe You could work that out either with my feet or the shoe people...)

I want to be deeply cherished, protected, part of a team, respected, trusted, loved passionately- chosen above all. More than that, I want to find someone to partner with that is worthy of my trust, respect, passion, and family.

I want to forgive myself for my failures, to expect less perfection...

...to do justice, to love mercy, to walk humbly with You.

Sincerely,

Collene
(The one that You love)

One of 100
Collene James
Monument Valley, AZ

Darkness Within

Father in Heaven,

I stand before You, asking for Your help.

I have confessed all that I know to You.

Yet, Lord I am asking You to search my mind, desires, and thoughts for any dark and wicked thing that continues to offend You as my King and Creator.

Shine Your light on those things and show me exactly what You see that I may repent and turn away from them.

I don't want any sin between You and me. In Jesus Name I ask this. Amen

"Search me, O God, and know my heart: try me, and know my thoughts: 24 And see if there be any wicked way in me and lead me in the way everlasting." (Psalm 139:23)

Shawn Carter

Overwhelmed
Collene James

118

Clouds

The hour was early, the beginning of dawn.
Daybreak would come; it wouldn't be long.
Dark puffy clouds in the sky could be seen.
It was then that I noticed a red in the east.

The vision changed quickly in front of my eyes
As the red seemed to spread and covered the skies.
Dark clouds became brilliant, and then changed again,
As the color receded and morning began.

Though the sun was not seen, it was plainly the source;
And I heard a voice speaking; Jesus of course.
"The color belongs to the sun, not the clouds.
But the clouds reflect glory, and in it they shout."

"Your life has its clouds that seem dark and so gray,
But the Son has His plans to lighten the way.
It's the trials and sorrows that loom up above,
The storms in your life that reflect beauty and love."

(Adapted from *"Jesus Said, When the Coffee's Gone"* by Nancy Bowser)

Nancy Bowser

Psalm 103:15-18
Collene James
Bear Lake, UT

"The life of mortals is like grass, they flourish like a flower of the field; the wind blows over it and it is gone, and its place remembers it no more. But from everlasting to everlasting the Lord's love is with those who fear Him, and His righteousness with their children's children— with those who keep His covenant and remember to obey His precepts." (Psalm 103:15-18)

Isaiah 43
Collene James
Southern Arizona

"Remember not the former things, neither consider the things of old. Behold, I will do a new thing; now it shall spring forth; shall you not know it? I will even make a way in the wilderness, and rivers in the desert." (Isaiah 43:18-19)

Play Time is Right-eous?

March 10th 2012

My Grandma Joyce, who passed away several years ago, told me when I was thirteen or fourteen years old:

"Collene, make sure you laugh- A LOT. When you are old, your wrinkles will not lie about the kind of life you had. If you laugh, you will look happy when you're wrinkled."

She had a cute, bubbly, infectious laugh. Her face even rested in a half smile.

I'm sure that I did not laugh as much in my previous 34.25 years, as I did in the last 6 months.

That being said, I will say that since the divorce, these questions have plagued me:

"What do YOU like to do Collene? Who ARE you when you're not a mom or business owner? What are your hobbies? What do you do for fun when the kids aren't around?"

Fun? Uhhhhhhhhhhhhhhhhhhhhhhh, can I get a definition? Can you repeat the word? How about using it in a sentence?

Last summer I started remembering how to play. It was uncomfortable at first. I was a bit anxious. I had a nagging feeling that I was forgetting something BIG. I felt a little insecure putting aside my stress, planning, and organization... How do you just "let go" and smile when life is falling apart around you?

I'll tell you how it started, actually:

I was getting ready to buy a house and was supposed to close July 15th. Prior to the closing, I had about six weeks of wait time. The loan was complicated, somewhat, requiring more prep time for the lender than usual. Then, my loan got audited, which complicated it further. To make things more interesting, I had to be out of my rental home two weeks prior to closing. Everything had to be moved to storage and I was homeless- for AT LEAST two weeks. As a mom, I was most definitely not allowing myself to exhale, much less dream about paint colors...

My friend, the one you're starting to know well, who knocks me around when I need it, essentially told me that I was sucking the fun out of everything.

She said "You are always waiting for the worst, and never enjoying the now! This is FUN, we should be dreaming about how you'll decorate. Instead, you're so certain it won't happen you aren't having any fun. Besides, you get to live with ME for at least two weeks!" (Did I ever mention that I have incredibly gracious, generous friends?)

Soooooo, late one night she made me go for a walk to the park down the street. Then she invited me to swing with her on the playground. Do you remember the feeling of going so high on a swing that you float for a second on the return, before the chains catch you again? I had forgotten. Then, as we were swinging and talking and laughing, the park sprinklers came on, surrounding us in a bevy of sprinklers! I felt like I was about nine again...

Later during my stay with her, she forced me to try a boxing class with her, way too early in the morning... However, there's something about punching stuff really fast that makes this girl grin...

I closed on the house, on time. Simultaneously, I started trying other new things as well as stuff I had let fall by the wayside when I became a wife and mother. I found my grin. I heard my giggle again. I even, literally, danced in the street! Play became more than a one- or two-hour event- I spent whole weekends, then even a week, dare I say it: a whole month, "letting go."

...but, it seems, I've done it again. For nearly two weeks, I have slipped back into the all-too-serious business of adulthood. I've started feeling old again too. My head is again full of worry. My brow tense with those secret fears (creating lines my grandmother would disapprove of). My joints are even aching as I struggle with sleep and restlessness. Again. The weight of the world has never felt more squarely placed on my shoulders. I'm beyond irritated, at myself, to be feeling this way- especially since "feelings" are so stupid. It's okay, though, because at least it's familiar territory, right?

NO!

My biggest fear throughout this life transition has been forgetting what I'm supposed to be learning, having to endure the painful relearning. So, what is it that's slipping?

"I'm supposed to be His daughter, His princess"... was the thought on my mind while I cleaned all day today. Thoughts about God as a loving Father flickered again...

It's trust again, that's lacking. "Is God still in control?" I again find myself asking. My friend's response still comforts: "...trust Him...you just have to get past yourself first." This week I'm forgetting what I learned, God help me with my unbelief.

Children trust. They live in dependence. They do not need to be in control. They are carefree. They play! This is right, the way it should be...

Faith Like a Child
Collene James

The Refresher
Collene James

"...David would take a harp and play it with his hand. Then Saul would become refreshed and well, and the distressing spirit would depart from him." (1 Samuel 16:23b)

Swimming Hole
Collene James
Lizard Lake, CO

Guilty

March 13th 2012

I told you several weeks ago that I didn't completely finish my first set of challenges. The love and wrath sections had me hung up in just about every way. My understanding of those concepts is being completely turned upside down.

Love as I understood it 15 years ago, 5 years ago, 5 months ago, was... well, a misunderstanding. "Wrath," it seems now, has been corrupted in my mind too... I have been skillfully avoiding writing about it, mostly because I don't fully have a firm grasp on the new "wrath" concept yet. So, like everything else in this process, there's been a gentle, persistent, undercurrent of pursuit in my soul and a flickering word over these weeks.

It occurred to me tonight: I get a firmer grasp WHEN I write, which is the whole point of this blog. (Duh, keep up Collene!) So, bear with me, while I prove to you that I know nothing, because I REALLY want to be changed by "love" and "wrath"...

The flickering word is "GUILT." Even in print it's a completely aesthetically displeasing word. When you grow up with an over-abundance of rules, and you have perfectionist tendencies- like I do... and you have no problem creating more rules- you tend to always feel guilty about everything. On paper, I can see it is nonsense, really. I can remember as a kid feeling guilty when a teacher or parent simply asked, "who did_____?" I felt this way whether there was trouble coming, or not or whether I was even involved, or not. I had the same feeling when a police officer would pass me, whether I was speeding, or not. (Back then I usually wasn't speeding, but I've managed to get over myself in that way.)

As an adult, guilt has been the undercurrent of my life in other ways. Add to that "desire" ... either I do desire the "wrong" things, or I don't desire the "right" things.

Uggh, what a prison. What about this "freedom we have in Christ" I keep hearing people sling around. Whatever, bumper-sticker!! This is miserable. God hates this, God hates that. Clearly God hates me because I LOVE that. So, you see where I'm coming from with this "wrath" topic right?

I'm already hopelessly a loser. Guilty. Condemned. Deserving of WRATH.

It's probably not necessary to define the word as I've always understood it, because I'm willing to bet the majority of the world understands it the way

I always did. But I'm going to, because it's my blog journal and I need to, for me, not because I think you're simple-minded. "Wrath" to me meant extreme anger, rage, fury, passionate distaste, emotional punishment-often irrational.

Maybe it's the English language that lacks. There are five words for "love" in the ancient Greek language. Is it so far, a stretch of the imagination that our use of the one word "wrath" in translating as it pertains to God is also lacking depth? It hadn't occurred to me before, but I'm listening...

I'm not asserting that we should "tweak" stuff in the Bible to make it fit our ridiculousness. I'm just struggling with the disconnect between what I've understood to be true and what actually works out in the testing of real life. So, I'm finding myself open to new thought patterns.

J.B. Smith says: *"Love is the desire for the well-being of another, so much so, that personal sacrifice would not stand in the way. It is not that God's love for us is dispassionate...it is just not an emotion that waxes and wanes... In the same way that God's love is not a silly, sappy feeling but rather a consistent desire for the good of His people, so also the wrath of God is not a crazed rage, but rather a consistent opposition to sin and evil... it is a mindful, objective response. It is actually an act of love. God is not indecisive when it comes to evil. God is fiercely and forcefully opposed to the things that destroy His precious people..."*

The guy goes on to use MADD as an example of that kind of "wrath." Mothers Against Drunk Driving is a group that fiercely opposed to people hurting themselves and other people...

Okay, it's starting to sink in. Guilt is not God's tool, it's the other guy's... In fact, some of the "wrong" things I desire can be good. As my Father who loves me, He wants me to have it all! He just doesn't want me to have any of those things in a way that will hurt me or others, or keep me from coming to Him as my Daddy.

It also occurs to me that this version of the word is necessary for true justice, which I love. Ultimately, I wouldn't respect a god who was emotionally unstable, indifferent, or played a partiality game when it comes to moral evil.

Okie doke, firehose thoughts tonight, right? I need sleep. But first, can I just say: I love you people and my grasp on these things just got firmer!

Weathered
Collene James
Front Range Mountains, CO

Sunset Just Brings Darkness

March 21ˢᵗ 2012

Solar Flares. That's what I'd like to blame it on. It has actually kind of become a joke between a few of my friends and me. While there may be some validity to the idea that magnetic storms on the sun have an emotional and physical effect on animals and people, this is not that.

I spent some time tonight in my spot, on my table by Lake Josephine at Riverfront Park. I've been craving solitude today, which is unusual for a people-person like me. I have to get to a place of understanding on this thing I can't figure out in my head. Avoidance isn't working. Neither is sleep. Over-analyzing is not my friend. I was hoping that the peacefulness of the park would bring peace to my heart. I brought my journal, hoping to write until I saw the answer. I didn't. So now, I'm reviewing my journal entry and giving it a second shot...

I pulled into the lot just before the sun dipped below the trees. The air is still a bit chilly, the day gray. Yesterday, allegedly the last day of winter, it snowed- slushy and heavy and somewhat deep. That's melted today. The calendar says it is spring now, but with the chill in the air, the park is disagreeing. The sun is casting long shadows now as I sit on the corner of my table. Ducks are breaking the stillness of the water as they make their way to shore. Behind me there is a parked car with two young people kissing. I don't want to see that. Not today. I return to my car and drive a bit further.

This is where my first exercise in solitude took place. That tree is starting to get buds on it. New growth. Hope.

Funny though, a few of the leaves that I saw last fall are still clinging to the branches. Something in me still feels like them. Did they spend the winter afraid to trust the winds? Huh. Yeah, I completely get it: new growth and hope, still with distrust...

My heart is sad today. It's been a rough month. I figured I'd be farther along in the "caring less" about certain things plan by now. It seems I care more. I feel foolish. Too foolish to even spell it out for you. It's okay though, because this process is for me and I'll look back on this and remember who, what, where, when... it's the WHY I can't work to some sort of understanding.

The presumed futility of asking "why?" has still never stopped me from asking. When I was a kid, I HATED the "because I said so" response. I loathe "that's just the way it is."

Why?

I can't learn, change, or grow unless I understand. Is it protection? Discipline? Laziness of the one in authority? As a parent I've said no for all three reasons... God is not lazy. God is good and gracious and loving by nature...so, what am I missing? Still there is silence. The silence leaves room for the guilt. I messed it up. I know, because I have this hindsight vision thing that accuses and points out a million things I should have said and done differently.

The sun is mostly set now. The ducks and geese are teaming up in couples to take care of their spring families. That's nice.

The colors are perfect in the sky. I snap some more pictures, still looking for something that gives my heart peace. This still doesn't add up. The pieces don't fit. I have no idea how to walk away from what I feel, what I know. Try as I might, I cannot kick it, push it, redefine it, loathe it, smash it to pieces... It seems that God hasn't released me from it either. It turns out I suck at trusting still. I stayed until dark. 'They' say faith is blind, right? Yeah, well faith has been just plain uncomfortable this month; I don't like not seeing the answers.

As I'm re-reading my heart on paper, I'm starting to think that I need to stop being frustrated at God for other people's choices. I need to be slower to make excuses for people, to hold them directly accountable, when those choices hurt me. Forgiveness with accountability.

I can't wait for sunrise.

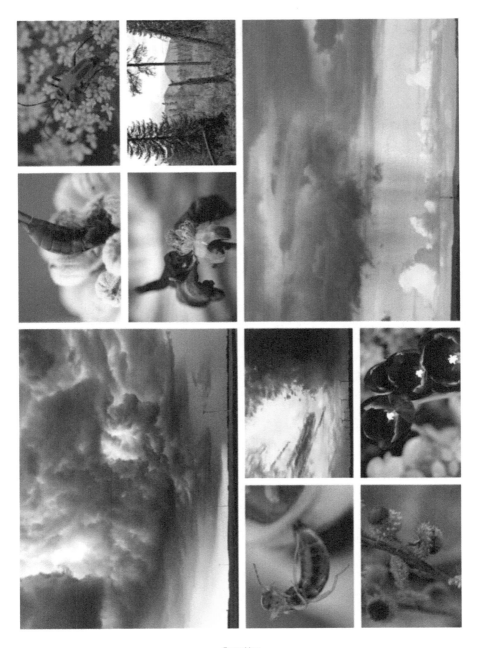

Fear Not
Collene James

"Fear not, for I am with you; Be not dismayed, for I am your God. I will strengthen you, Yes, I will help you, I will uphold you with My righteous right hand." (Isaiah 41:10)

132

Breakthrough
Collene James
Denali, Mount McKinley from Flat Top Mountain
Anchorage, AK

Listen

G   C
1.   There are days when darkness overcomes the sun;
      G   C
      The doubts increase and all I want to do is run.
                  G   C   G   C
      I cry, Jesus. Jesus. I cry, Jesus.

                        G   C
Chorus: All I have to do is call on You today;
             G   C
             I choose to yield to You, and trust You with my way;
                      G   C   G
             And just listen. I'll listen and obey. I'll listen.
                      C   Am7
             You're never far away.

                    D
2.   The truth's revealed and I see the light;
            C   Am7
      Your arms are open and your plans are bright.
      G   C   G   C
      Jesus. Jesus. Jesus.

                        D
Bridge: The love You give, it's changing me;
                  C   Am7
             The life You give is flowing free;
                  D
             I have Your mind; You're in me;
                  C   Am7
             You have my life and I've been set free
                  G   C   G   C
             To follow. Follow where You lead. Follow.

      G   C
3.   You are sovereign God and Lord over all;
      G   C
      You're my master and I'm listening for Your call;
            G   C   G   C
      So lead on. I'll follow where You lead. Lead on. Lead on.....

END: I'll follow where You lead me;
       So lead on..... I will listen.

A Song of Nancy Bowser

Murder of the Facade

April 12th 2012

Tonight's insomniac mental movie brought to you by the US Navy, NASA, and me. Prepare yourself, I have a jam-packed little mind... Although I've been wrestling with a blog/journal topic for weeks, I didn't imagine it coming together like this, and it still might not. Let's see if I make any sense, shall we?

Dad was a military man- a Naval pilot, briefly. He separated from the Navy before I was born, but he told us a couple of stories. For my whole life, he displayed a little orange and white model airplane on a bookshelf or his desk. Somewhere along the way I learned that it was a model of the training plane he had learned to fly in. The fact that his instructor had also crashed in that plane, with Dad on board, seemed like an insignificant fact to my young mind. No need to take note, he's safe now and not flying, so I barely gave that any thought as a child. Tonight, as soon as I closed my eyes, the image of the field and crashed plane as I had imagined it as a child, was front and center...

Dad was, apparently, unique as far as pilots are concerned. He loved to fly. His body did not. He never seemed to go up without, what had gone down, coming back up as well... As a result of his, um... gifts and abilities where airsickness is concerned, he was selected to spend roughly six months being tested and studied at NASA. Delicious, I know, but bear with me. These thoughts tonight tie into the topics already weighing my mind...

I first acknowledged them last fall, just before I started writing this blog journal. Back then it was subtle, a flirting idea- with two alternating flickering questions barely holding my attention, really...

Recently, I spent some time visiting some friends out of state. I'm not sure I've met a more perfect couple. Maybe I'm intrigued by them more than most other couples I know because both have personalities similar to my own. As a couple they challenge each other, they effortlessly understand each other (for better or worse), they have the same sense of humor, they are both motivated, hard-working, passionate, intelligent people. He's type A, a military guy- Special Forces stuff... and she's the PERFECT self-sufficient, supportive wife for that kind of man. Individually, they possess incredible strength and depth; as a couple, well in my mind, the term "Power Couple" applies. Together, they are deeply and intimately known. Okay, so they're not perfect and neither is their marriage, but they are perfect for each other. I would have been suspicious of the validity of that kind of chemistry and connection as an onlooker, had I not briefly stumbled upon something similar once, a million years ago.

As usually happens when we all get together, a few other people showed up at the house, creating somewhat of an adult slumber party, complete with a movie and pizza. Eventually the lights went out, but the other couch surfer and I kept talking. This one was the same caliber of guy as our friend. I am intrigued by, and in some ways can identify with, what makes these people tick: they are never satisfied, never good enough, never finished with the job, their questions are never completely answered.

We talked for a while and quite honestly, I don't recall exactly how we got around to it, but I do remember the statement he made:

"Well, Collene, no one REALLY wants to be known."

What?!! That perspective had never occurred to me. Insert one of those alternating, flickering questions I've been wrestling with, increasingly, over the past few months:

"Does anyone really know me?"

I hear my voice telling this stranger in the dark, out loud and maybe somewhat aggressively, "I want to be known fully, then accepted completely. I crave it. Not by everyone, but by the people that matter."

All I can think about since that conversation is that I'm so sick of having my guard up, constantly presenting the "best of me" to everyone. It's mind numbingly exhausting. I'm eager to murder the facade.

Now, married in my mind with question number one, is the second... Earlier this week, I further confirmed: I'm "that" girl. A dumb, emotional, ridiculous, embarrassing girl. These emotions are so uncomfortable for a girl like me, who's never been comfortable with 'girly-girl' ways. Sometimes, the unresolved conflicts and destroyed relationships in my life weigh on my heart and nearly succeed in drowning me with grief. In my mind a couple of them are worth redeeming, but I am powerless to resolve the mess on my own.

The other flickering question resurfaces: "What makes these people I have loved so deeply, been so open with, walk away so effortlessly... one after the other?"

My assumption has been that once they really started to know me, they opted out.

I called my dad. He knows me, right? I'm hoping to hear something encouraging.

Nope.

Just more misunderstandings... stress, anger, hurt... dumb girl.

Oh, and words. I said words to him that I used to never use at all, but now they seem to apply to situations more often than not. He was less than proud. To him it was completely unacceptable. Even more so now, I feel incredibly unknown, not accepted. I care, but I don't have the energy to fight for it anymore. I lack the ability to pretend in any aspect of my life anymore. I know I'm not a complete treasure. I've got all kinds of ugly and nonsense to sort in me... I worry that there will be more loss.

Dad called me the next day to reassure me that he loves me. Unconditionally. I believe him, for now, but I still feel misunderstood at a fundamental level- altogether, unknown.

Utterly alone.

Sooooo, while I'm laying here replaying the grainy childhood mental image of my dad's Navy/NASA days, it occurs to me: I don't know him that well either. Does he want to be known? Our experiences shape us, I imagine those days for him were incredibly shaping. Just maybe, these people that so effortlessly walked away weren't doing so because they were getting to know me, but rather, I was getting to know them.

Whatever. It may not matter, but now I believe I'll sleep.

Come Out of Her, My People
Collene James
New York, Seattle, Jacksonville- USA

Destruction of the Gods
Collene James
Corinth, Athens, Oia, Sounion- Greece, Ephesus- Turkey

Unseen

And.
Belief,
it is the substance
of what is expected –
the proof of what is unseen.

Enoch was taken to You
because he pleased You.
His belief pleased You –
I want to please You.

Without belief it
is impossible.

If I come to You
Most High,
I have to have belief
that You are,
that You are
The Redeemer,
The Rewarder.
And to.
And for
those who believe,
who earnestly seek You –
for You are.

And.
Belief,
it is the substance
of what is expected –
the proof of what is unseen.

By it I want to inherit
the righteousness
to please You.

Call me out, oh Elohim.
Call me out
to a place,
to the place of
my inheritance –
to the land of promise.

I long for a better place.
The place
I look to with expectation,
to the place of gold foundation –
the city built upon
a Rock.
The city unseen.

And so.
Belief,
it is the substance
of what is expected –
the proof of what is unseen.

Hebrews 11
Ashley Fugleberg

Turning Corners

April 16th 2012

"He is jealous for me, loves like a hurricane. I am a tree bending beneath His wind and mercy...and heaven meets earth like an unforeseen kiss. And my heart turns violently inside of my chest. I don't have time to maintain these regrets..."

There are no less than 35 directions I've thought about taking this blog today. Words are going to fail me tonight; I know this because I am already stammering in my mind. I am freakin' excited! *"My heart turns violently inside of my chest"* are the only words that feel applicable and I'm not sure I can even explain why. Except this:

Today was a new day.

Do you ever wake up and just know, you've turned a corner? I've been living in a maze of sorts I think, because this is the third corner I've been around in twice as many months. The view is no less exciting the third time...

I was up late. Or early really, grabbing breakfast with five new friends at Denny's. Very cool people, really. Although the company was great, the location was really what got me thinking. Denny's was the location of my first date after my divorce. Classy, right? Um, well, about as classy as the guy.

That date was 11 months ago. It was a 5:00 a.m. coffee date since we were supposed to be meeting up with one of his friends to build beds for his garden and plant stuff later that morning. I figured that was a safe time of day for a respectable date. Nope. It turns out the time of day doesn't matter. I've told the entire date story a few times, however since I'm already getting off topic, I will save the excruciating details for chapter one of my first "how-not-to" book. There is no doubt that there is a "man-wound" in me that must get addressed. When is God going to intervene and raise up and restore to the world His kind of men?

Anywhoooo, I woke up way too early this morning for a girl who doesn't ever sleep and has no motherly responsibilities for the day. I could not help but feel heavy-hearted. What is the point? What am I doing with this life? Images of moments and people of the last year flicker in my memory. The feeling that I'm waiting for life to restart takes over, yet again. I've got one shot and I know it, but weeks and months have turned into a year... and more. I'm still passively waiting- for what exactly? I don't have a clue, but as I pour my coffee, I know that TODAY things have to change.

I haven't been to church in a month; I decided to go. At least I won't be alone with myself here...

Here's where the words are failing me. The topic today was on leadership and was directed specifically at the men. This fact, alone, caused an emotional reaction in me that I was unprepared for. Meanwhile, my already heavy heart was soothed in a way I cannot explain. Through the river of tears and snot that poured off my face I wrote these notes:

"The eyes of the LORD search the whole earth in order to strengthen those whose hearts are fully committed to him..." (2 Chronicles 16:9)

"Look carefully then how you walk, not as unwise but as wise, making the best use of the time, because the days are evil. Therefore, do not be foolish, but understand what the will of the Lord is." (Ephesians 5:15-16)

"But if serving the LORD seems undesirable to you, then choose for yourselves this day whom you will serve... But as for me and my household, we will serve the Lord." (Joshua 24:15)

A firehose of soothing, confirming, hopeful words... Then, the MOST encouraging thing: The men were challenged to be leaders, at church, but more importantly and dear to my heart, at home.

Aggggh, amazing. Someone, a man no-less, is speaking out to a group of males the words that are the very cry of my own heart!

I can't describe the atmosphere in the room this morning, but I know this: God is going to answer my heart's cry and I get to watch; even more importantly, so will my boys. I think I'll keep going.

Meanwhile, the roaming words "Integrity" and "Faithfulness" are not accidental in the timing of their placement in my mind. I plan to continue trudging along, picking up the pieces and moving through this mental maze, resolutely turning as many corners as it takes... I don't have time to maintain these regrets.

Full Steam Ahead
Matthew Bailey

Thrive

April 25th 2012

Words bubbling up in my head and heart have not found their sentences yet. Still, I feel like I need to put something on "paper." This week I must remember that God- that silent, urgent, persistent, pursuer- moved here, is still unwrapping this gift for ME...

An urge, turned into action, sparking reciprocation, breaking a dam that had restrained love, forgiveness, understanding and grace. Now, like a river it moves, getting stronger by the hour, engulfing me and not a moment too soon. Forgiveness. Restoration?

I already told you about Marie and her leaving, but now together with my cape and my sidekick, we will face twenty years lost. Pain beyond belief, flooding further than I had imagined. Healing comes? Death at the door. These emotions are too much, crushing individually, but together they are weaving a tapestry of hope and peace. It cannot be denied: This is bigger than me, than us.

He is here. He makes all things new.

The song in my head today, *"Thrive"* by Switchfoot. I couldn't have said it better myself:

"Been fighting things that I can't see in
Like voices coming from the inside of me and
Like doing things I find hard to believe in
Am I myself or am I dreaming?

I've been awake for an hour or so
Checking for a pulse but I just don't know
Am I a man when I feel like a ghost?
The stranger in the mirror is wearing my clothes

No, I'm not alright
I know that I'm not right
A steering wheel don't mean you can drive
A warm body don't mean I'm alive
No, I'm not alright
I know that I'm not right
Feels like I travel but I never arrive

I want to thrive not just survive
I come alive when I hear you singing
But lately I haven't been hearing a thing and
I get the feeling that I'm in between
A machine and a man who only looks like me

I try and hide it and not let it show
But deep down inside me I just don't know
Am I a man when I feel like a hoax?
The stranger in the mirror is wearing my clothes

I'm always close but I'm never enough
I'm always in line but I'm never in love
I get so down but I won't give up
I get slowed down, but I won't give up
I want to thrive not just survive"

Thriving in Dry Places
Collene James
Somewhere, AZ

146

Surprise!

May 14th 2012

Take six. The previous five attempts at writing my heart out here have failed. I'm bursting with news and growth and am increasingly frustrated to be unable to give it all words... This morning, I thought I was grasping it, but it got muddy again this afternoon. It wasn't until I was able to verbalize some of these thoughts with my rock-solid dad tonight, that I had the encouragement I needed to try again:

The song continually leaving my lips today is *"Amazing Grace (My Chains Are Gone)"* by Chris Tomlin. This song, specifically, brings me back in my memories to three or four years ago- the beginning of this process of destruction-for-the-sake-of-restoration. In fact, "restoration" is the flickering word that has become part of my, recently non-existent, but now intensifying prayer life. The song of the day fits perfectly with the mental topic of the week and seems to be hand chosen, by Someone, for the verse I found earlier in the week:

"In my anguish I cried to the LORD, and He answered by setting me free." (Psalm 118:5)

Some acts are unforgivable, right? Yup. And that's where I've been living for a while now. I've spent years coping with pain by rewriting history in my head, avoiding certain thoughts, people, places, things- shoe shopping instead.

Aside from the shoe collection, I had always felt that I've maintained a fairly healthy life, despite myself. Since I've been thrown head-long into the restoration phase, it's become apparent to me that this 'coping' has really done nothing positive for me. In fact, the injuries I have ignored have been incredibly destructive to me and have played a huge role in the ridiculous narratives I've bought into for so long. Now, I personally feel like shouting from the proverbial mountain top, all that I know and remember. However, this mentally revised-to-the-truth history is not my story alone to tell, so I'll continue to remain vague here. I think the truth of the matter will remain no less clear...

It never ceases to amaze me when conversations and little moments that are completely unrelated, string together behind the scenes to become strong enough to be a theme. In 32 days between April 1st and May 2, my feet touched the soil of 11 of these United States. As a result, because I'm a teeny bit social and a lota bit chatty, I've had my share of incredibly insightful, and seemingly completely unrelated, conversations over the last month. They all have been instrumental in bringing me to this place, on the corner of my couch, in the finally calming swirl of my mind tonight.

During that month of gallivanting, my 35th birthday happened. Because I have, somehow, fooled a LARGE number of people into being my friend, the well wishes, flowers, cards, meals, surprises and gifts continue to pour in... I am completely delighted, yet in awe of this phenomenon. I have literally NEVER experienced such an outpouring of love, and I cannot say I'm disappointed!

The actual day of my birthday was awful and wonderful all at once. The day was spent assisting in the planning of and preparing for a funeral, actually. Because those emotions are unprocessed and don't seem socially acceptable for public consumption, let's move on...

That day also brought connections with a friend as well as a family member I've been REALLY missing... Along with those connections, came the realization that forgiveness is completely possible, even in some of the most unforgivable situations. Because the fingers of forgiveness are far reaching in every direction of my life, I will have to take the time to contemplate and then explain all of that some other time.

Okay, so all these little birthday gifts and surprises have reinforced the fact:

I LOVE surprises!!

Also, during this month, a sweet friend of mine is preparing a REALLY big surprise to give her husband for their wedding anniversary in August. I'm her assistant/cheerleader. She's BAD at surprises. In fact, she's been giving him hints already and we're only in May. All of this ties into one of this week's little spiritual revelations...

I started thinking about how frustrating it was for me, as a child, when birthday or Christmas surprises got ruined. I NEVER wanted to know what was coming and even resented those who couldn't keep their mouth shut.

I realized this week that, for a long time, I have been trying to control and anticipate, by guessing ahead, what God is up to and why He's allowing certain situations.

It separately struck me the other day also that, more often than not, I do actually trust God in this process of putting me back together. I've decided it's time for me to quit trying to figure out the surprises awaiting at the end of this journey. Additionally, it seems urgent that I grasp the understanding that simply 'coping' is ripping me off. Instead, I desperately need to get over myself, and lean into my heavenly Father, in faith, emotionally, not just intellectually. I will hover in the discomfort of whatever it is I'm feeling whether positive or negative, and allow the emotions to just be present until there is closure, reconciliation, understanding... I am going to go ahead and let the Master Giver take His time and plan my surprise, His way and in His time.

The specific lyrics I cannot seem to listen to enough are:

"My chains are gone
I've been set free
My God, my Savior has ransomed me
And like a flood His mercy rains
Unending love, amazing grace"

I AM FREE.

Help
Matthew Bailey

Returning to Egypt

May 19th 2012

Some days you just know what you know, even when the visible evidence appears to be contradictory to what you know. This week was full of those days! ***"Now faith is the substance of things hoped for, the evidence of things not seen,"*** from ***Hebrews 11:1***, is the roaming sentence of the week- which has made "faith" and "hope" the flickering words of the week...

I recognize, even as I type, how churchy this blog journal entry is starting out. Bear with me, because although it is, it's no less genuine. Some stuff is getting really real in me now as things I've always known in my head, make the long, arduous journey the full 12 inches to my heart...

Being a hater of churchy bumper-stickers like I am, I've recently been repulsed by the five-letter recipe that makes up the word F-A-I-T-H. People sling the word around in every situation, mostly (in my mind, at least) referring to some mystical, unicorn riding, fairy loving La-la Land dweller.

"Just have faith, Collene, everything will be great."

"Life is beautiful, if you just have faith."

Nonsense.

Life is messy and ugly mixed with moments of beauty and pleasure, for EVERYONE. The faith-full do not get a free pass. Furthermore, faith for faith's sake is stupid, empty, a waste of time and breath. Faith in WHAT is my problem and deepest question. The "promises" that I always thought were true, didn't work out so well for me, even with a fairy-dusting of "faith."

So, since I'm still thinking, pretty much daily, about these false internal narratives that started this whole blog thing, I've been re-reading my earliest writings. It turns out "faith" was a roaming word in November too, with my new friend "trust."

As a side note: HOW COOL IS THIS? I am a whole different girl than I was in November!! Yay, but I'm still working it out....so back to the "F" word...

Okay, so I Googled the Hebrews verse and decided to read the whole chapter. There's obviously lots of stuff there. It's a wealth of information about people in history who had faith...I'll get back to this, because what I did next was Google the word "hope." The first link brought me to some excerpts of something C.S. Lewis wrote about "Hope," "Desire," and "Longing." The guy is deep and I'm a hairstylist, not a philosopher, so I've left the tab open all week to read and re-read what he wrote. The thing that sticks in my head is:

"Most people, if they had really learned to look into their own hearts, would know that they do want, and want acutely, something that cannot be had in this world. There are all sorts of things in this world that offer to give it to you, but they never quite keep their promise.

The Christian says, 'Creatures are not born with desires unless satisfaction for those desires exists.' A baby feels hunger: well, there is such a thing as food. Men feel sexual desire: well, there is such a thing as sex. If I find in myself a desire which no experience in this world can satisfy, the most probable explanation is that I was made for another world...

If none of my earthly pleasures satisfy it, that does not prove that the universe is a fraud. Probably earthly pleasures were never meant to satisfy it, but only... to suggest the real thing. If that is so, I must take care, on the one hand, never to despise, or be unthankful for, these earthly blessings, and on the other, never to mistake them for something else of which they are only a kind of copy, echo, or mirage."

Go Mr. Lewis!! Okay, mixed in with his words on that particular website were a few other verses, so I looked 'em up:

1 Peter 1:3- never mind, just read all of *1 Peter* when you get time, most of it applies... Also, ***"The Lord is good to those whose hope is in Him, to the one who seeks Him"*** (*Lamentations 3:25*)

What "good" means here is yet to be understood by me. However, for the first time ever, I'm blind to the plan, uncomfortable in the emotions, unsure of my ability, and completely confident that I can trust that He will be good to me in the end- because of the desert I find myself in... Here's why:

All these things I read, coupled with some pretty insightful conversations with my fake big sister this week, brought me back to the faith of Moses. He was resolute in his belief that God is trustworthy, faithful. He placed his hope in God's promise of freedom, so much so, that he led an entire race of people out of slavery in Egypt (impressively, I might add) to one-day-at-a-time living in the desert. The people were pumped and trusting of the situation, briefly. Then stuff got unclear, uncomfortable, ugly... they got sick of the bread that was provided every single day, just enough, with no inkling of provision for tomorrow, and started longing for the predictable and known days of slavery in Egypt. Hindsight and history tell us it all worked out in the end:

God kept His promise, He was trustworthy...

I spent the week identifying in myself, the knee jerk reaction to some uncomfortable stuff in my desert. The dysfunctional prison of lying thoughts, unhealthy relationships and waste-of-time coping mechanisms have appealed to me recently, even as my daily needs are being met emotionally, physically, financially. Thank God for weeks like this, and friends like mine, and that hope that won't disappoint!

Impotent Idols
Collene James
London, England- U.K.

Psalm 8
Collene James

O Lord, our Lord, how excellent is Your name in all the earth, Who have set Your glory above the heavens! Out of the mouth of babes and nursing infants You have ordained strength, Because of Your enemies, That You may silence the enemy and the avenger. When I consider Your heavens, the work of Your fingers, The moon and the stars, which You have ordained, what is man that You are mindful of him, and the son of man that You visit him? For You have made him a little lower than the angels, and You have crowned him with glory and honor. You have made him to have dominion over the works of Your hands; You have put all things under his feet, all sheep and oxen— Even the beasts of the field, The birds of the air, and the fish of the sea That pass through the paths of the seas. O Lord, our Lord, how excellent is Your name in all the earth.

Psalm 77

Elegy

Audible words hit ether,
swallowed up in the veiled brume, plastering these four walls,
closing in on me like a siege of befogged soldiers
come to occupy my mind.
My soul refuses comfort,
it melts like wax 'neath the blazing brow of flickering flame,
igniting sparks dry as memories of mercies faded;
my murmuring spirit weeps.

Endless days, moonlight dismissed;
anxieties, like tent pegs, stretching weary eyelids wide.
I reminisce upon those long-forgotten lullabies—
a balm to my heart, forlorn.
Will God forever ignore,
his compassions caged like rain within storm clouds during drought?
Could his affections quicken and from grave clothes be unbound,
or is love decayed, deceased?

I will not forget your deeds!
The sight of you widened the blue oculus of the sea;
the clouds cried out in terror, releasing thunder and tears;
the earth, it trembled and shook!
Path cut through a sea of glass
with bolt of lightning wielded by lapidary unseen;
chiseling hidden footprints in barren floor of the sea,
on dry ground, I follow thee.

Vicki Joy Anderson

Ancient Strongholds
Collene James
Mikonos, Athens, Aegean Sea, Corinth, Greece

Unparallel

we walk in straight lines
– usually –
but at times it means
we can't turn
to the right –
to the left –
even when there is a line
running
right next to us,
parallel.
and there it goes
off to the right
making its own path,
its own way,
and we want to go –
to turn right,
to stay parallel
with a line like us –
keep company,
be together.
but we shouldn't,
we can't,
we mustn't
sway left or right.
so we stay where we are
and keep to the way
and remain straight –
unparallel.

Ashley Fugleberg

Waiting

May 30th 2012

I woke up suddenly, thinking it was morning and I was late for my day... but it wasn't, and I wasn't. Maybe my phone buzzed; I checked it- nope. It confirmed the time, 1:31 a.m. Now wide awake, I realized I felt sick. Headache, tummy ache... oh and heartache. I'm irritated. Now I'm going back to sleep, this is a stupid interruption.

"Did you do something wrong?" The voice in my head was clear and familiar.

"NO!" I closed my eyes again. I want to be asleep; this is still stupid.

"Did you disobey Me?"

"No, I did everything I was supposed to, and I didn't do anything extra."

Now I don't care about sleep.

"Well, Collene, do you trust Me?" I might have thought a feeble "yes," but the truth is, I'm not sure.

Now it felt urgent that I get out of bed, find my tattered blue notebook, and write. This time not for the online blog journal, but just for me. I was being encouraged, mentally I guess, to write my story.

I have this understanding in me that is built on nothing but little flickering thoughts. I need to write them down. Is this the part of the assurance of things hoped for, I've been reading about all this week? It doesn't matter, I can't sleep, I'll write.

The clock approached 3:00 a.m. I have come nowhere near finishing all I remember, but my eyes are so heavy. My only choice is to trust, hope and wait...

"With arms high and heart abandoned
In awe of the One who gave it all.
So I'll stand
My soul Lord to You surrendered
All I am, is Yours"
(*"The Stand,* "written by Antonio Romero, Joel Houston, Tania Braun)

These lyrics roll through my thoughts as I drift off to sleep. Now, as I'm writing this here, I'm convinced that **1 Corinthians 13:13** is more directly for me. The previously avoided and loathed "Love Verses" no longer repulse me. Instead, I was initially confused by their interruption to marinating thoughts on "Faith" and "Hope," which have been the words for this blog twice since November. Now all three are tying together:

"...and now these three remain: faith, hope and love. But the greatest of these is love."

I'm not sure I'm ready to put it all together for you here, but I'm positive I'll need the reminder of these things while I wait. Oh, and while I'm standing here with my arms high and heart abandoned, waiting, this is my new heart song.

I'm waiting
I'm waiting on You, Lord
And I am hopeful
I'm waiting on You, Lord
Though it is painful
But patiently, I will wait

I will move ahead, bold and confident
Taking every step in obedience
While I'm waiting
I will serve You
While I'm waiting
I will worship
While I'm waiting
I will not faint
I'll be running the race
Even while I wait

I'm waiting
I'm waiting on You, Lord
And I am peaceful
I'm waiting on You, Lord
Though it's not easy
But faithfully, I will wait
Yes, I will wait

I will serve You while I'm waiting
I will worship while I'm waiting
I will serve You while I'm waiting
I will worship while I'm waiting
I will serve you while I'm waiting
I will worship while I'm waiting on You, Lord

("While I'm Waiting" By John Waller)

Hush
Andrea Fugleberg

The Season of Darkness

July 11th 2012

Well, this has been a wild week. If I'm being honest, it's been a wild six weeks. Aside from the constant internal work going on in me, a crazy little freakish accident with one of the other stylists resulted in elevated work-load insanity for me at the salon. It seems I'm barely taking a breath these days.

I have about four half-written blogs in cue and chapter after chapter of scribble in my blue "raw journal." Nothing is scrubbing clean enough for public consumption yet, but I've got lots of unfinished thoughts roaming around inside me, so I'll try again.

To attempt to wrap those unfinished thoughts into something cohesive for you here, it may be notable to mention that Tenth Avenue North is the band I've been listening to recently. I can't seem to get enough of the lyrics for two of their songs, *"Hold My Heart" and "Empty My Hands."* If you take a few minutes to at least read the lyrics, and listen to a sampling of the gentle persistence of those words set to their music, you'll potentially see how they have been mingling together with the roaming word of my thoughts for the last month and a half:

"Sufficiency."

Sufficiency in Christ. Christ alone? How? How do I find ALL of my or my family's needs met in Him? How does HE compensate for what I lack when it comes to parenting my children? This month it has been well documented that I absolutely cannot do it all. I don't want them simply to grow up because enough time has passed. I want to raise them- with standards, and insight, and hope, and discipline, and warnings, and examples, and truth...

"Take care of what's important to you."

This was the final text from a friend who left too soon, to marry someone else. His words pinpoint my current anguish.

"I can't" was my reply. I know with devastating acuity that I'm not capable. Last week, a man made the off-handed comment to me:

"If we know what needs to be done, yet don't do it, the consequences fall squarely on us."

I feel like I'm watching a train move steadily for the washed-out bridge. I can't stop it, but I see the consequences of my own insufficiency pending... I am completely unable to *"take care of what's important to me"* and still unable to completely trust Him to fill the gap, only because I can't see how it could possibly work out in every facet. It feels urgent, yet I am in the dark. The plan isn't clear. Is there a plan?

Furthermore, how does He cover each specific loneliness and want- or dry the tears that seem to leak, WAY too often, from the corner of my eyes until I drift off to a fitful sleep?

I feel like my questions are "wrong" to ask. They seem faithless and ignorant. It's not Christian "PC" to ask. But then I'm not exactly a politically correct Christian these days, either. So, I'm asking anyway.

With the new situation at work, the truth is I'm physically more exhausted than ever before. It turns out I wasn't built to work 9-15 hours a day, 5-6 days a week, in the summer, with the absence of a seven-hour school day to help with the feeding, entertaining, encouraging, disciplining, correcting, teaching, and enjoying in relationship, a 9-, 12-, and 13-year-old.

I had a green yard; it's 85% brown today. I bought a ridiculous amount of gorgeous annual flowers and potted them this spring. They are 96% dead. I have a dog; I think he hates me, but desperately wags his tail and licks me, reminding me of his attention starvation, every time I walk in the room. I have enough dust bunnies under my furniture to make a sleeping bag. I am certain there is nothing green (that should be green, at least) in my refrigerator. I have amazing friends; I couldn't tell you what one of them has going on this weekend, or last weekend, or the one before. I have no idea what their voices even sound like anymore. The "check engine" light has been on in my car for weeks. The oil change was due about 1200 miles ago... (Dad, relax, I'll get to it... tomorrow...?) This is all temporary, I know, but are the effects going to be long-lasting?

Those who know me well know that for me, physical exhaustion leads to an overactive mental gymnast. I've done my best to reign in my mental performance on the uneven bars, but alas, I'm the Nastia Liukin of the 2012 Mental Olympics. It's actually quite impressive, however, gold medals are not awarded at the 2012 Mental Games, only silver hair, forehead wrinkles, frown lines, short tempers and elevated blood pressure.

I desire nothing more than to truly understand "sufficiency in Christ, alone." My prayer is that the darkness I find myself in is simply the shadow of His hand and not the very long, very cold, winter months of night, in a frozen, arctic, abandoned wasteland.

In Too Deep
Collene James

Dare

O, the courage it takes to dare
to believe a holy God could care
to take a spark and flame a fire
from out of every heart's desire.

O, the foolishness required
to be, in angel's eyes, admired;
to run towards danger and not flee
because it is with eyes of faith you see.

O, the joy that it must entail
to shake hell's gates so they don't prevail;
for the works of darkness cannot raze
when we lift voices to our King in praise.

O, the sacrifice expected
once idols in our hearts erected
are drowned in a flood of tears
or lacerated by the Pruner's sheers.

O, the death that so soon awaits,
to ensure that all corrupt abates;
so when our Savior's face, we behold,
we are presented, pure as gold.

Vicki Joy Anderson

Cold Climbing
Collene James
Flatirons Mountain- Boulder, CO

Cloaked
Collene James

The Crucible

August 6th 2012

The 2012 NFL pre-season kicked off tonight. What a relief! Fall is coming.

I guess I'm not writing tonight to talk about football, but this is a seasonal change I'm not afraid of. I have made a strong connection between the NFL, Thanksgiving, giving thanks, beauty, trees, trust, restoration, and the art of giving since I started this healing journey. All of this put together in my mind feels like progress as I mark the calendar changes since I started this work last year.

For tonight's blog journal entry let me try to hoist you up onto this moving train of thought I'm conductor and engineer of:

Call it what you want, the summer of 2012 has been another intense mashup of seasons: The Fallow Season, The Season of Darkness, The Season of Crossroads, The Drought Season... Although I didn't write about all of them for you, you can trust my fake big sister when she referred to it as my Crucible Summer. She is as usual, perfectly accurate:

cru·ci·ble (krs-bl)n.
1. A vessel made of a refractory substance such as graphite or porcelain, used for melting and calcining materials at high temperatures.
2. A severe test, as of patience or belief; a trial.
3. A place, time, or situation characterized by the confluence of powerful intellectual, social, economic, or political forces.

I should note that the "crucible-ed-ness" of the summer is not anything like the "destruction-for-the-sake of-restoration" season I had come out of prior to beginning this blog. Rather, the Crucible Summer, in hindsight, is shaping up to look more like an end-of-the-quarter test in each of the classes of Trust, Faith, Hope and Love.

With that being said, let me get back to this train of thought we're trying to catch:

Thanksgiving:

Although I'm not blogging much this summer, I'm still scribbling in my tattered blue journal. Actually, I filled that and started to tatter a red one, but I digress... I've poured my heart out and relentlessly presented my requests to God. Quite honestly, I've been convinced at times that I live in a soundproof, padded cell. I still ask, seek, knock, trust- without comfort or understanding for days sometimes. I've had no choice. I can't go back to Egypt, yet I haven't arrived at my Promise Land... There's a story in **Luke 18** about a persistent widow, so I'm feeling like I'm in good company and not wrong in my own persisting.

Lately I've felt I need a shift in focus- a change of season. I'm sick of me. Sick of fear thoughts and emotions. Sick of the mourning in me. Sick of restlessness and despairing thoughts. I begged God to give me a new focus...

He did. This time "Thanksgiving" has been the flickering word and with it this set of verses:

"And we urge you, brothers, admonish the idle, encourage the fainthearted, help the weak, be patient with them all. See that no one repays anyone evil for evil, but always seek to do good to one another and to everyone. Rejoice always, pray without ceasing, give thanks in all circumstances; for this is the will of God in Christ Jesus for you. Do not quench the Spirit. Do not despise prophecies, but test everything; hold fast what is good. Abstain from every form of evil." (1 Thessalonians 5:14-22

Beauty:
This summer is hot and extremely dry. A little over a month ago most of the Western United States was, seemingly, burning down. Montana was no different. Between June 26th and June 29th, 73 homes and countless livestock and out-buildings were consumed by a wildfire, locally.

Those numbers mean very little until they're personal. They became quickly very personal yesterday as I was given the opportunity to work side-by-side with the owners of one of these homes. As I stood, knee deep, in the ashes of all that remained of my friend's lifetime of memories, I was nothing short of overwhelmed.

We spent the day sorting, sifting, stacking, digging. Most of the time I busied myself with identifying which of the pipes, wires, and chunks of metal I found were copper, steel, or aluminum... and hoisting them out of the basement pit. From there they were piled in their appropriate piles for recycling.

Occasionally, I could identify something recognizable: A Kitchen Aid bowl, a stack of mostly shattered coffee cups, a melted sewing machine, a bicycle- steel of course, the aluminum one was completely incinerated... There were melted clumps of gold, formerly a pair of her special earrings, she thinks... one of her husband's hammers, well, the steel head of it...

Now and then, I would glance at my friend. Strong. Tall. Tired. Hurting-inside and out. She's been sorting, sifting, tossing, digging for a month and there's still so much to do before they can bulldoze this foundation and begin to even lay a new, safe foundation to rebuild upon.

A verse-turned-song kept crossing my mind, soothing my heart, escaping my lips... I sang quietly while we worked. *"He gives beauty for ashes, strength for fear, gladness for mourning, peace for despair. He gives peace for despair." ("Beauty for Ashes" by Crystal Lewis)*

Later we sat around covered in black ash, sipping iced tea, serenading the men with a variety of poorly sung songs, (sung in rounds, I might add) as they dug a trench for water run-off. Our little female quartet does not have classically beautiful voices; we will not be touring soon. We couldn't stop laughing...

Life really can be so sweet, even covered in ashes of destruction.

Trees, Trust, Restoration, Giving:
This morning I was thinking about this blog and its title "Seasonal Allergy." Originally, I named it this based on my fear of the changing seasons of my life. A million years ago I heard some churchy lady talk about seasons of the tree referenced in *Jeremiah 17:7-8*. I didn't give her words much credibility back then because of my church-lady wounding, but they come to mind again now:

"But blessed is the one who trusts in the Lord, whose confidence is in Him. They will be like a tree planted by the water that sends out its roots by the stream. It does not fear when heat comes; its leaves are always green. It has no worries in a year of drought and never fails to bear fruit."

On that day, I knew I wasn't that tree. I feared the drought. Tonight, I don't like the Drought Season, but I trust the One who has charge of the rain, and I continue to sense restoration. I am encouraged to finally be strong enough to be the encourager of friends and a giver of myself to others again.

Colliding with the Healer

August 10th 2012

"Breathe
Sometimes I feel it's all that I can do
Pain so deep that I can hardly move
Just keep my eyes completely fixed on You
Lord take hold and pull me through

So here I am
What's left of me
Where glory meets my suffering

I'm alive
Even though a part of me has died
You take my heart and breathe it back to life
I've fallen into your arms open wide
When the hurt and the healer collide"

Yep, that sums it up. I'm not sure I can move, but the clock ticks, the day beckons. Suffering can wait. This song (*"The Hurt and the Healer"* by Mercy Me) was the alarm's soundtrack that started my day.

I'm not sure why I insist on doing everything the hard way, but tonight, here I am again. The kids are having sleepovers, my friends are busy, my phone is nearly dead... (I've mentioned that comfortable solitude isn't my strength, right?) As long have I have an ounce of energy in me, and there's something uncomfortable or painful to address in the depths of me, I have the tendency to evade, run, distract, invest in anything or anyone but that topic. Finally, at the end of a grueling week, I've exhausted myself to the point that I lack the ability to run away from myself mentally. As usual, I can't sleep. I'll write.

Wednesday sucked. No, you don't understand, it SUCKED. The night before was full of dreams again. Not just dreams, but the kind that I can't escape. The informative kind, I guess. I went to work a little "off."

The Crucible-ness of the Summer is grinding on. Brutal decisions to be made with no good choices and the consequences falling only to me, nagging health concerns, excruciating personal losses, incredible physical demands, clients to fire, "friends" I can't trust anymore, parenting pressure, people I love with even greater needs than mine, perfectionism left unchecked, spiritual, and emotional frustrations, questions with no satisfying answers... I want my bed. Actually no, there's no air conditioning, therefore no sleep; besides I now dread the recent randomly specific dreams... I want a coma... well, no not that- aren't those expensive?

I got to work early and planned to fortify my emotions by busying myself. My day wasn't going to end officially for 10 more hours, and I needed to pull Professional Collene up by the bootstraps. Unfortunately for Professional Collene, I was sweetly greeted with a hug by one of my co-workers who knew the details of my tough decisions and recent personal losses. Great, now we're going to need a mop to sop the tears and possibly a spatula to re-Spackle my make-up back on before my first client. I am no longer going to be Professional Collene for this particular day. My client schedule started mostly on time, yet somehow by the second client, I was already 20 minutes behind. The third client arrived a half hour late. Ummmmmmm, that almost works now though, if I skip lunch; her color can process while I start client number four... "I could still get out of here tonight by 8:00," I thought... Will Wednesday ever end?

Meanwhile, I had broken my resolve. I sent a text. Okay, more than one... The dreams and restlessness were too real. The recipient of the texts responded, confirming one of the dreams. Weird, I know. This is starting to be a pattern with that specific friend. Our friendship has always had a connection unlike any I've ever known. Still, I can't seem to communicate everything I feel I need to...

My exhaustion, fear, sadness, pressures of the day and of life sat heavily on my shoulders as I escaped work, (miraculously on time, I should add) and fled to one of my favorite places after work. One of my most trusted friends, my fake sister-in-law, joined me on the patio. We guzzled iced tea in silence for a while. My tears streaming, her heart catching each tear as she waited for me to talk. What I love about her is that she is a digger. She is not afraid to go deeper than the words I'm saying and expose the heart of why I'm saying them. This is an important quality for one to have in a friend and it perfectly explains *"faithful are the wounds of a friend." (Proverbs 27:6)* Most of us tend to be our own worst enemies when it comes to the truth of what is buried in the thoughts and motives of our own heart.

Why is my heart broken? No really, WHY? What is it that I'm hanging on to that won't heal? If God is real and His Words are true then *"The LORD is near to the brokenhearted and saves those who are crushed in spirit" (Psalms 34:18)* and *"He heals the brokenhearted and binds up their*

wounds," (Psalm 147:3) are not just meant to be cute little bookmark phrases.

Again, her probing questions reveal an area of distrust still in me. Is God good? Yes, always, duh. He may have forgotten about me though.

Does God hear our prayers and promise to give us the desires of our heart when we seek Him and ask? Yes, I can show you a million examples in scripture and in life- your life that is, not mine.

Does God love you? Yes, in the way a parent lovingly cares for the neighbor girl that attends a sleep-over with their daughter all weekend... but then I'll have to pack up my pillow and leave, I'm sure of it...

We sat there until after dark hashing through example after example of God's loving, faithfulness to me in the last year, six months, one month. Okay, now I see... but there is still an area or two where healing hasn't begun. Somehow the project seems bigger than all the others, more impossible to reach into, even by God.

Here's what I know:
  a)   I can't heal myself.
  b)   He says He can.

I guess I only have a plan A here because the only thing left in my mind to declare tonight is this:

"He who began a good work in me will be faithful to complete it..." (Philippians 1:6)

Goodnight.

Vulnerable
Collene James

Balloon Time
Andrea Fugleberg

Darling

My darling,
My darling,
I see the locked door, your mouth.
Chains, I see them cut your chest.
My darling,
My darling,
do you know
I would you Mine,
I, yours.
There, your pain.
A panel blocks your breath.
I AM balm to confusion.
I AM a calm to convulsion.
My darling,
My darling,
do you hear.
I AM Chainbreaker.
I AM Breathmaker.
You only need to search so far:
look to Me.
My darling,
My darling,
turn your eyes
upon Me,

and
      I will free you,
      walk My Way

and
      I will teach you,
      sing My praise.

Ashley Fugleberg

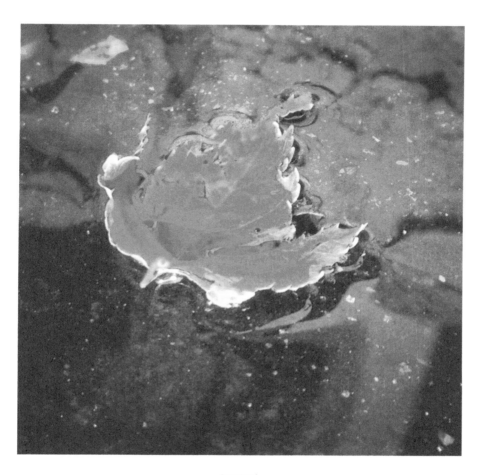

Baptized
Collene James

Stripped of All Defenses

```
    C              G
Stripped of all defenses
            F              G
Standing there before my Lord,
     C         G
Feeling fear and insecurity
     F                    G
He turned me toward His Word.
C                      G
The lie that once held splendor
           F              G
Has been brought into the light,
       C            G
The sin that once consumed my life
       F        F/G
Has been set upon a flight.
```

Chorus 1:
```
C         Am7                    F        F/G
Never to return again to the person I once was,
C         Am7              F              F/G
Running from reality, Now I'm running to Him because
C         Am7          F          G
Jesus my Redeemer, The healer of my heart,
C                  Am7        F              G
Washed away the misery, Gave me a brand-new start.
```

```
C              G
Stripped of all defenses
         F              G
Standing there before my Lord
     C         G
He took my burdens on Himself,
    F                  G
Replaced them with His love.
C                 G
Hearing words of wisdom
    F        G
Spoken from above
          C          G
Being changed into His likeness
F            F/G
Knowing Jesus' love.
```

Chorus 2:

```
C          Am7                    F           G
```
Never to return again to the person I once was
```
C              Am7              F            F/G
```
Running from reality, Now I'm running to Him because
```
C          Am7            F            G
```
Jesus my Redeemer, The Savior of my soul
```
C              Am7                    F                G
```
Set me free from guilt and shame, His love has made me whole.


```
   C              G
```
Stripped of all defenses
```
         F              G
```
Standing there before my Lord,
```
      C              G
```
He clothed me in His righteousness,
```
      F            G
```
And He made me His own.
```
      C              G
```
I'm standing on His promises
```
      F            G
```
To help me be so bold.
```
      C                  G
```
The hope He gives has freed my soul
```
         F            F/G
```
And the story must be told.

Ending:

```
C              Am7      F  G
```
Jesus, my Savior…..
```
C              Am7      F  G
```
Jesus, my Redeemer….
```
C              Am7      F  G
```
Jesus, my Deliverer….
```
C              Am7      F  G
```
Jesus, my Healer….

A Song of Nancy Bowser

175

Why Did I Doubt

August 22nd 2012

Something incredible happened last week. I've spent the weekend mulling it over, trying to figure out how much of it to document on the world-wide-web and how much of it to keep to myself. Although I'm finding it extremely encouraging to re-read my thoughts from last fall and winter, there are certain things not worth telling EVERYONE...

It was another one of those turned-a-corner moments that I was not in charge of. The moment, like any life-changing moment, peaked after a few days of buildup. Here's what happened:

I spent the last two weeks working less and playing more... I even danced- a lot! Also in the last week, there was a nice dinner with a good friend and her husband, a baseball game, late night patio chats, a weeknight street dance accompanied by one of my favorite local bands, late-night breakfast and apple pie ala mode with friends, a rodeo, more fair wanderings, karaoke (not me), long walks in the dark, more new friends, deep conversations over rounds of lemon water and a baseball game with strangers. Oh, and laughter, lots of laughter.

Along with the dancing and the laughter, there were also a few tears. Deep conversations tend to bring about those unresolved things in my heart...

So, Wednesday night and Thursday morning I was again back to the internal work, thinking about the three "R" words that have been flickering all year:

Repentance, Redemption, Restoration.

I've been SO selfish as it pertains to my actions. Although I know for a fact now that I've changed my mind about what I want for myself and how I want my life to look, I had never considered how my decisions or resistance to making them may have impacted people around me at their deepest, internal, level.

Although I would never intentionally hurt someone in ways that I can see, it didn't even cross my mind that I may be hurting someone in ways no one can see...

I've thought for hours about what Redemption and Restoration would look like for ME because of Repentance, but did I cause a delay in the process for someone else while I waffled back and forth in insecurity and distrust?

Suddenly it made sense. As the specifics started fitting together in my memory like a puzzle, I was overwhelmed with grief. I had made decisions, went against my conscience, in the face of that still-small-voice warning... In fact, I remember thinking "whatever, I'll deal with the consequences, I want this..." In hindsight, I see that the still-small-voice was as much about protecting people around me as it was me. I trampled all over it, quenched it and rebelled against it, selfishly.

Friday just happened to be the day I was supposed to attend another concert with a couple of friends. Tenth Avenue North is the band. I'm smiling a little as I think about the "me" that I was this time last year; I wouldn't have been caught dead at a church concert. Although for my whole life prior to the last two years, I had participated in every church event known to man. I had come to the realization that very few churchy people were gracious or merciful and I've had my fill of that kind of hurt... However, recently a song or two by this group has found its way into my heart. I was excited to have the opportunity to go.

Before the concert I prayed that my heavy, grieving heart could find encouragement at the concert. Then I internally rolled my eyes. "It's just a bunch of musicians, showing off their talent, right? Keep your expectations low, Collene."

Okay, so my friends and I had front row seats. The first two groups were good. I hadn't heard of them, but it's easy to have fun in the front row. Then T.A.N took the stage. The first several songs were good, familiar even, upbeat. As they were getting ready to start the next song, the lead singer stopped. He turned to the band and said *"I don't think we're supposed to do that song yet. I really feel strongly that we need to play one of the new (then, unreleased) ballads. I can't shake the feeling that God wants us to do that song for someone in here tonight. Maybe I'm crazy, I've NEVER changed the set like this before..."*

The band scrambled to figure out what he was doing, then played these lyrics:

"Let me see redemption win
Let me know the struggle ends
That you can mend a heart that's frail and torn
I want to know a song can rise
From the ashes of a broken life
And all that's dead inside can be reborn
Cause I'm worn"

(The song, *"Worn,"* on the album, *The Struggle*, was since released...oh, and the album cover feels a bit apropos for me these days too; check it out!)

I sat. That man has read my journal?!? The lyrics continued, some of them nearly word-for-word quoting my blue tattered journal. HOW could they know? This is my gift, I'm convinced. Of all my memories from the summer, THIS is a defining moment. The lump in my chest that has sat heavy since Wednesday night, dissolved- released by tears of thankfulness. God had heard my cries and was sending me a little "hug" through these strangers and their lyrics.

I stayed after the concert and met the guys from the band. I thanked the lead singer for his obedience to change the set, then explained briefly that my journal, the tattered one, was supposed to be private...

If there was doubt- and there was- I now experientially know this: God is personal. He deals with me individually. He loves me; I am convinced. I have no doubt. He will redeem, restore, rebuild, remake- forgive.

Okay, there's just a few more lyrics from another T.A.N song, that have been roaming my head since Friday:

"You are more than the choices that you've made,
You are more than the sum of your past mistakes,
You are more than the problems you create,

You've been remade..."

(*"You Are More"* from *The Light Meets the Dark* album)

"Immediately Jesus reached out His hand and caught him. 'You of little faith,' He said, 'why did you doubt?'" (Matthew 14:31)

Safely Harbored
Collene James
Seward, AK

Phoebe
Collene James

*"...How often I wanted to gather your children together, as a hen
gathers her chicks under her wings, but you were not willing!"
(Matthew 23: 37b)*

This Momma's Grace

September 22nd 2012

I held a newborn today.

I inhaled his sweet, fresh baby fragrance. I felt him stretch his teeny bum and then re-tuck his scrawny legs under himself- to my chest. He grunted and squirmed and peeked at me through one barely open eye. He stuck his lip out and tucked his face to my neck. Oh-my-goodness, I'm in love! For a few minutes I stared at his sweet, innocent, perfect face and features. Wild dark hair, perfect ears, button nose... He has NO idea the tears, prayers, faith, hope, and intense love his sweet little life is responsible for. He may never.

I tried to remember my own newborns, but my mind is cobwebbed and dusty; those days are long-gone. So, I watched his new momma. She, in her sleep deprived, postpartum fog, watched her little boy with pride and love-filled eyes as he passed from one set of arms to the next. I can't decide if my favorite thing was holding him or watching her...

As we chatted, laughed, cooed, told stories about our own babies, pretended not to have a lump in our throats, and imparted bits of hard-earned mothering wisdom to our newest mom-club member, I couldn't help but hear again one of the flickering words of September:

"Grace."

Incidentally, accidentally, it's my daughter's name- twice. Her first name, Hannah, means "Grace" or "God has favored me." Her middle name is Grace meaning "God's favor or blessing."

Mr. Webster uses synonyms for grace, such as: forgiveness, charity, mercifulness, lenity, leniency, reprieve, kindness, kindliness, love, benignity.

I thought, briefly, about the billions of mistakes I've made in each of my children's lives since they were 7lbs. I tried not to project the millions more I'll make before their 18th birthdays. Instead, as I watched this baby sleep and thought about my own children's tiny fingers tucked into mine and later, their chubby arms around my neck, I marveled.

"Be gracious toward yourself," I told the new mom. "You've never been a mom before."

Huh. I hadn't either, before I had an infant, or a toddler, or a kindergartner, or a teenager... maybe I need to take my own advice.

I don't deserve it, but I've got It too- access to this same grace He has offered to this new momma... For that, I am beyond amazed and forever grateful. Meanwhile, their, less-chubby arms still willingly hug my neck, and their less-tiny fingers still wrap around mine.

Birth
Collene James

Construction Season

September 26th 2012

The "crucible-ed-ness" of the summer has waned, leaving more time for the internal construction zone, that is my heart and mind, to pick up the pace. In fact, the work is being done around the clock. If you've ever had to remodel a portion of an old house, you'll understand the excitement I feel. Here's why:

I told you the other day that I've had "Grace" mingling with a couple of other words in my head all month. "Mercy," and "Kindness" rounded out the trio. My old friends, "Redemption" and "Repentance," made cameo appearances again too.

There's nothing more frustrating than living in a house that desperately needs repairs. Tearing out a kitchen or a bathroom and still being required to function daily in those spaces is frustrating and crippling.

I told a friend the other day that I feel somewhat like my heart's kitchen is torn out. The refrigerator is still in there, along with the food and necessities for daily living, but the sink is missing. The water is turned off, the counters and cupboards are not set. I've been making do with random utensils and even eating out, a lot. Thankfully, I've gotten a glimpse at what the Contractor has ordered for me. I. Can't. Wait! When I'm up and running, my heart's kitchen will be bigger, more beautiful, more functional, and completely able and willing to host some fantastic shindigs.

This week, I wandered through the pile of fixtures that have been torn out of my heart's kitchen. UGLY! Survivable, maybe, but ugly. While I took stock of what exactly is being changed in me, I started trying to recall just how it all started. It's been a year exactly, this week since I called on the Contractor to begin His remodel. Let's skip over most of the details of how, for now, and proceed to the why...

Prior to that week last September, I was stupid. No- really, really, stupid! I was also defensively constructing walls around my stupidity, even though I knew, fully, that I was being stupid. I knew that my thoughts, decisions, and actions, would never hold up under the scrutiny of, well... anyone. I didn't want to keep being stupid, but I didn't know how to correct my stupidity. Defensiveness was my only option.

Until... Somewhere in the recesses of my heart a barely audible pulse of hope started beating. A conversation that started with "God would never_____ for someone like me," was proven to be a false statement. God did that thing, for me, that week. Then there were soft whispers in my mind and heart that formed sentences that I recognized. Bible verses, actually. Rusty memorization from decades before, with no references, started to permeate my thoughts. Then conversations with a virtual stranger, laced with the compassion I had always craved, but never dared to seek... I was challenged. I was changed. I was shown mercy. I was safe. I started to crave bold honesty about my stupidity. For the first time in my life, I didn't feel like I needed to justify my mistakes; their power over me began to lose its grip.

This week, as I mentally walked through the old part of my heart, I'll admit I briefly forgot about the remodel going on inside. The powerful grip those things had over me tried to condemn me again. As usual, because of the Kindness of the Lord, that led me to Repentance in the first place, I was reminded that those chains are broken. There's no going back. No other kind of life will do, anymore.

Build
Matthew Bailey

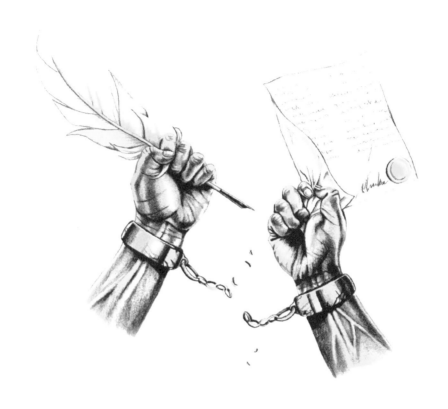

Freedom
Andrea Fugleberg

You Are the One

Verse 1:

        Dm   A
You are our God. We are Your people.
  A   Dm
We seek Your face; and humbly do we pray.

Dm   Gm   D
You are the one that our hearts long for. You're the one that we love.
Gm   D
We'll seek You with all our strength.

Verse 2:

        Dm   A
We call on You, O Lord. We come into Your presence.
      A   Dm
We humbly seek the Spirit of the Lord.

Dm   Gm   D
Salvation reigns; He's overtaken sin and death.
          Gm   D
You've set us free by the power of Jesus blood.

Bridge: *(From Isaiah 45:8)*
Dm   Dm/C   G
Shower, oh heavens, from up above,
          Dm   G   Dm   G
And let the skies rain down righteousness.
Dm   Dm/C   G
Let the earth open and salvation come forth,
    Dm   G   Dm
And righteousness.

Verse 3:

        Dm   A
Send forth your Spirit, Lord, and breathe on us new life.
      Dm   A
Anoint us Lord and fill us with Your love.
        Dm/A   A
Rain down Your righteousness; Cover us with Your holiness,
      A   Dm
And fill our minds with the power of the truth.

      Gm   D
Help us to stand firmly in our faith,
      Gm   D
Raising our shields against the enemy.

Verse 4:

Dm   A

Take up the Sword, the power of the Living God;

     A   Dm

Destroying strongholds of the enemy.

     Gm   D

Give us your peace, As we follow in your holy ways;

     Gm/D   D

And let us daily lift our hearts in praise.

     Gm   D

You are the one that our hearts long for. You're the one that we love.

Gm   D

We'll seek You with all our strength.

Repeat Bridge

End:

Dm   A

You are our God; We are Your people.

     A   Dm

We seek Your face; and humbly we do pray.

A Song of Nancy Bowser

Tender Strength
Collene James

Sitting on the Edge of a Dime, Swinging My Legs

October 22nd 2012

Have you ever had a day that you felt so small, so low? I lived a lifetime this week, feeling like I was sitting on the edge of a dime, just like that. I'm irritated to admit, but try as I might to avoid them, his incredibly insightful words kept echoing through the empty silences of my week... again.

So Low
Collene James

"Do you ever wonder, is God in Control?" I had asked.

"He is, you just have to trust Him."

"What if I can't anymore?"

"You can, you just have to get over yourself first."

His response both soothed and cut me. What does he know about me? Besides "he" is just someone-I-used-to-know now anyway. Between you and me, I'm relieved that I won't ever have to tell him he was right, or that he had me figured out before I even figured myself out.

Tonight, it seems my buddy Oswald Chambers agrees with the stranger-I-used-to-know too:

"Why doesn't God reveal Himself to you? He cannot. It is not that He will not, but He cannot, because you are in the way as long as you won't abandon yourself to Him in total surrender."

Welllllll, that's just weird. I don't usually look up his stuff before bed. Tonight, couldn't have been more perfect timing for those words. I've wrestled, hand-to-hand combat style, with the "getting over myself" concept all weekend. Until today, I couldn't figure out what that's supposed to look like on a daily basis. Here's how it finally made sense, but I'll have to back up a few days:

Last week there was a trip. Nope, not a vacation, there's a difference, trust me. The whys and details aren't important to the story, but the timing is. I already told you that this time of year is tough on me, with dates and whatnot... Prior to the trip, I had felt myself slipping into disappointment, lethargy, discouragement and teetering on despair. Circumstances and conversations pushed me over the edge, and I allowed myself to embrace a full-on depression.

So, in that mentality, I decided to re-read something I wrote in August about a project of healing in me that seems impossible even to God. As I was reading what I wrote then, I realized that I may have accidentally given God permission to reach into that impossible place and do something about the insecurities and deep injuries I've held closely guarded and bound securely.

Is it possible that current emotional turmoil is evidence that those deep things were exposed to the light and air, dramatically and all at once, and by my own permission?

Well what good is exposure if there won't be healing? The lyrics of *"You Do All Things Well"* by Tenth Avenue North became my source of comfort and hope:

"You break me to bind me
You hurt me, Lord, to heal me
You cut me to touch me
You died to revive me"

There's a paragraph that I've typed here about four times. I can't seem to make it publishable, so I'll jump to the end. Today **Luke 9:23** is what finally made sense of all this nonsense I've been wrestling for months- no, years. Yup, it's a bumper-sticker, turned real-to-me verse:

"Then He said to them all: "If anyone would come after Me, he must deny himself and take up his cross daily and follow Me."

So, there it is. Oswald, the Stranger Friend, and the good doctor, Luke, agree. I must get over me. My rights, desires, hopes- including the God-given ones, my capability and self-sufficiency, what I perceive to be my deepest needs, even my fears- will have to die, every day, if I want to follow Him- and more importantly if I want to see that He's in control... and I do. It's a well-documented fact that I make such a mess when I lead.

The good news is that He's still writing my story with Mercy's pen. Nearly every day, I am being reminded, in outrageous ways internally and externally, that I am unconditionally loved, a precious treasure, extremely valuable, a daughter of the King, more valuable than the birds of the air or the flowers of the field...

One of these days, I just might fully believe it myself.

Dry Places
Collene James

190

Dark Family

Father God, I ask You to help me overcome the darkness of my family lineage. We have offended You and defiled Your creation through our disobedience, ignorance, and rebellion. I repent and renounce any and all of my family's sins that have been passed down to me through teaching, habit or consequence.

I ask You God to make null and void any and all rituals, curses, or family traits of sin that have been handed down to me, or put on me, by any member of my family whether biological or legal through adoption or fostering.

I am asking You, Jesus to end all generational sin, habits, vows, and covenants, and their curses, that came from any part of our lineage or people-group. I am also asking that these sins, rituals, vows, covenants, and agreements not only be null and void for me, but also for my offspring. In Jesus name I humbly ask. Amen

"You shall not bow down to them or worship them; for I, the LORD your God, am a jealous God, punishing the children for the sin of the parents to the third and fourth generation of those who hate Me, but showing love to a thousand generations of those who love Me and keep My commandments." (Exodus 20:5-6)

Shawn Carter

Goat by Nature
Collene James

Psalm 91

(With 1 Peter 5:8 and 1 John 4:4)

Verse 1

A
He who dwells in the shelter of the Most High,
    Bm   Bm E
In the shadow of the Almighty;
  E   E7
Will say to the Lord, My refuge, and my fortress,
    A   A7
My God in whom I trust!
D
He will deliver you from the fowler's snare
    C#m
And from deadly pestilence.
 F#m
He will cover you with His feathers
    E
And under His wings you'll find refuge.

Verse 2

    A
You will not fear the terror of the night
    Bm   E
Nor the arrow that flies by day,
  E   E7
Nor the pestilence that stalks in darkness,
    A   A7
Nor destruction at noonday.
  D
A thousand may fall at your side,
    C#m
Ten thousand at your right hand.
    F#m
But it will not come near to you,
     E
You'll only look and see the reward of the wicked.

Verse 3

    A
Because you've made the Lord your refuge,
    Bm   Bm E
The Most High your habitation,
  E   E7
No evil shall fall on you, or plague come near your tent.
    A   A7
His faithfulness is your shield.
  D
Satan's like a roaring lion

C#m
Seeking to devour.
    F#m
But greater is He who is in you
        E
Than the one who is in the world.
A   Bm   E
We know Your Name, We praise Your Name, We cry out Your Name- It is
  A   F7
LOVE.

Verse 4

Bb
He will give His angels charge of you
    Cm   F
To guard you in all your ways.
 F   F7
On their hands they will hold you up
        Bb   Bb7
Lest you dash your foot against a stone.
Eb
You will tread on the lion and the serpent
      Dm
And all of the enemies
Gm
You will trample under foot
      F
When you walk with the Prince of Peace.

Verse 5

Bb
Because we cleave to God in love, (He says,)
 Cm   Cm   F
"I will deliver him.
F   F7
I will protect him cause he knows my Name.
        Bb   Bb7
When He calls to me I'll answer him.
Eb
I will be with him in trouble;
Dm
I will rescue him.
Gm
With long life I will satisfy
     F
And show him my salvation."
Bb   Cm   F
We know Your Name, We praise Your Name, We cry out Your Name- It is
Bb
LOVE.

A Song of Nancy Bowser

Lady in Fig Leaves
Andrea Fugleberg

Fig Leaves Are So Last Season

October 23rd 2012

Exposure was the main character of my day. Nobody likes that guy, seriously! Well, wait. I started thinking about various personalities of Exposure and- boom- before I knew it, I could almost imagine him becoming a dear friend.

It all started with me relaying to one of my nosy pastors, some of the specific details about the insecurities and pain I left out of yesterday's blog journal entry. Well really, he's not nosy; I did give him permission once to dig and he's not the kind of guy to turn down an invitation. He was annoyingly accurate and seemed to be teaming up with a few of my friends, a sibling or two, and a parent in his assessment of me.

The craziest place I could think of in all of scripture for the guy to take me would be the Garden of Eden in *Genesis 3*. We read the story. Then he re-read it, substituting my name for Adam's and using the details I had just given him about my situation in place of Adam's specifics. It made sense to me...

Adam was exposed. He was afraid and didn't trust God with his exposure. So, he covered himself his way, with a few fig leaves; then he hid from God. Huh. That's a familiar action and reaction. As the story goes, God lovingly leads Adam to a confession, despite his resistance, then makes him a better cover in the form of fur and leather clothes. This solution required some blood, pain, and death, but Adam's exposure was covered- without earning it or deserving it- perfectly, comfortably, and completely.

Exposure brought access to real love.

Before I left our meeting today, I asked my sweet pastor to tell me how I can fix this natural-as-breathing reflex I have to sew myself a few fig leaf outfits. I don't even know when I'm doing it for crying out loud.

His response, my big follow-up fix-it action?

"Stop doing."

Uhhhhh, I'm a do-er. How does a do-er not do? Apparently, *"by taking their hands off the situation,"* whatever that means. Soooooo, he tells me, we're going to be praying for illumination and understanding this week on those types of situations. This means my uncomfortable, exposed injuries will remain open to the air and the light and potentially be a whole subject in the classroom of life this week. Ughck, I'll let you know how that goes.

Meanwhile, at lunch, I had more food for thought. I'm a visual learner and find myself using illustrations to tell a story. As I was discussing, with my fake big sister, the events of the weekend and the morning's conversation with my pastor, I summed it up for her kind of like this:

I feel like somewhere along the way I had a broken bone. Maybe not an arm, but something deeper and more vital like a spine. I spent years putting gauze and ace bandages on it while treating it with ibuprofen. Eventually the pain subsided, and the bone healed in an unattended way. Now I'm crooked and crippled, but the pain is lessened- unless I try to stand up straight or move forward in any way.

Recently, it occurred to me that I would like to stand straight and walk correctly again. The physician offered to cut me, to heal me- to break me, to bind me. He'll have to cut through my flesh to the bone, re-break it, set it correctly, then suture and bandage me with His plates, screws, staples, and gauze. His medicines will be prescription strength and His tools sharply precise. Somehow, I keep arguing with the surgeon about how to do the procedure. In His patience, He is waiting for me to say I'm ready. In His mercy, He'll cause me to heal and function the way I was intended to before the injury. Exposure is merciful.

Finally, it's no secret I love photography. I admire "real" photographers and am not afraid to admit that the more I learn about it, the less I really know. I spent the afternoon alone, playing with some of the pictures I've taken, trying to salvage some of the ones that had low exposure by using certain filters during the edits. Hmmmm, there's that word again. Exposure. In photography, it refers to the amount of light allowed to fall on an object or area in a shot, and is usually controlled by a shutter. Without Exposure, we would have no photographic art. Exposure is illuminating.

Okie doke, I'm getting it. This acquaintance, Exposure, is begging to be my friend. I suppose I'll look for the illumination and understanding this week that the good pastor is praying for me. Like Adam, I might just find real Love. Besides, fig leaves are so last season.

Clarity

Matthew 6:33:
Seek first the Kingdom of God and all these things will be added to you.

Sometimes we feel lost,
When in fact the Savior knows exactly where we are.
When we see only darkness,
The Light is just ready to break through.
When things appear uncertain,
Truth gives us His eyes that wipe away the doubt.

When we don't know which way to go,
The Spirit is waiting to be our Guide.
When we are fearful,
Security is there to wrap His arms of Love around us.
When we sense hopelessness,
The Author of Creation is prepared to do great and mighty things.

When we hear silence,
The voice of the Shepherd is waiting to speak.
When we are battling,
The Mightiest Warrior ever is at hand to fight on our behalf.

When we are bound, Jesus sets us free.
When we are consumed with guilt, the Savior washes us clean.
When we are suffering, Mercy comforts us in our affliction.
When we are broken hearted, Jesus is very close.
When we cry for help,
The Faithful Father shows us the way of escape.

When we are hurt or sick, the Healer makes us whole.
When we come to the end of our resources,
the Provider meets our needs.
When we are lonely, Jesus, the Companion satisfies our soul.
When we are weak and don't know how to pray,
The Spirit is interceding for us.

All these things are there for those who seek first His Kingdom.

This is Clarity.

And this is Truth.

Nancy Bowser

Apprenticeship of Love

October 24th 2012
"Collene, do you trust Me?"

His question continues to challenge my spirit. Sometimes, I'm not sure...

"In the same way the Spirit also comes to help us, weak as we are. For we do not know how we ought to pray; the Spirit Himself pleads with God for us in groans that words cannot express. And God, who sees into our hearts, knows what the thought of the Spirit is; because the Spirit pleads with God on behalf of His people and in accordance with His will." (Romans 8:26-27)

I woke up that way again this morning. What once felt like a baby elephant playing on my chest, now feels like a massive, full-grown pachyderm has firmly seated himself directly over my heart. The hours, days and months have not lightened the load and the nights are getting darker. Initially, it was easy to turn the burden over to God. I could fill pages and hours with very specific, heartfelt prayers. Now, with the thick darkness and confusion of this jungle, most of the time all I can utter is "Jesus, help."

Thank God for **Romans 8** this morning. Thank God that the subject of my deepest aching burden doesn't have to depend on my faithfulness, understanding or skills. Thank God that He pursues us, despite us, all the while inviting us to participate in His pursuit of others. Thank God that He is using this situation to teach me a hands-on class about true love. Pray that I graduate, would you? Here's the syllabus:

"If I speak in the tongues of men or of angels, but do not have love, I am only a resounding gong or a clanging cymbal. If I have the gift of prophecy and can fathom all mysteries and all knowledge, and if I have a faith that can move mountains, but do not have love, I am nothing. If I give all I possess to the poor and give over my body to hardship that I may boast, but do not have love, I gain nothing.

Love is patient, love is kind. It does not envy, it does not boast, it is not proud. It does not dishonor others, it is not self-seeking, it is not easily angered, it keeps no record of wrongs. Love does not delight in evil but rejoices with the truth. It always protects, always trusts, always hopes, always perseveres. Love never fails.

But where there are prophecies, they will cease; where there are tongues, they will be stilled; where there is knowledge, it will pass away. For we know in part, and we prophesy in part, but when completeness comes, what is in part disappears. When I was a child, I talked like a child, I thought like a child, I reasoned like a child. When I became a man, I put the ways of childhood behind me. For now, we see only a reflection as in a mirror; then we shall see face to face. Now I know in part; then I shall know fully, even as I am fully known.

And now these three remain: faith, hope and love. But the greatest of these is love." (1 Corinthians 13)

Light in Your Darkness
Andrea Fugleberg

Hold Me in Your Arms

  C
1. Take me in Your arms
       F
And hold me tenderly and tight.
C
Hold me through the darkness
     G
And on into the light.

C
  Here in Your arms
    F
I am safe and secure.
    C
Your love is my armor
   G
And there is no fear.

    C
2. So hold me in Your arms
      F
And do not let me go.
   G
Your Beauty surrounds me
    F
With the warmth of Your glow.

C
Lord, You're my Savior
    F
And my hope is in You.
 G
I choose to surrender
   F   C
And place my trust there too.

    C
3. So hold me in Your arms
      F
And let me rest in You.
G
Touch me with Your Spirit
   F   C
Transform me through and through.

C
Here in Your arms
F
My soul is at rest.
G
I can face the fire
F   C
And I can pass this test.

C
4. Take me in Your arms
F
And hold me tenderly and tight.
C
Your Word will lead and guide me
G
As I battle through this fight.

C
Your holiness consumes me
F
Like the wave of a flood.
G
I'm covered by Your grace
F   C
And by the water and the blood.

END:
C
Take me in Your arms
F
And hold me tenderly and tight.
G
Hold me through the darkness
F   C
And on into the light.

C
Here in Your arms
F
I am safe and secure.
G
Your love is my armor
F   C
And there is no fear.

A Song of Nancy Bowser

Fight Club

October 31st 2012

The other day I planned to tell you about my love letters- the tangible evidence of true Love being shown to me directly from the Father. I have written and re-written about them at least six times. The concepts churning in my heart have gone in a dozen directions and nothing seemed complete. I had the sense that I had yet to take another end-of-quarter exam. I took some notes about the Sunday through Saturday events and the incredible love that I was shown. I was surprised by the extraordinary examples and blessed to note the ordinary examples...

Then came Sunday, again.

The morning started as usual. I have started making it a habit of not only attending church but going early for a class as well. I am the "baby" of the group, which I really like; the people have proven themselves to be genuine. That in itself is quite healing...

The church I've been attending is seven miles away, so I decided to multi-task by calling my dad on the way there. My parents have been on my mind heavily lately, for various reasons, and it had been a few days since I checked in with them. Mom answered Dad's phone and told me he'd have to call me back. He had spent the whole night awake, in pain.

The previous week, we had been together in Arkansas to support my grandmother as she went through a difficult heart surgery. When I left, Grandma had just been moved out of the ICU and everyone else seemed perfectly healthy.

Days later I called my dad for an update on Grandma's rehab progress. *"Little Girl, I can't talk; I hurt too much. Can I call you back later?"* had been his response that day.

Uhhhhhh, okay. I called Mom. She informed me that Dad had suddenly started experiencing pain that he had decided must be kidney stones. The pain passed quickly, and he returned my call. Days passed. A few bouts of pain and 1,100 miles later, he was home safe and returned to his normal routine.

This time, on Sunday, Dad didn't call back. Hours passed; the day uneventfully slipped into evening here as I wrestled with my own internal challenges.

Bedtime came; then Mom called- effectively signing me up for a club I never requested membership to.

"Collene, your dad's pain never went away this morning like it has the other days. I took him to the ER in Flagstaff this afternoon. They're running tests, but they've ruled out kidney stones."

The doctor had suggested to Dad that he may have pulled a muscle in his lower back... Uh, if you've ever met my dad, you know that he doesn't go to the ER with a pulled muscle. He was insistent, *"I'm 64 years old. I've pulled muscles, this isn't that. Try again."*

A CT scan and some bloodwork were ordered. We should know something in 30 minutes, they say. Thirty minutes later the nurse arrived, announcing that it would be about 30 minutes before the doctor would have the results. Dad teased her that her time was up already, she needed to give him answers now. She knelt next to him and with her face resting on her folded hands said, *"I'm so sorry, you must be in so much pain. The doctor needs to talk to you, but he needs more time."* This was the first indication that his "pulled muscle/kidney stone" wasn't going to be so simple.

The doctor returned, with pictures. My daddy's bones are full of holes. His hips are both fractured, his ribs and spine are splintering off into pieces that free float in his abdomen. This man has been fighting forest fires all year all over this entire nation. How is this possible?

Sunday night he was admitted to the hospital with bone marrow tests ordered for Monday morning.

The night took forever to pass.

Monday morning came and went, there was some disagreement among the doctors... Finally, after reviewing his tests, a new doctor assigned to his case decided a bone marrow test is too risky. He believes my dad's spine could shatter, just from the needle. A lymphatic biopsy is ordered along with additional blood work and more scans.

Monday reluctantly drug on.

One brother was unreachable, working in Africa. Another was not directly contactable- as a member of the U.S. Marine Corps, located in AnUndisclosedDangerousLocation (it's a real place, trust me). A third had no cell service and no power, living in New York with his new pal, Hurricane Sandy. The rest of us, remotely desperately clung to each other, from every corner of this country, for encouragement and even a few laughs to break the tension...

Monday night the doctor finally returned. Even without the biopsy results, it is obvious:

My hero, my rock, my adviser, my daddy, Superman himself- has rapidly growing, Stage IV, full-skeletal metastasized, incurable cancer.

I hate this club I've been forced to join.

This morning when I woke up with tears already (still?) streaming out of the corner of my eyes, I realized that I am changed forever. I thought I was acquainted with Grief, but yesterday, Grief started unpacking his boxes to live with me forever.

Yet, already this club has it's comforts. So, so many of my friends and loved ones are members here. I am no longer going to be watching them from across the fence. They've already started to show me around. My five days of love letters look puny in comparison to the flood of specific love evidence that has already filled pages of my red tattered journal since Sunday. Yes, God is still good. Yes, He loves even me.

Three things were already in place inside my heart before this week and for now, this is all I have:

1. The recurring words on my lips, as I waited for news on Monday, were actually lyrics to *"Don't Stop the Madness,"* another Tenth Avenue North song:

"All I hear is what they're selling me: "If God is love there can't be suffering, have a little faith and prosperity."

But, oh my God I know there's more than this! If you promised pain, it can't be meaningless. So make me poor if that's the price for freedom...

Do whatever it takes to give me your heart and bring me down to my knees Lord."

2. I had already been reading in **Romans 8**, you might remember this from the other day. A few verses before those I mentioned that day it says this:

"I consider that our present sufferings are not worth comparing with the glory that will be revealed in us." (Romans 8:18)

3. I had a conversation, completely unrelated to this situation, on Monday morning... My friend, who embraced Grief years ago, gave me these words of wisdom:

"Shake hands with Sadness, he'll visit often and stay for a short while. However, when Grief knocks at your door, welcome him and embrace him, for he has moved in to stay."

Finally, if you don't know my dad, you need to understand this about him:

He has just rallied. He plans to, in his words, *"...get the pain under control, start a treatment, talk to a few more specialists, cut some firewood, do a few chores around the house and get back to fighting fires."*

I don't doubt that. With his excellent health, physical strength, and spiritual and emotional fortitude, he will have longer than most with his diagnosis. This is likely to be a long, grueling race...

Leaving Paradise
Collene James
Santorini Island, Aegean Sea- Greece

205

Every Party Has a Pooper

November 13th 2012

If you don't appreciate a toddler tantrum thrown by an adult, you should go now.

If I could throw myself to the ground and toss my sippy cup and bang my head- hard, onto the concrete- all the while wailing and rolling around, I would. If I could kick someone, hard, in the shins and run away as fast as possible, I would. If I could beat my tiny fists against someone's broad chest and kick at the air until I ran out of steam, I would. If I could lay my head on someone's shoulder and sob until they tucked me into my crib for the night- with my soft footy pajamas, I would.

But I'm a big girl, with no sippy cup, no soft footy pajamas, no broad chest to beat, no shoulder to sob on, no shins to kick, and a headache that wouldn't find relief slamming the ground. There's no security within the four slatted walls of a crib and really, I'm all out of steam anyway.

Today, I'm afraid. I literally, physically hurt in chambers of my heart I never knew existed. I found that even breathing in too deeply released tears at stupid times today. I'm angry. I want to pick a fight with someone, anyone. Yes, I am immature and ridiculous, embarrassing even. What I really want is just to be held, to be reassured that it will all be okay.

"It" won't be okay. None of it. I don't want to do this anymore.

I don't want to **DO** this.

I don't want to do **THIS**.

Most of them are stuffers, my ancestors that is. When situations are complicated, emotionally speaking, the family handbook prescribes an ignore-it-it'll-go-away remedy. However, I'm only a recessive carrier of that gene, an anomaly. I need direct, head-on information. I need a plan. I need "why" to be understood. I'm irritated that I'm so different than all of them. In some ways I feel like I don't belong. I can't find comfort in coping the way most of them do.

I am more alone than ever.

Last week I took the pre-planned trip back to Arkansas; my third visit since April. The timing of the trip could not have been more perfectly orchestrated. My grandmother had just had heart surgery and was about to be released from the hospital. The trip was planned before Dad's diagnosis. My dad had told his mother about his cancer, but spared her grave details, concerned for her own health. In some ways, I spent the week reassuring her of what I'm not convinced myself. She seemed naive about the entire situation until the day she point-blank asked me: *"Do you know where they plan to bury your dad? Is there a nice cemetery near their home?"*

I **DON'T** want to do this. I don't think his mom does either.

The other parts of the week were sweet. And bitter. Grandma told me about her fighting depression since Grandpa died in April. She told me she clings to the happy times, of which she had dozens of stories. She says she is writing a book; I told her I'd try to help her. Who wouldn't want to hear about my 83-year-old, semi-driving, itty-bitty grandma who "used-to-could" do just about anything? This woman has a plethora of one-liners.

She assured me several times that she knows, very well, some of what I'm going through and that she understands how hard my daily life is as a single, full-time working mother. I believed her because she willingly shared a few of her own experiences along with a few regrets and heartaches she has.

I found myself deeply loving and appreciating this woman in ways I didn't think possible only six months ago. I found a little of myself in her and then I found myself feeling very sad. And very mad. And fighting complicated emotions and doubts and hurt and frustration and years of confusion. And then I found myself, on the return plane, coming to a place of acceptance without understanding. I hated leaving, wondering if I'd see her again. There are so many places I need to be and only one of me and never enough time or resources...

If I had the energy, I'd tell you about the other pressures I can't quite escape. I will say that if I'm being honest, today fear, doubt, distrust, loneliness and the physical sensations of grief are ruling my heart.

"What I feared has come upon me; what I dreaded has happened to me. I have no peace, no quietness; I have no rest, but only turmoil." (Job 3:25,26)

Will someone please send me to my room?

~~Angry~~ Blessed

November 26th 2012

Last fall, when I started this blog, a friend called me to express her concerns about it. She has always been on the lookout for potential destroyers of my heart and saw this as a huge risk. She was right, it was and continues to increasingly be risky. What neither of us could have known is that despite the vulnerability of exposure, the risk has paid off in unexpected ways.

Writing here, unlike writing in my tattered journal, has helped me process years of experiences and nonsense internal narratives. I am being forced to confront the inconsistencies in myself while being held to a certain amount of accountability by my readers- whomever they may be. This has made it nearly impossible for me to turn back and get comfortable again in the ridiculous lifestyle of my "Egypt." I am being changed.

I have not spent the entire last two weeks being angry. The truth is, after I wrote last, I regretted letting you see that deep into me and nearly deleted the Party Pooper post. I would have, except for the conversation I had with a reader the next day. *"You just summed up the entire two and a half years of life after my dad died, unexpectedly, my senior year of high school,"* she said. Later, another reader sent me a reassuring message. His grief also resonated with my ugly thoughts and emotions. He went on to tell me more about his experience. These conversations are invaluable to me, so I press on.

For months I've been arguing with myself about whether to tell you more of the "everything" I committed to working through. Mentally, I have written that blog 1,000 times since May. Yet, each time I sit here to type it, I don't. I continue to feel that I am at a loss pertaining to a specific experience this past year. In some ways, I feel despair that I can't work the situation to a comfortable, healthy place of understanding in my head and heart simultaneously and make it "pen-sure" for all of you. Instead, I'll tell you about Thanksgiving this year.

Anger is exhausting. I threw my fit, asked my "whys," retreated to my bed, sobbed barrels of tears and then, I drove.

Fifteen hours of road noise, kids happily chattering in the background, my iPod on shuffle, and my own noisy thoughts, brought me to my first destination. I concluded that don't have time or energy to be mad. I have worked my heart into a place of forgiveness and, if it were possible, I'd owe an apology or two. By the time I arrived in Albuquerque my head and heart had shaken hands in a cease-fire agreement, for now, and I was able to enjoy my visit.

She and I have three decades of friendship experience, most of which have been spent communicating by pen and paper. (It seems that I'll have to take my kids to the Museum of Natural History, past the Atari and Pacman displays, to the room of Ancient History to show my kids a postage stamp...). She has known my family nearly as long as I have and has such sweet memories of things that I had forgotten or taken for granted. Lately these kinds of conversations are deeply important to me. Although we were surrounded by five of our offspring, most of the time, I didn't feel a day older than ten. We reminisced and shared perspectives, updated each other on the current life state-of-affairs and then shared plans for the near future... I am so blessed.

Before I left New Mexico I had come full circle. The "I don't want to do this" mentality of the days and weeks before was replaced with the understanding that I absolutely don't have to do this, but I need to. I am aware that I have "outs," distractions, escapes. Instead, I am committed to finishing the course and earning my degree. Pain is an excellent teacher and experience is what gives meaning to ideology.

I finished my vacation in northern Arizona. Three of my five brothers met me there, at Mom and Dad's. There was a sister-in-law, two nieces and a nephew thrown in the mix, along with my own kids. I can't define it, exactly, but the visit was different than usual. "Simplicity" is the only word that describes it. I have decided that these people I was assigned to share life with from birth are the exact people I want to do life with when things get tough. We could not be more different. We could not be more perfect for each other.

Dad feels healthy. I noticed a few (unacknowledged) pained expressions, from time to time. He looks tired. He has changed his diet and, somewhat, his daily routine. He is softer. Mom is too. I have thought a lot about the reality that he, like all of us, is dying. Sometimes I want the specifics. Do we have two months, ten years? Ultimately, it doesn't matter. No one knows, except God- and He's not saying. For now, I have today, and I am blessed...

Standard

(Isaiah 59)

Dm   Am   Dm
We raise up a standard in this place (2 x's)

Dm   Am   Dm
We raise up the standard of the name of the Lord.
Dm   Am   Dm
We raise up the standard of the love of God.
Dm   Am Dm
We raise up the standard of salvation.
Dm   Am   Dm
We raise up the standard of Yeshua's blood.

Dm   Am   Dm
When the enemy presses in hard do not fear.
Dm   Am   Dm
We raise up a standard in this place.

Dm   Am   Dm
The Lord's clothed in righteousness, vengeance and zeal.
Dm   Am   Dm
We raise up a standard in this place.

Dm   Am Dm
When the enemy comes in like a flood.
Dm   Am   Dm
We raise up a standard in this place.

Dm   Am   Dm
The name of the Lord shall be feared from the west.
Dm   Am   Dm
We raise up a standard in this place.

Dm   Am   Dm
And His glory will come from the rising of the sun.
Dm   Am   Dm
We raise up a standard in this place.

Dm   Am   Dm
We raise up the standard of God's justice.
Dm   Am   Dm
We raise up the stan-dard of God's truth.
Dm   Am   Dm
We raise up the stan-dard of God's Word.
Dm   Am Dm
We raise up the standard of intercession.

Dm   Am   Dm
Yeshua Hamashiach we raise You high!

A Song of Nancy Bowser

Dasani Me

November 30ᵗʰ 2012

I had a conversation with a client today about llamas. That turned into a conversation about camels, which got me thinking, again, about desert wandering.

Deserts have been on my mind all week, along with the "sufficiency of Christ" concept. I've never been thirsty in a desert, even in the slightest, but I have been extremely thirsty in less dramatic locations. So, are you with me? Llamas, camels, desert, extreme thirst- each are the cars on this thought train tonight.

The other conversation of the week that I plan to marry with that train of thought is the one I had Monday at the Benjamin Meeting. That's what I'm calling my weekly Monday morning sanity hearings with my counselor/pastor/mentor/friend/person. I'll tell you about the thought train marriage in a minute, but first let me tell you about Benjamin.

I like Ben. He's experienced in EVERYTHING. He's a long-time boxing coach/trainer, former altar boy, former electrician, former dairy hand, veteran of the Navy, father of 8, and husband to the coolest lady alive (to hear him tell it). He has theology degrees, counseling degrees, compassion, patience, and insight. Okay, that's a scratch of the surface, but it's enough to give you tonight.

The BEST part about the Benjamin Meetings is that he came to me and asked to meet with me. Weird. I was putting off the strange urge to call him all summer. Sooooo, the result has been a couple of months of me sticking my toe in the waters of trust, testing their depth and trying to figure out what exactly the result of our friendship will be.

Ben is the first church leader I have felt completely comfortable around, especially when I don't like what I'm hearing. More than once I've told him that he or "it" p*$$*s me off. I may or may not have used the phrase *"so what you're telling me is that what I think/want is @$^&%*$$?"* He is always calm, always even tempered. I'm pretty sure his blood pressure never rises. Which is good, because I'm (at times) highly, frustratingly emotional. He doesn't get personally offended at my faithlessness or doubt. While I'm not proud of my messy mouth or the emotions that fuel the words, it is extremely comforting to know that a pastor, a direct representative of God Himself, is willing to accept me right where I'm at-without condemnation or criticism. I know the ugly words are temporary as my preferred vocabulary, but right now they seem to be the only ones strong enough to express the strength of my distress.

So, Monday we were discussing the idea that I'm supposed to somehow, magically, find my "sufficiency" in Christ alone. I was again mad that those words are SOOOOO bumper-stickery and the perfect Christianese example of why I HATE being around glossy, church people. No one can give me a satisfactory example of how that meshes with real life, especially in the life of a worn-thin, tapped-out, mostly penniless, stupidly idealistic, overly trusting, weakly hopeful, massive-hearted, divorced mom of three. More than a few numbers went up on my blood pressure that day, as well as the pouring of a few dozen jugs of tears and snot.

Ben and I had come up with a list of five of my harshest daily realities. They all started with "P." Okay, all but one, but we changed it to a "PH" for the sake of the list. At the end of the problem solving/perspective gaining session I told him about my current grief-category anger as it applies to the list:

"I feel like my whole life I've been excruciatingly thirsty, standing alone in the middle of an enormous desert. In two of those categories I was recently offered a glass of water. Before I could grab it and drink, the glass was torn from my hands and a teaspoon of that water was trickled onto my lips. Now, I've tasted it. What I've craved, no NEEDED for survival, tasted sweeter than my exhausted, treacherously parched soul could have ever dreamed up. It's beyond cruel. Actually, I believe that this is worse for me than if I'd never known water existed."

We sat at his table and argued about semantics for a while. I told him that my understanding is that I'm not supposed to want or need anything. In fact, how dare I even try to ask for a "want," when "needs" are constantly in my face? I'm supposed to care less about the frivolity of asking for Dasani water, when swamp water isn't even an option.

He let me rant. He tossed a box of Kleenex at me and waited. Then he said, *"Collene, Jesus was a man. Even He said,* **'My grace is sufficient for you'***..."*

He went on to say, *"Don't you think that if He was physically sitting next to you in an actual desert, He'd give you actual water? He never just sat by someone with real-life needs and somehow magically became their 'sufficiency' just because He was physically present."*

He made me define "Grace," which was easy because it's part of my daughter's name- "God's Blessing." Okay, so then he made me define what a blessing is..."a gift," I told him.

"Yup."

So, if all that is true, then why in some of these areas, am I being tortured with barely moistened lips and I'm not even seeing swamp water in a mirage on the horizon? Is there some birthday party event I have to wait for to take even a teeny sip again? What happens if I die of thirst first?

I don't know. I'm still wrestling the narrative that stubbornly whispers, *"it's because you're bad and don't deserve it, Collene."* The truth is, it's entirely possible that I took that glass of water and threw it out myself, rather than having it taken away by someone else. What I know is that I can't see it, solve it, or repair it. I'm concerned that, that which I destroyed, although now that I know it CAN be, WON'T be salvaged or replaced by Him... Tonight, I'm clinging to the last shred of belief that says He will.

I'll end by telling you, mostly for me to refer to again in the future, what Ben told me last. Apparently, from his perspective, I am not a mess. I am surrounded by messiness, but I am *"very well adjusted, intelligent, grounded, thoughtful and even sane."* I am an *"unusual woman"* (a compliment, I think) and *"incredibly deep- relationally."* In addition, I am *"a very good mom who parents with purpose and foresight"* and oh, *"any man with half a brain could see that I am a catch."* Uhhhhhhhhhhhhhhhhhh, all of that is even uncomfortable to type. I can't see it quite that way, but whatev, it's his opinion and it felt good to hear.

Goodnight.

Door of Hope

C
In the Valley of Trouble, there's hope for your soul.
    G   F   C
In the Valley of Trouble, He can make you whole.
      C
The pathway is praise that leads to the Son,
    G   C
His name is Jesus, He's the One.

        G   F   C
He's the Door of Hope and the Bread of Life;
    G   F   C
The Lamb of God and the Sacrifice.
    C
He died on the cross, He's paid the price;
    G   F   C
So let's worship the King now and give Him your life.

      C
He's the Living Water and we'll never thirst;
      G   F   C
When we drink from His well and put His kingdom first.
      C
This is the work of God that we believe in Him;
    G   F   C
His blood it can cleanse us and forgive us our sin.

      C
There's a love that can conquer the greatest of fears;
    G   F   C
Turn ashes to beauty and dry all your tears;
      C
Heal the hurts that are binding, set the captives free.
    G   F   C
His name is Jesus, so come and see.

(Hosea 2:15; 1 Peter 1:3-5; 6-9; Psalm 22; John 1:29, 6:35; Revelation 5:12; Hebrews 12:2; 1 John 4:18; 2 Timothy 1:7; Isaiah 61:1-3; John 4:10, 6:29, 7:37; Matthew 6:33; 1 John 1:7,9)

A Song of Nancy Bowser

Wave Shaped, Rescue Ready

December 6th 2012

I had been dropped. Somehow my feet left the floor of the sight-seeing helicopter, and I was falling. Even still, I'm still not completely sure if I was pushed or if I jumped; it doesn't matter anymore. It was a free-fall with no time to tuck and curl and certainly no parachute. I hit the water, flat on my face, the air sucked from my lungs, the cold night closed around me, the cold water rushed every pore.

When daylight broke, I was still twisting in a somersault, trying to make heads or tails of where I was. Was that ocean bottom or sky? It all looked the same, the pressure was intense, the saltwater stung every gaping wound.

It took nearly a year just to get my head above water. Even still today, the cold nights fall on me fast and drag on forever; the days are hot and long. Sunsets and sunrises are the hope and beauty my tired body and mind crave as I tread the deep water. My swimming skills are lacking. I should have spent more time in the pool, I think.

Then, late last year I saw the beach. My soul was revived. I pumped my tired arms and legs to swim faster. In the distance I saw white sand, warmth, rest... I thought I felt my toes touch the bottom of the ocean.

The whipping, bitter, wind picked up again early this year. The waves feel taller than ever as they crash over my head; the current is dragging me back to sea. The vision of the beach is a faded memory, replaced by the reality of the immensity of this ocean. I relaxed a little lower in the water. I'm tired of the fight. It's lonely. It's painful. It's cold and desperately dark. The days turn to weeks, then months, and now, three years. Still, somehow, I don't drown.

I'm starting to sense strength in my body like I've never known. These waves are shaping it, toning me. I realized this month that the sunrises have lasted a little longer, and the sunsets have seemed a little warmer.

This week I caught a glimpse of what I couldn't see before. What I once thought was a hallucination is really a lifeboat, full of friendly faces. It is now clear to me, some of the tugging I feel is a thick rope fastened securely around me. Together they are paddling slowly to shore, pulling me with them, screaming encouragement into the wind, whispering love to me in the cold, still darkness. I have not been alone in this, not for a day.

It is becoming apparent to me: I am a recruit. I am part of a team. I was dropped or pushed or allowed to fall, as a part of the program. All of this training has been disciplining and shaping my body, mind, emotions, will and spirit- for a real eternal purpose.

We will eventually get to the beach. My feet will feel the warmth of the white sand. I will sit, briefly, and soak up the sun. I will laugh and play and rest... I hope to spend a day or two there, but the beach isn't where I'm from, nor is it where I want to live.

One day, very soon, I will have a boat of my own. It will come with a rope, and I will have the strength, willpower, understanding, wisdom, insight, and experience to help paddle another fallen swimmer to shore.

"In this you greatly rejoice, though now for a little while, if need be, you have been grieved by various trials, that the genuineness of your faith, being much more precious than gold that perishes, though it is tested by fire, may be found to praise, honor, and glory at the revelation of Jesus Christ, who having not seen you love. Though now you do not see Him, yet believing, you rejoice with joy inexpressible and full of glory, receiving the end of your faith—the salvation of your souls." (1 Peter 1:6-9)

Wave Shaped
Collene James
Nags Head, NC

Rescue Ready
Collene James
Outer Banks, NC

217

Pillows and Parachutes

Creator looked at me,
smiled, and handed down
a soft, fluffy bundle.
How soft, a pillow.
I thinkingly thought as
I held my new toy.
Hello.
A different voice,
I looked up,
who are you, I wondered.
I'm Doubt,
I'm here to ruin your life.
Your pillow looks sleepy,
Here, hug me instead.
Quiet arms wrapped me up and
I yawned a lean into a
pillow that was a parachute.
I was meant to fly,
– you see –
but my new friend's embrace
was warm and nice,
so I rested my head
and doubted what he said,
he couldn't possibly
ruin my life.

But there and then there,
it was a pain
too uncomfortable to sleep.
I stood and looked down
to find what bothered me so.
There it was on my pillow,
a beautiful golden buckle
and another and another.
This is no pillow.
I thinkingly thought
as I skipped a leap
off a ledge
labeled *Faith.*
I was meant to fly
– you see –
and my pillow was a parachute.

Ashley Fugleberg

Perspective

F/A   Bb2
  Give me Your eyes to see
F/A   Bb2
  I need Your ears to hear

F/A   Dm7
  Your heart to love
               Gm7   C
  And never to fear

  F/A   Bb2
I draw near to You
F/A   Bb2
  I give up my rights

F/A   Dm7
  I'll die to self
            Gm7   C
And live for Christ

A Song of Nancy Bowser

Seen
Collene James

220

Praise

O Yahweh, God of all. I give You all and want to shout out loud, how great You are!

Your love for me has set me free!

I want You to hear me say how much I am thankful for all that You have done for me. You O God, have brought me to life again, with this life I will worship You.

Everyone, know this,

Yahweh is the life giver,

He is the greatest power, and none can compare.

Your love shines forever and never ends. Though I have not seen Your face, I can feel Your grace upon my life.

I want to bless You Lord with my life's actions. In Jesus' wonderful name, amen.

"The LORD bless thee, and keep thee: The LORD make his face shine upon thee, and be gracious unto thee; The LORD lift up his countenance upon thee, and give thee peace." (Numbers 6:24-26)

Shawn Carter

Part I- Avoiding Hagar, Sacrificing Isaac

January 8th 2013

Have you read about Hagar? Hagar got a raw deal. I've thought a lot about her this week, and I want nothing to do with her! I'm sure she was nice enough, but I've decided "nice enough" isn't good enough to pattern my own life story after her.

I'm guessing Ms. Hagar isn't front and center in your short-term memory, so I'll do the catching up for you:

Back before Father Abraham had many sons, many sons had Father Abraham... God had given him a vision and a promise about those "many sons." Abe was 85-ish. He, being a communicative husband, left his little moment with the Almighty and went home to tell his wife Sarai about the direction their life was now apparently heading...

Well, Sarai (soon to be Sarah) was intelligent. She had no problem with the math, or the biology, and according to her own understanding, she wasn't about to imagine her AARP eligible body cranking out any infants anytime soon. She was also an economizing wife. She already HAD house-help from a maid (Hagar) and decided that she'd be the "safe bet" pertaining to getting on with the baby dream. She, as only a wife can do, gave specific instructions to Abe: *"The LORD has kept me from having children. Go, sleep with my slave; perhaps I can build a family through her." (Genesis 16:2)*

Abram (who had not had his name changed to Abraham yet) obeyed his wife. Hagar readily conceived. Obviously, because Sarah didn't do much THINKING before she did her speaking, she was surprised to find that she was jealous and angry. She pouted then got downright ugly about it. Apparently, she didn't want what she wanted. Wives!

So, Sarai was mean enough to Hagar that the maid ended up running away. God, the pursuer and restorer of people and situations, sent an angel to Hagar. After a little chit-chat that included some encouragement, a few promised blessings and a command to return to Abram, the pregnant Hagar went home. Abe was 86 when his illegitimate firstborn son, Ishmael, was born.

Eventually, about the time Ishmael started his junior high home-school courses, God came back to Abe and reminded him of His promise, lengthened his name (from Abram to Abraham) and got then got really specific: *"As for Sarai your wife, you are no longer to call her Sarai; her name will be Sarah. I will bless her and will surely give you a son by her. I will bless her so that she will be the mother of nations; kings of peoples will come from her." (Genesis 17:15-16)*

Abe's reaction? He hit the ground laughing. Then he said: *"Will a son be born to a man a hundred years old? Will Sarah bear a child at the age of ninety?"* And Abraham said to God, *"If only Ishmael might live under your blessing!"* Then God said, *"Yes, but your wife Sarah will bear you a son, and you will call him Isaac..." (Genesis 17:17-19a)*

Long story short, God didn't stutter or mince words. It happened EXACTLY that way-- 25 or so years AFTER the promise was declared...

Now flash forward a few years. Get this: God comes back to Abraham and very clearly tells him to take Isaac up the mountain, build a fire, and sacrifice him as an offering to God. Uhhhhhh, what?! Yep, that's the request: *"Take your son, your only son, whom you love—Isaac—and go to the region of Moriah. Sacrifice him there as a burnt offering on a mountain I will show you." (Genesis 22:2)*

By now Abraham trusts, completely, that he legitimately heard and now recognized the voice of God. He trusts that voice. He trusts the love of his God and he responds the only way that makes sense to him anymore. He got up, got his boy, grabbed a donkey, cut some firewood, and headed out. THREE days later, Abraham reached his destination. I wonder if he did much thinking on that little three-day jaunt with his sweet, trusting, son...

As he started unpacking his wood and preparing his fire, Isaac asked: *"Hey Dad, what are we doing? This looks a little like a sacrifice of worship, but I think we forgot the lamb..."* (A Collene paraphrase.)

Abraham confidently responded, knowing that he knew what he knew even after the visible evidence, once again, contradicted the promise he had heard: *"God himself will provide the lamb for the burnt offering, my son." (Genesis 22:8)*

Abe continued obediently. Alter built? Check. Fire started? Check. Knife sharp? Check. Son bound? Check. He placed Isaac on top of the wood and raised his knife.

"Abraham! Abraham!"

The shout came from heaven, an angel of the Lord.

Abraham answered, *"Here I am."*

"Do not lay a hand on the boy," He said. *"Do not do anything to him. Now I know that you fear God, because you have not withheld from Me your son, your only son." (Genesis 22:12)*

WHEW! Abraham looked up and saw a ram caught in the bushes. God provided a sacrifice, restored the promise, and carried out His original plan through Abraham's legitimate offspring, Isaac.

Unfortunately, as is always the case, there's a cost associated with catching the "vision" from God and sprinting ahead to make it happen. Ishmael was also blessed with a big ole' family. If you like history, look it up. Abraham's little sprint ahead of God cost him and continues to rip violently through the family.

We've all seen that puppy, the one someone calls "come" to. He speeds to his master, but then blows right past. Where the heck is that dumb dog going?! I am that dog. *"Wait, isn't my master running after me? I had the vision, I thought we were going!"* My Master is shaking His head in the distance. *"Collene, I'm the one that knows where we're going, come back to Me and heel..."* It seems I still may need more training.

My new woulda-been-a-friend-except-he's-dead, Oswald Chambers, put it a different way in his January 4th entry for *"My Utmost for His Highest."* I've probably read it a dozen times in the last four days. Like Oswald says,

"At first you may see clearly what God's will is— the severance of a friendship, the breaking off of a business relationship, or something else you feel is distinctly God's will for you to do. But never act on the impulse of that feeling. If you do, you will cause difficult situations to arise which will take years to untangle. Wait for God's timing and He will do it without any heartache or disappointment. When it is a question of the providential will of God, wait for God to move.

Peter did not wait for God. He predicted in his own mind...Peter...was honest but ignorant... (Jesus had) a deeper knowledge of Peter than Peter had of himself. He could not follow Jesus because he did not know himself or his own capabilities well enough. Natural devotion may be enough to attract us to Jesus, to make us feel His irresistible charm, but it will never make us disciples. Natural devotion will deny Jesus, always falling short of what it means to truly follow Him."

Good Lord! Considering that, I pray I don't restlessly look for a Hagar to fulfill God's vision for me as it pertains to my own understanding! I've experienced, one too many times, the *"it will take years to untangle"* scenario Oswald warned about. I sense the call to pack up my donkey, my altar building supplies and some fire-starter and to grab my dreams and sharpen my knife.

Burning Bush
Collene James
Carbondale County, CO

Part II- Loosening One Fist, Tightening Another

January 9th 1013
Last night I couldn't find a natural segue and I had a lot more to think on... The idea of sacrificing my "Isaac" isn't new, although it's a little awkward to imagine since I literally HAVE a son named Isaac. The whispering urges to *"let go"* and *"empty my hands"* and to *"wait with arms high and heart abandoned"* trace clear back, on this blog journal, to May for sure and possibly earlier in 2012.

Like Peter at the Last Supper, (If you missed it in yesterday's entry, see the January 4th entry for *"My Utmost for His Highest"*), I have honestly felt like I was and am wholeheartedly abandoning myself to God's plan for me. Just like Peter, I feeeeeeel myself reaching, searching, hoping, trusting, and losing sight of my own agenda. I also find myself feeling love and gratitude more than ever before; I now have a deep desire to *"lay down my life"* for this Jesus I see... I've spent this past year with a bit of a strangle hold on certain characteristics about God that I desperately want to be true. Loving, Faithful, Pursuant, and Trustworthy are all concepts I am clinging to for dear life. But, like Peter, it seems I don't know myself as well as Jesus does...

Because the *"Let Go"* theme keeps playing through my mind, I am aware that there must be something I'm supposed to release, but I have been unable to figure out what, exactly. I sort of know "what," I just don't know what parts of "what." The concepts of *"presenting my requests to God,"* *"praying without ceasing,"* *"faith being the assurance of things hoped for but unseen,"* and that *"he who asks, but doubts is double-minded and unstable in all his ways..."* all have had me tripped up as they pertain to my "what." *(See Philippians 4:6, 1 Thessalonians 5:17, Hebrews 11, Luke 11:11, Matthew 7:10-11, James 1:2-8* to see those concepts for yourself.)

How does a girl *"pray boldly"* and *"without ceasing"* all the while *"letting go"* and sacrificing the dream called "Isaac" without it falling under the category of "doubt."

Incidentally, have I told you I still get accused of over-thinking, often?

Okay, soooo with the Friday (January 4th) Oswald Chambers entry still fresh on my mind, Sunday came. I was in a less than "godly" mood that morning. My youngest sister is visiting, so she got to be my pre-church sounding board. The experiences and conversations and nightmares and heartaches of the last two weeks had reached a boiling point. To say the least, I was ready to tap out and surrender to the fear, doubt, distrust, and disappointment. After I vented, she gently told me a few of her frustrations as well as a few of her realizations about herself in the midst of them. We headed to church.

Oh good, the freakin' bulletin handout is splattered with bumper-sticker phrases! I internally rolled my eyes, then reminded myself that my pastor is one of the most genuine, big-hearted, spiritually grounded people I know. I'd stay. I can't deny the church-wound in me is still gaping.

"...And God has an abundance...in mind for you..." were the words that stuck out most.

"Abundance" is such a frustrating LIE, in my experience. I've never had an abundance of anything. Well, except shoes, and even that is debatable and certainly not God's fault.

I'm not a preacher and I certainly do not intend to parrot the good pastor's sermon here. I will say that he, without knowing it, had a verse of scripture that addressed nearly EVERYTHING I had been complaining to my sister about in the privacy of my kitchen an hour before, and those were just in his opening paragraphs. DANG! Now, I have to listen.

What if I recklessly believed God when He whispered His promise to love me perfectly? What if I recklessly believed that God meant it when He said He has **"plans to prosper and not to harm"** me? What if I trusted His voice and believed His promise to fulfill the exact request I presented Him with, my "Isaac" if you will, and trusted that He would not give me a stone when I need bread or a serpent when I need a fish? (See **Matthew 7** for context clues.) Would that trust last long enough for me to haul that very same "Isaac" the entire three-day journey, up to the mountain, to sacrifice it- all the while knowing, in the depth of my soul, that God would still provide the very thing I put to death?

What if I believed Him enough to stand, with arms high and heart abandoned- fists unclenched, while I waaaaaaaaaaaaaaaaait, indefinitely, for Jesus to move first? What if that wait is 25, or 40 years? What if I gave up my dreams and my needs according to my own understanding, and in exchange, grasped the hand of my Abba (Father) long enough to follow Him to the viewing window, where dreams incubate, to catch a glimpse of HIS dreams for me and HIS understanding of my needs?

I remember the Sunday, not quite a year ago, when I made it through an entire church service without melting into a sobbing mess. That was a good day. This past Sunday was the first one since that day that I couldn't get through one song, or one bullet-point on the handout without a river of tears washing my cheeks. I am being asked to give up even more. After all the loss and pain and devastation of the previous four years, I find myself at the altar again. Will I trust enough to place the rest of myself on it?

I didn't come this far to stop here. The answer is, yes.

As I worked my way through my heart and each of the things that are so dear to me, acknowledging my deep wounds and fears and hopes, I again remembered Oswald's Friday words:

"...you will cause difficult situations to arise which will take years to untangle. Wait for God's timing and He will do it without any heartache or disappointment."

The picture I took of my, minutes-old, new baby niece flashed in my mind. She is me; I am her. I am not intentionally, rebelliously, gripping that which will cause heartache and disappointment. I am not intentionally sprinting past Jesus when He calls *"come"* and gives me a vision of His life for me. I am desperately reaching for Him clinging to His finger, crying out for His comfort, all the while pulling my own hair out and causing my own discomfort...

Father, help me let go of that which is causing me pain, while tightening my grip on the comfort that can only come from You...

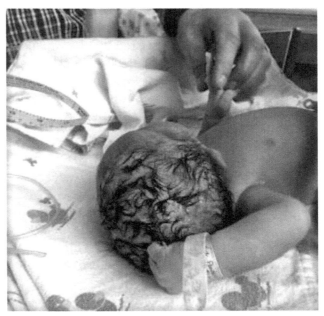

Who's Got Your Keys

January 15th 2013

I've been thinking and discussing stuff with a plethora of people. The best thing about my job is that I get to meet an endless array of personality types. People that come from a broad spectrum of childhood experiences, religious perspectives (or lack of), senses of humor (or lack of), and relational awareness. People fascinate me.

The theme of most of my conversations today centered around "people pleasing." It's interesting how themes emerge some days. My last client today is one that has taken almost two years to get to know with any depth. She's super polite, intelligent, well put together, gorgeous. I am her polar-opposite as it pertains to initial presentation, but her perfect match as it pertains to the gears and guts of how we think and what makes us 'tick.' Both of us have a "people pleasing" bent to us, which greatly interferes, at times, with the "God-pleasing" directive we both desire to fulfill...

Anywho, she and I have had similar experiences pertaining to parents, in-laws, mothering and relating to "church people." As a side note, if you consider yourself a "church person," it's entirely possible I will offend you in this blog from time to time. I'm almost sorry, except not really. I've been one too, I'm afraid, so I feel pretty good about calling you and "old me" out on certain stuff.

As my client and I talked tonight, I found myself once again feeling the familiar blood-pressure-raising, sick-to-my-stomach-knot, frustration-turned-pain, I ALWAYS feel when I hear, yet another, example of "church people" slaughtering their own while maintaining an air of piety and judgement.

Aren't we so glad God had mercy and grace and died for Ms. So-n-So so that she could then turn and point her fat finger in some wretched sinner's face and demand perfection? Oh, but don't forget Mrs. Sunshine-n-Roses! You know her, she's full of bubbles and fairies. Isn't it suuuuuuuuuuch a blessing to be near her? *"Oh, your daddy has cancer? Oooooooh, honey, God knows best! He'll be better off with Jesus anyway, let's thank Him for the fact that you HAVE a daddy in the first place, it could be so much worse."* Or, *"that sixth miscarriage just means the timing for a family isn't right yet, remember, God's timing is always perfect."* Mrs. Sunshine-n-Roses always has the ready-made bow to package up your "ugly" with her "pretty" to make it more palatable. God fits neatly in both Ms. So-n-So and Mrs.

Sunshine-n-Roses's boxes. Seriously, I have words- strong, off-putting words- which express more concisely how I feel, but you get my drift and I'm trying to be classier in 2013.

Oh, while we're on the subject, "religion" to me is a four-letter word. I don't care what branch you're sitting on; religion seems to be merely man's way of controlling other men. (Not to leave you ladies out of it, "women trying to control other women" is the subtitle.) Okay, now that I've established how I feel about all that, I'll catch you up to speed. Twice last week, once yesterday and three times today, this very topic came up. It's safe to say I've got a little work to do in the area of forgiveness as it pertains to some specific "church people," but the ultimate frustration for me is this:

I want a BIG God. I have come to despise the god that so many of "His" people present and claim to represent.

I want the Guy that parted the sea to bring His people out of slavery. I want the God who fed thousands of people with a couple of fish and a little bread. You know, the One who put a little spit in the blind guy's eyes and gave him sight. I want the One who made the walls of Jericho fall at the sound of a trumpet and shouting, the One who delivered victory, over the giant, Goliath, to a kid with a stick and a rock. I want the Guy who called a decaying Lazarus out of his grave...

I am a slave to what I know; I am starving and needy and blind. I have thick walls of insecurity and pain. I'm small and insufficient but have giant battles that need a victory. I am in desperate need of life. If God is not still that guy, what's the point? If He fits in a definable, palatable box that some pious, hoity-toity, perfect church person is comfortable with, I don't have time to waste on this.

I'm guessing a BIG God like that can handle my four-letter words, my doubting, my anger, my fear...

So, the incessant self-analyst in my brain has finally come to terms with the fact that I am the one I should be most frustrated at. I spent somewhere just over 30 years looking to these "church people," in varying degrees, to define for me who God is- accepting their definitions and understandings while never looking any further. Technically, I've only known God vicariously, not personally, for the vast majority of my spiritual journey. I've gotten angry and frustrated and disillusioned when leaders, teachers, parents, and friends contradicted each other, or failed in their assessments, or unfairly judged me. Maybe it's because of laziness or the "people pleaser" in me, but I finally see:

I am the one who gave them the ring of keys to look for a way to unlock all that is such a mystery for me...

Tonight, with all that in mind- along with a few wrestling thoughts pertaining to the "business" and "programs" and pressured "requests" for everyone to take-a-turn-in-ministry-mentality (as defined by the committee) that has become church in America- I brought my swirling thoughts and the day's conversation remnants to bed with me tonight. The lights went out and, predictably, the whir of my mind's processor hummed louder...

Good gravy, I hope no one is currently looking to me to unlock those doors. Please do yourself a favor and bypass this hot mess of a blogger-friend for perspective or guidance. Let's both go straight to the Almighty Himself, shall we?

Standing in Pleasant Places
Collene James
Crystal Mill, CO

Is Your Love An Illusion?

Is your love an illusion?
Or can it possibly be real?
It's hard to believe that You desire me;
This truth is hard to feel.

You are Creator God,
The Holy, Righteous One.
I don't know how it's possible
That for me You gave Your Son.

Like diamonds in the water on a sunlit afternoon,
When the sun begins to wane
And the diamonds disappear;
Will Your love remain?

Based upon Your Word,
Oh Lord,
This I choose to believe:

It's not what things appear to be,
For I know Your love is real.
It's what I know is true,
Regardless how I feel.

Nancy Bowser

God Cries
Collene James

233

Be Still, Be Still

February 9th 2013
"Do you not know? Have you not heard? The Lord is the Everlasting God, the Creator of the ends of the earth.

He will not grow tired or weary, and His understanding no one can fathom. He gives strength to the weary and increases the power of the weak.

Even youths grow tired and weary, and young men stumble and fall; but those whose who hope in the Lord will renew their strength. They will soar with wings like eagles; they will walk and not be faint."

Well, lookie there! Would you look at that? Just look at it! *Isaiah 40:28-31* is putting the last month in a nutshell!

I was given homework at the Benjamin Meeting three or four weeks ago that I completely failed to even start. Tonight, as I look back and assess the month, week and day I can't help but be drawn back to the assignment...

"Collene, BE STILL," he told me...

Sure, I'll do that... right after I cram three weeks of company, bronchitis, a new baby niece, a 6,000 mile trip with three kids, a family wedding, a few friendship mending conversations, a relationship-altering (ending?) conversation, a concussion-causing health concern, a hit-and-run involving one of my children, a cat surgery- technically two, but I don't have a punch-card so who's counting, a teenager's first crush, first girlfriend, first break-up, first school dance, a close friend's emergency situation, a cancer-marker-increase-scare, a trip back to "Egypt" in my head-n-heart... all the while working 13 of the last 15 days- on my feet, in deep conversations with amazing people I deeply care about and as well as some I barely know, hour after hour...

You get it: life is happening. How does one simply *"be still?"*

December's bustle built into January's cry for help and has already crescendo-ed into February's earth-shattering scream for relief.

"BE STILL and KNOW that I am God...," I hear in my mind.
It's persistent and loud enough to cause me to look it up for context:

"He makes wars to cease at the end of the earth; He breaks the bow and cuts the spear in two; He burns the chariot in the fire.

Be still and know that I am GOD; I will be exalted among the nations, I will be exalted in the earth. The Lord of Heaven's Armies is with us; the God of Jacob is our refuge. SELAH" (Psalm 46:9-11)

In fact, if you're at all like my sweet friend, who's going through her own tailor-made desert wandering, you'd hear it twice: *"be still, be still..."*

You would cry aloud, like us- in the shower, or alone in your car, or from your sea of pillows at night, into the dark: *"Jesus, show me mercy in this..."*

The quiet voice that whispers *"be still,"* washing your heart with the promise of peace, would pierce your darkness with *"please, little girl, know that I am God. I've got even this. My mercies are new EVERY morning... do you trust Me?"*

And then, tonight, you too would understand: He has collected those tears and kept a record of each one in His ledger and they are not wasted, according to **Psalm 56**.

He has not missed a thing. He has not even slept, according to **Psalm 121**. Additionally, He *"quiets you with His love and rejoices over you with His singing"* according to **Zephaniah 3:17**. Don't forget that He loves you perfectly, defined in **2 Corinthians 13**, and because of that- His *"perfect love casts out all fear"* as found in **1 John 4**...

Also, *"He who began a good work in us is FAITHFUL to complete it,"* according to **Philippians 1**. For tonight, that is enough. Tomorrow, because of the mercies that are new every morning, I have been given a homework Mulligan. I will *"be still, be still."* I will begin to grasp that He really is the BIG God I crave.

Today, He met me with unfathomable proof that He sees, hears, and feels me- and not only that, but has surrounded me with protection, support and love. Furthermore, He has used me- called me into the battlefield. The last three years of desert wandering have not been wasted. All that He has taught me has not been in vain. I was, finally, the comforter, the truth speaker, the promise bearer. My experience was used as salve for the sweet, injured, discouraged soul on the other end of the phone. The Truth that has taken root in me, has been a source of Life for a friend... in short- I see that there has been purpose in my suffering that reaches beyond myself *(2 Corinthians 1:4)*.

Tonight, I will rest...

Twice
Collene James

Part I- I am loved, Fear Be Gone

February 23rd 2013

It's been an eventful month. Like I told you last February, this time of year is packed with memories- not the good kind. Although I have avoided writing for a variety of reasons, the relentless words, sentences, and paragraphs have not ceased to scribble themselves out on the pages of my mind.

As usual, I have roaming words. "Love" is not new, in fact it was the I-think-I-just-threw-up-a-little-in-my-mouth concept that has plagued me, taunted me really, since well before the beginning of this blog journal. Unfortunately for you, I'm slow at learning things I resist. Fortunately for me, the good Lord is patiently persistent in His pursuit of me and is not willing to flunk me out of the class. I guess, like it or not, I've been signed up for Summer School. (Shhhh, I think I'm starting to like it. Don't tell anyone.)

"Fear" is the newest word being added to the theme being woven through these writings. "Be Still" is still the inescapable concept being stirred into conversations, texts, songs, and books I'm reading. It's starting to feel like a conspiracy!

Three weeks ago, the pastor at my church started a six-week series on Love. Seriously??? SIX WEEKS is a long time to discuss something I feel soooooo.... well, on the outside-of-looking-in. It's not that I don't understand what it takes to really love someone, I do. It's just that the kind of love I have poured out on most people is at such a slow drip rate returning. My well is bone-dry. Obviously, there's an engineer/operator error and I'm just plain too tired to figure it out. I'd like to throw a tarp over it all and wait for a downpour to fill that bad boy up...

The theme the first week was about loving the "unlovable." Great. I can do that. I DO, do that. If there is one thing I know, it's that God gave me when He made me, an insight and understanding of people. Even the ugliest of personalities are lovable and, usually, I seem to easily figure out the root cause of their "ugliness."

Week two confirmed what I already know and believe at the core of me: Love Matters Most. ***"There are three things that will last- faith, hope and love. The greatest of these is love." (1 Corinthians 13:13).*** Yup, you are my witnesses, I've been in that chapter a time or two this year. I get it- love and relationship are all that matter in the end of this life and for all time hereafter. With every cell in my body, I believe that. Let's face it, no dying person ever asked to see their financial statements or property deeds from their death bed. Trophies, wardrobes, and stamp collections mean very little as we lie there anticipating our final breath. People want people in the end.

"Loving like Jesus loves me"- the theme for last week- really defined for me, my discomfort with the series. We went on to discuss the Accepting, Valuing, Forgiving, Believing-In nature of Christ. Oh, I "get it" in a million ways as it pertains to YOU. I see you. I get you. I accept you. I value you. I forgive you. I believe in you- until I'm made a fool a bazillion times and then, once more. That's not the problem. The question getting louder every day is:

"What would it look like if I loved ME the way Jesus does?"

From there it's time to make an abrupt dive to the "fear" thread of this woven theme. Sometime in January the whisper of the words *"Perfect love casts out fear, Collene"* would randomly cross my mind. I shoved them aside because they made no contextual sense.

In general, I'm not a fearful person. I am an adventurer. I am a professional at bootstrap pulling and carrying myself with confidence, whether I emotionally feel like it or not. I don't fear the night, or being alone, or heights, or death. Still the words of **1 John 4:18** filtered through my days. *"What am I fearing,"* I wondered... so, He showed me.

A few weeks ago, I was encouraging a friend. *"God is soooo gentle when He heals us,"* I told him. *"We fear that He's going to rip and tear the whole deep, gaping wound and expose our mess in its entirety, causing unimaginable pain and embarrassment. He's not like that. I'm finding Him to be a gentleman, always. He quietly points out where He'd like to start His work and asks if He can 'have that yet.' If I say 'no,' He waits. If I say 'yes,' but continue to grip it tightly, He waits. He persists, asking often, displaying His trustworthy character, bathing me in grace and mercy, until I release the thing I'm hiding away. God is gentle."*

I'm realizing that which I fear, He's been gently asking for, for a long time. Once upon a time, I was sick. I was married and therefore not solely responsible for providing for my family. Although he didn't always like it or understand it, my husband was- for the most part- helpful and patient with me during the search for a diagnosis.

Last month, on the morning I was to be flying home from my Alaska trip, I passed out, dramatically, for a second time. I came to, in a pool of blood, with a potentially broken nose and a mild concussion. As I type the bumps are still painful on my forehead and nose. Let's just say I got more than a few double glances on the flights that morning...

In the weeks since I've been home, my body has returned to the all-too-familiar aches and exhaustion. I fear doing THIS again, this time alone. I fear the progression to what I know is possible. I fear a life of having to rely on someone. I fear having no one reliable. Ultimately, just like I did last fall, I continue to fear "being still."

"Perfect love casts out fear."

God, who loves me perfectly, has surrounded me with tangible, practical, wisdom, expertise, and support in a variety of ways. Additionally, I have hope and peace and a downright good attitude about this.

I realize now that I have not been taking care of me physically (or emotionally) in a loving way, the way Jesus would. The flight attendant instructions to put your own oxygen mask on before assisting others has come to mind so often this week. It's the phrase I told myself as I crawled into bed for the second nap of the day last Saturday, and what I reminded myself of when I said "no" to just one more client, on an already fully booked day. If I am not able or willing to take care of me, I will continue to be a bone dry well and utterly useless to everyone...

Abundance
Collene James
Teton Mountains, WY

239

Part II- Fear Be Gone

February 24ᵗʰ 2013

Today I wanted to be around people, but I had no real energy for interacting with anyone most of the day. Since I live only a few blocks from a lively coffee shop, I chose to take my thoughts and do some reading there. People interest me, motivate me, and make me think. I absolutely love watching-studying people. Because I was so long-winded in yesterday's Part One, I needed to gather my sputtering thoughts and develop what it is I'm really trying to say, without letting it take the negative turn that's easily produced by an exhausted mind. We are, after all, discussing fears- the deepest darkest ones at that.

By now, you know that I've been reading the daily devotionals of Oswald Chambers' *"My Utmost for His Highest."* The guy doesn't let me get away with anything, which is fine, I suppose. I do want to be "called out" on my nonsense and to be sharpened, deepened, made wiser, healed. I guess it's less personal or risky when the one doing the challenging of my deepest thinking has been dead for 95 years.

Anyway, the "love," "be still," and "fear" words were echoed in two of this week's writings. In fact, the ***"perfect love casts out fear"*** and the ***"be still and know that I am God"*** verses were BOTH used in them. At this point, I'll just add that it's a teensy bit creepy that, that keeps happening. The words were already a woven theme in every other aspect of my life, I suppose it shouldn't surprise me that Oswald would join in the fun, or that God make His point a hundred ways in a week- a million in a year- for someone as slow, resistant, prideful, injured, and untrusting as I've been. Two points from this week's readings stand out:

1. *"If what we call love doesn't take us beyond ourselves, it isn't really love. If we have the idea that love is characterized as cautious, wise sensible, shrewd, and never taken to extremes, we have missed the true meaning. This may describe affection... but it is not a true and accurate description of love." (February 21)*

2. *"Perseverance...is endurance combined with absolute certainty that what we are looking for is going to happen....it means more than just hanging on, which may be only exposing our fear of letting go and falling... Perseverance is our supreme effort of refusing to believe that our hero is going to be conquered. Our greatest fear is not that we will be damned, but that*

somehow Jesus Christ will be defeated. Also, our fear is that the very things our Lord stood for- love, justice, forgiveness, and kindness among men- will not win out in the end..." (February 22)

Well, thank you Oswald, I couldn't have said it better myself. Not only do I fear that Jesus may not win out in the end, but I'll take it a step further: I fear that Jesus will say He loves me, show me a few dozen examples of something that feels like love, get my guard down, and then ultimately reject me. Silly? Maybe, but for me it's not completely unfounded.

I'll give you the ridiculous example I gave my friend, who joined me late at the coffee shop tonight:

Imagine a timid little girl whose daddy asked her if she wanted dessert. She said *"yes,"* so her daddy pressed her further, *"well what kind of dessert would you like?"* She shyly asks for ice cream. *"Sweetie, be specific, tell me what kind of ice cream you want. Do you want toppings?"* So, the little girl musters up her most heartfelt hopes for her dessert, she's specific with flavor and toppings and includes a request for it to be served in her favorite bowl. Then, as though the conversation never occurred, the father sends the little girl to her room to sit, quietly, alone, seemingly all night. There's no ice cream, with or without toppings. There's not even a cookie or a piece of fruit. In fact, the father doesn't even talk to her again. So sits a timid, confused, little girl alone in the dark- feeling rejection, hopeless, foolish...

If that daddy is like God, and God's character is good and kind and loving, then he has gone out to buy the highest quality ice cream and most lavish toppings available. He has not forgotten her request, and remembers every detail, right down to her favorite bowl. But, if that little girl is like me and she is familiar with a lifetime of feeling rejection, she can't help but be crushed and fearful that she has been forgotten.

My friend and I agree: To put these fears to death, I am going to have to persevere in every sense of the word. I will have to actively believe in the Jesus of scripture. It will require me to replace fearful instinctual thinking with intentional reminders that He is BIG, victorious, true, kind. I am going to have to shrug off timidity, self-protection, and selfishness to love Him back- to get to the place of my full surrender, like only He deserves.

The Joy of Suffering

March 3rd 2013

"I just want this to be over!"

I can't tell you how many times I've breathed these words under my breath, sobbed them in my shower, shouted them in the face of a friend, begged the Almighty- literally face down on the hardwood floor of my home, muttered them from the driver's seat of my car, sent them as a text to the masses, scratched them into the pages of my tattered blue journal- and then when that was full, the red one... It has become the anthem of my heart.

"I know you want to squirm to a place of comfort, away from the pain, but there just isn't a such a place or position- you just have to do this." The nurse's gentle words of truth echo through my mind over and over, nearly every day of these last nine weeks. The labor pains were too intense, she couldn't catch a breath, she couldn't cry, she couldn't speak, she couldn't move... until finally, mercifully, she could. The intensity had subsided for a few minutes of rest. The messy relief of cold washcloths, sips of ice water, words of encouragement, strokes of love... just enough mercy and comfort to suffice for the next round of suffering...

Labor is like that. There is hope in the peaceful moments between the suffering of excruciating pains. There is renewed energy and re-focusing... A woman never fully forgets the suffering of her labor. As she cradles and cherishes what it produces, she finds meaning and makes sense of the pain.

Because a million flashing stories, concepts, verses and analogies are firing relentlessly as I write, I'm positive I'm going to fumble tonight's journal entry. I literally started writing myself notes to try to map it out. I'm also convinced that with the clarity this week will come a few clouds of confusion, so I've got no choice but to fumble through this and get it on "paper." Care to join me?

I could see no way out. This was like one of those tangled metal puzzles you find at the check-out counter of touristy gift shops. There HAS to be a way of solving it, but no amount of thinking it through would bring resolution.
It was one of those situations that would free itself, accidentally almost, as I continued to wear a rut over the well-worn pattern of thinking this week. Then, the puzzle fell open. Simply put, I had a moment of clarity, a brief sunrise of understanding. The ever-so-gentle murder of a nightmare that I had been calling a dream.

Beginning on October 7th this year, residents of North Pole, Alaska, began experiencing 163 solid days of absolutely no sun. As of Tuesday, and for the next consecutive 11 days, they will experience a few hours of navy-blue, pale, twilight. Navy-blue is dark, but black is darker. Twilight brings hope of a seasonal change that no one has an "allergy" to! Then, on March 18th, the actual bright, golden sun will peak over the horizon and stay there, within sight, for the full 24 hours of that day as it curves its horizontal path around the sky. It will provide warmth, illumination, vitamin D and, ultimately, a very good reason to praise God and party! As the days go by, it will gain strength as it gradually rises above the horizon, casting full light and warmth on the frozen tundra.

This week I had a similar sunrise of my own! There have been navy-blue twilight hours of understanding and acceptance, followed by the familiar darkness of confusion, anger, heartache, wrestling, questioning, suffering... Like my friends in the northiest of north places, I know my winter is not over until the Son pours a full dose of His Light on the subjects I've suffered through. As His Light shines on this thing, it climbs higher, erasing shadows of doubt and distrust and fear. I will experience my own version of the 189 sunset-less days of the arctic summer season regarding these things! Light and life and warmth and nutrients will turn my fallow season into a period of usefulness and bearing fruit!

By now you understand that "Suffering" is the word of the week. The topic is quite difficult to discuss with most people in detail. The specific definitions are extremely personal and have no boundaries as it pertains to internal, external, spiritual, physical, mental, emotional and, for some because of love, vicarious suffering. In fact, "suffering" tends to be redefined even within an individual from season to season as life happens and circumstances change us.

Instead of embracing the word and the reality of the weight that it carries, I have dodged it, scolded myself for feeling it, and measured it up next to the brands of affliction a handful of my friends are experiencing. In short, I've wasted precious time assuming mine was of a lesser quality, therefore making it useless and invalid.

It turns out we all have a mandatory pass to the fire-pit of suffering before we are allowed to leave this life. Mine is tailored to me. It is lovingly and mercifully intended to be just heavy enough to show me my own strengths, weaknesses, and insufficiencies. It is just harsh enough to soften me. It is just long enough to take me to the very edge of me- where all that is left to cling to are the sharp edges of Trust, Faith and Promise as I hover over the abyss known as Despair.

A few of us will allow ourselves to be consumed and destroyed by our tailor-made affliction. Hordes of us will paste on a smile, adopt a coping mechanism, and answer life's *"how-are-yous"* with an *"all's well"* every time.

However, there is a kind of person that will embrace the circumstance, allow the grief of it to wash over every cell of their being. They will allow themselves to feel the terror and the anger and the hope and the heartache. They will scream the unanswerable questions into the darkness and toil and sweat and strain to keep meaning alive while fighting with bloody hands, broken teeth and torn fingernails as they grasp for joy.

And now it hits me! There it is. The barely audible word- whispering through the conversations and scriptures while quietly flooding the recesses of my head and heart this week:

Joy.

If we are willing, if we daily choose to march ahead into the darkness-searching for the light of Truth and Hope and Love and ultimately, Faith in the One who is Faithful- then this ugly fight to survive our circumstance and make some sense of it that would be worth earning, in the end, produces Joy.

These scriptures, which I've collected over the last 500 days or more, finally make sense in a way that is not just a hope, but a practical reality:

"In all this you greatly rejoice, though now for a little while you may have had to suffer grief in all kinds of trials. These have come so that the proven genuineness of your faith—of greater worth than gold, which perishes even though refined by fire—may result in praise, glory and honor when Jesus Christ is revealed. Though you have not seen Him, you love Him; and even though you do not see Him now, you believe in Him and are filled with an inexpressible and glorious joy, for you are receiving the end result of your faith, the salvation of your souls." (1 Peter 1:6-9)

"Humble yourselves, therefore, under God's mighty hand, that He may lift you up in due time. Cast all your anxiety on Him because He cares for you. Be alert and of sober mind. Your enemy the devil prowls around like a roaring lion looking for someone to devour. Resist him, standing firm in the faith, because you know that the family of believers throughout the world is undergoing the same kind of sufferings. And the God of all grace,

who called you to His eternal glory in Christ, after you have suffered a little while, will Himself restore you and make you strong, firm and steadfast. To Him be the power for ever and ever." (1 Peter 5:6-11)

"I remember my affliction and my wandering, the bitterness and the gall. I well remember them, and my soul is downcast within me. Yet this I call to mind and therefore I have hope: Because of the Lord's great love we are not consumed, for His mercies never fail. They are new every morning; great is your faithfulness, I say to myself, 'the Lord is my portion therefore I will wait for Him.' The Lord is good to those whose hope is in Him, to the one who seeks Him. It is good to wait quietly for the salvation of the Lord... no one is cast off by the Lord forever. Though He brings grief, He will show compassion, so great is His unfailing love." (Lamentations 3: 19-26, 31-32)

And finally, I can offer to you an answer to one of the "whys" of my particular tailor-made suffering:

O·B·E·D·I·E·N·C·E

Now, if you know it, sing it! *"Obedience is the very best way, to show that you believe..."*

Hebrews 5:8 tells us that through the suffering of Jesus, He learned obedience. I used to think that everyone who was not being obedient, was being disobedient. Now I know that sometimes obedience is a learned behavior through the discipline of suffering. I also used to think that "discipline" was for naughty little boys and girls. Now I know that discipline is always just a tool for strengthening and training while building or revealing character.

Through the obedience of marching one-step-at-a-time through this pain, I am learning the unforgettable, real-life-applicable principles of who Jesus is through His proven character as He relates to me. That brings me joy. And although I am under the realization that this, always-so-brief, "summer" season of light will eventually be followed by another twilight of a different kind, and that the labor of this affliction has yet to completely give birth to my greatest, cherish-able joy, I will leave you with **2 Corinthians 4:16-18**- which sums it up best:

"Therefore, we do not lose heart. Though outwardly we are wasting away, yet inwardly we are being renewed day by day. For our light and momentary afflictions are achieving for us an eternal glory that far outweighs them all. So, we fix our eyes not on what is seen, but on what is unseen, since what is seen is temporary, but what is unseen is eternal."

Spring's Reward
Collene James
Beartooth Pass, MT

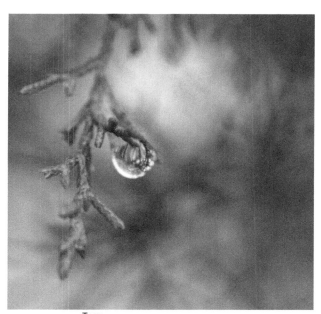

Tear
Collene James

Torn
Collene James
Yukon, British Columbia- Canada

247

The Scarlet Letter

I'll proudly wear Your Scarlet Letter;
And I'll gladly bear Your name.
Your love, it led You to the cross;
Your blood was shed, but was no loss
For You bore my sorrows and my pain.

I'll proudly wear Your Scarlet Letter;
In humility I'll bear Your name.
Your power conquered death and sin,
You've overcome, You win.
In You there's no more guilt or shame.

I'll proudly wear Your Scarlet Letter,
And I'll gladly bear Your Name.
I'll worship in prosperity
And I'll worship You in pain.

I'll proudly wear Your Scarlet Letter,
I'll live Your life of love.
I'll tell the world about You,
My Father up above.

Nancy Bowser

If Not For Freedom, Then What For

January 18th 2015

Well, it has only been a solid 21 months since I cracked the curtains for you to view into my world. Please don't think I have not wanted to before now, but truthfully the things I processed over the last year and a half were too closely woven with other people's stories and they weren't fully mine to tell. Let me briefly catch you up to speed on a few details of my life so that my chatter tonight has a shot at making a lick of sense.

Sometime around the publishing of my last blog journal post I became engaged, then married. He had absolutely no trouble accepting my three Bonus People. In fact, he blessed me with three of his own Bonus People. Even if you're marginal at math, you've probably counted SIX young-uns, with a tally of three boys and three girls. As it stands tonight, we have three high schoolers, two middle schoolers and a preschooler. These simple facts alone will possibly reveal a clue as to why I've chosen not to journal here in my "down time." I can further explain...

Maybe the best way to put this is that we are a multi-career family. You're probably aware that I own my little booth-rent salon business. My husband is a (semi-retired?) recording artist, high school English teacher, doctoral student, Young Life student ministry leader, theater director, English Mastiff breeder, semi-professional cyclist, non-profit founder, race organizer, online professor, and-something-else-I'm-sure-I've-forgotten...

We have gymnasts, swimmers, wrestlers, basketball players, bike shop employees, track stars, softball players, new drivers, up-and-coming drivers, volleyball hopefuls, trumpet players, saxophonists, clarinetists, choral members, and folks that plain just want to be heard, from time to time. Between the practices, training, workout plans, concerts, counseling appointments, games, lessons, work schedules, meetings, races, back rubs, occasional broken bones, school dances, first dates, heart breaks, weekend trips, grocery shopping, meals, new puppy litters, car accidents, and more than one devastating loss.... I. Can't. Think. Straight.

That brings me to tonight.

I have chosen to take a hard look at my "Be Still" directive from 2013. It is a concept I have thought about tattooing on my forehead, except Mom, Dad and the Mr. would potentially, strongly, object. It seems that I'm sort of bad at obedience to "Be Still" when the seven other people I live with don't have the same convictions and- quite frankly- I've personally lost direction. In response to all 'o that, and because my auto-immune issues so kindly reminded me in a catch-your-attention-or-else kind of way, I've chosen to take a little mini sabbatical of sorts to re-organize my priorities and re-balance my skew.

If you're following my journal entries, you'll be happy to know that my thinking has not become over-thinking and my perfectionism is still firmly behind me. I promise I am a MUCH less "stressy" woman to live with, trust me, I do it 24/7 and I have a backstage, all-access pass to me. I like being in my own mind most days. After a little research, I am pleased to discover that the woman who started this nonsense in 2011 is truly not the woman I am today.

Buuuuuuut, that's not to say I don't still have a few things to address internally:

If I only had one emotion that I was allowed to assign these past 18 months, I would truly say JOY sums it up nicely. I will not type foolish, Pollyanna-esque drivel without first giving you a glimpse of the other side of that coin. Fear, grief, heartache, anger, frustration, exhaustion, and suffering all have made their visits and continue to be the undercurrent emotions that attempt to flood out the flow of Joy most days. Had you asked me last month I might have minimized Joy and maximized something less accurate. It has never been truer:

Nothing worth having comes without WORK.

I think it's vital that I do not toss "Happy" in the mix of emotions that characterize my days. Although there has certainly been happiness, Happy herself is fickle. She requires things to be "just so." No, Joy is my companion of choice and I've fought hard to earn her.

I don't know what is "normal" in terms of how the Lord works His truth through a person to cause genuine, lasting change. However, for me there's always a theme. Sometimes it's a word or a phrase that echoes the silent spaces of my day- at the shampoo sink, in the shower, in the silence of an occasional lonely commute, in the darkness just before drifting off to sleep, as I stir a pot on the stove or take out the trash....

For me, MANY of these words and concepts end up fully circling back to a larger theme: the story of Moses and the Exodus.The enslaved Israelites, Egypt and the hard-hearted Pharaoh, the plagues, the sea-parting, the desert wandering, and the Promised Land, the consequences for disobedience... I mean FOR YEARS, this story is the rich soil that has grown incredible truths for me about the character of God, the power of faith in something, or rather, Someone BIG, hopefulness, hopelessness, provision, grumbling, ungratefulness, thanks, a desire to run headlong back into slavery, fear, harshness, softness, insufficiency, sufficiency, impossibility and the miraculous... oh, and I'm hoping a plethora of yet un-earthed treasures.

There is simply no way, for time's sake and for privacy's sake, to explain the ins and outs of how, but on this day and because of this week, I, with one of my Bonuses, built a symbolic stone memorial in our 'desert,' just as the wandering Israelites did. The memorial was then and is now, to remember that God is GOOD, and He moved here. He is at work, He loves us deeply and when I pass here again in my own wanderings, I will remember. Yes, this is why- Joy. Circumstances are the same as ever, the desert is just as hot and dry, but this time there's a pillar to remember...

Oh hey! I almost forgot: When I BE STILL, guess what happens?! The Lord truly does the fighting for me, just like He said in *Exodus 14:14*! It cost me nothing- except the willful wrestling match between trust and fear, the act of taking rogue thoughts captive and making them obedient to Truth, Nobility, Justice, Purity, Excellence, Love and Praise, then being WILLING to say *"whatever you ask, I'll do"* to the One who asks for everything I have, am or hope for in my deepest places.

Freedom has never felt so free, and if I lose everything I think I have, it won't come close to having the power to send me back to the emotional, physical or spiritual slavery of "Egypt" or the bondage of fear or the exhaustion of misplaced "worship."

"It is for FREEDOM that Christ has set us FREE. Stand firm therefore, and do not submit yourself again to the yoke of slavery." (Galatians 5:1 Emphasis mine.)

Come On In, The Water's Fine

August 13th 2015

Hey Reader!

Although blogging has been the least of my concerns for the last couple of years, the tug has gotten stronger and has felt more urgent in these last few weeks. So today, I obey.

Oh, I've been journaling. This time not in my tattered blue or red notebook, but in a sleek hard-backed, spiral bound, big-girl notebook. It has the kind of paper that makes a girl want a high-quality pen and her best penmanship. There are no hard-written pen holes or snot-n-tear stains on any of the pages. I've been more-or-less polite in most of my entries. That is not to say content is any less messy, but I am simmering down a little in my relationship with Jesus and in my belief that God, my Father in heaven, is ALWAYS good, even when life's circumstances aren't. (By-the-way, this is a spoiler alert and a bit off tonight's topic, but despite what you feel, I found out through experience that fear really is a waste of time and energy. You're welcome, carry on...)

If you read anything I've written, you know by now that the story of Moses and the Israelites- their deliverance from Egypt, the parting of the Red Sea, the wandering, the trusting, the not trusting, the faithfulness of God, the unfaithfulness of man- has been the active theme that the Lord has used to reveal Himself to me. If you missed it, I now can tell you it all started when I bitterly told God that I was sick of the "Churchianity" and the ridiculous "stained glass masquerade" I was accustomed to participating in for basically my whole life.

I had found that the burden of out-of-context rules of American Church didn't work to better myself, my relationships, or my life. I told Him that if He is who He says He is, He'd have to come get me and I wanted nothing less than a Red Sea parting of my own. I was sick of head knowledge and rhetoric and cliche and hollow platitudes. I wanted gut-level, instinctual, life-altering belief, or nothing.

Interestingly, God didn't start with a big fat sea-parting miracle. He started with a gentle, undeniable, undeserved, pursuit of my heart. He used hushed-tones of mercy and grace which oozed over my then rebellious-born-from-pain lifestyle. During that time, multiple lessons were learned through the circumstances of Moses and his people.

Alrighty then, so life moved on. The calendar pages changed, kids got taller than me, the family grew, then shrunk... the lessons of Moses were never far out of mind. Busyness abounded. I forgot, then remembered, then forgot and was forced to remember "Be Still" again and again. Because of my personality, I am convinced it is going to be a never-ending reminder to rely on my WEAKNESS, which is stillness, so that the Lord will be my STRENGTH. I digress, but through it all I found myself once again, uncomfortable, and in the direct heat of the refiner's fire- August 2015.

Because of those discomforts and through a myriad of specific-to-me messages from the Holy Spirit, I have been challenged to assess the depth and specificity of my prayer life. As usual, themes are carried through from situation to situation, from year to year. Again, August 2015 being no different, a collection of prayer themed verses washes over me:

"Consider it pure joy, my brothers and sisters, whenever you face trials of many kinds, because you know that the testing of your faith produces perseverance. Let perseverance finish its work so that you may be mature and complete, not lacking anything. If any of you lacks wisdom, you should ask God, who gives generously to all without finding fault, and it will be given to you. But when you ask, you must believe and not doubt, because the one who doubts is like a wave of the sea, blown and tossed by the wind. That person should not expect to receive anything from the Lord. Such a person is double-minded and unstable in all they do." (James 1:2-8)

"Ask and it will be given to you; seek and you will find; knock and the door will be opened to you. For everyone who asks receives; the one who seeks finds; and to the one who knocks, the door will be opened. Which of you, if your son asks for bread, will give him a stone? Or if he asks for a fish, will give him a snake? If you, then, though you are evil, know how to give good gifts to your children, how much more will your Father in heaven give good gifts to those who ask Him!" (Matthew 7:7-11)

The depth of those verses is not lost on me. I presume a skilled teacher could spend a month of Sundays digesting all that is packed in each of those words. I am not that guy. What trips me up this time around is the repetitive word "ask." Cool. I ask. I don't really even doubt, per-say. But do I AAAAAAAASK? Do I specifically ask for the exact thing I'm hungry for (i.e., bread or fish) or do I just ask to be full somehow, even if it means eating rocks and snakes? Truly, the answer is no. Maybe I am lazy; I say global things like *"help me in this,"* *"fix that however you want, but only IF you want to fix it Lord."* For my whole life, my prayer life has been general, relatively dispassionate, saucer-deep, and with mild reservations. I haven't looked for the miraculous parting of the sea, because I haven't been so bold as to ask my Father for it directly, therefore I'm rarely at risk of disappointment... or for miracles for that matter.

Are you still with me? Okay, so to remedy my situation I spent the last month diligently, daily, boldly, specifically, asking for Red Sea parting, dry land crossing, and deliverance from my enemy- we'll call that ugly beast "Egypt" for today. Guess what?! Circumstances are the same, Egypt still hates me and would LOVE to devour, distract, disable, or destroy me, yet I am safely pitching my tent every day and night this month on dry ground! Make no mistake, Egypt has not been destroyed with the same drowning finality of the Egyptians in the Biblical story, yet. A night watch will still be required, but I KNOW now that *"He keeps those in perfect peace whose mind is fixed on Him" (Isaiah 26:3).*

So, this brings me to the rest of the story- to catch you up to real time. I started reading a new book tonight after work. I kind of liked having this new routine of intentional, structured, placement of my mind on higher things and I figured the 7 or 8 years the book remained marinating in dust, unopened and unread on my shelf was sufficient time to give it a whirl. The book is called 'A Quiet Heart' by Carla Jividen Peer and while I can't vouch for more than the first few pages, I think we'll get along just fine. I love the way Carla sums up a life experience I can relate to 100%:

"... I wanted to have mighty exploits so that people could look at me and say, 'God is real.' He is real, He performs wonders, and He intervenes in our lives.

The key to doing exploits is knowing God. However, there are two kinds of knowing. There is knowing about which is characterized by information and there is knowing of which is characterized by intimacy. For many years I knew about God. Knowing about God is an academic knowledge that begins with studying the Bible or hearing someone teach the facts and truths of the Bible. But there is a progression of knowing. Knowing of God grows out of knowing about God. Knowing of God is a personal, intimate relationship. The first the of knowledge- the academic is important. The knowledge of God goes deeper; it has to be learned experientially, and it is often costly."

Okay, so NOW, in light of the heat and pain of this current refinement and in light of Carla's words, major blocks of "knowing about" knowledge just fell like Tetris blocks into the "knowledge of" category- making this *Philippians 3:8* verse make sense:

"Yes, everything else is worthless when compared with the infinite value of knowing Christ Jesus my Lord. For His sake I have discarded everything else, counting it all as garbage, so that I could gain Christ."

Those words are no longer simply memorization fodder, cliché- or worse, ingredient number one in the recipe for major spiritual-frustration and "back-sliding" excuse making. I no longer feel like the jerk-of-the-world Christian who doesn't genuinely crave *"Christ alone to the glory of God alone."* Furthermore, I cannot seem to get enough of scripture, Old and New Testament, where previously crazy sentences such as *"All my fountains are in You"* and *"The Lord is my defender, my deliverer, my strong tower"* were nice sounding poetry but frustratingly empty-sounding promises.

Through a considerable amount of personal cost in almost every area of my life, along with my willing submission to His plan for me to enter the DEEEEEEP and scary Red Sea (I can't swim and I'm really more of a hot tub soaking kind of girl), and just a pinch of mustard-seed faith that *says "God is ALWAYS good to those who's trust is in Him"* (not surprisingly another nod to an afore-mentioned *Lamentations 3* theme), I learned this:

God is SO GOOD that He won't force you into the water; He also doesn't cease to invite you in. We get to choose submission, which is ALWAYS the case with any type of Biblical submission. Of course, if we don't step into the scary, uncomfortable place, we won't see the walk-on-water, parting-of-an-entire-sea, life-breathed-into-dry-bones, giant-killing, fiery-furnace-surviving, closed-mouthed-hungry-lion, virgin-gives-birth caliber miracles we crave, and that He is deeply desiring to display to us.

I must admit, I'm hooked. As of about two weeks ago, I know what it means to honestly say, "I hold nothing on this planet dearer than my hard-won, intimate knowledge of my Savior." I think I might have just graduated from warming the bench, Coach. *"I want to know Christ—yes, to know the power of His resurrection and participation in His sufferings, becoming like Him in His death, and so, somehow, attaining to the resurrection from the dead." (Philippians 3:10-11)*

I regret having wasted so many years fearing my part in the obedience/blessing exchange of scripture. Please pray with me that you and I don't lose sight of THIS and that we continue to experience our own "resurrection" of sorts...

Still Waters
Collene James
Clear Lake, IA

WINTER
BY COLLENE JAMES

Winter
Collene James
Montana

No Fun

It wasn't fun,
the day I learned people lie.
That they can lie those big ones —
not little ones, white ones,
oopsies and uh-ohs,
but the world stopping ones —
the soul tearing,
screaming into your pillow ones.
It wasn't fun when I knew
there was no going back:
when it would never be as it was,
when I would never again be
what I was before that lie —
that first time-to-grow-up lie.
It wasn't fun.
But I learned and did and
still inhaled, still exhaled and
I decided there was truth
somewhere and
somehow I would get back to that.
I would find a world and
a girl like I was in a place with
lies, yes, but with truth and
that Truth will set me free and that
just might, just might, just might
be fun and will definitely,
just definitely,
be real.

Ashley Fugleberg

Not a Fan of the True Selfie

February 19th 2016

February 19th 2016

Admittedly I haven't thought much about you all in quite some time. Life. Is. Busy. If I'm being honest though, I'd start by saying: Life. Is. Messy.

I started thinking about my blog journal, or lack of blog journal, a few months ago. My eldest, out of the blue, asked me why I don't write anymore... The question surprised me a little. I had no idea he was ever one of my readers in the first place. The answer to his question isn't so simple. There are reasons. Busyness is the easiest excuse. Seriously, though, life is MARCHING... but I've told you about all of that, the bazillion kids, activities, careers, businesses, ministries, hobbies, trips... It's A reason, but not THE reason.

A variety of observations have collided in my mind this week, so I've decided to sort the mess out here in front of you all.

Observation #1- I have an acquaintance. I don't have much interaction with my friend, but because it's-a-small-world-after-all, occasionally information about my friend's life crosses my virtual path. I usually smile and silently cheer life events as I interpret them, and then click my way back to something more relevant to my life. Recently, when this friend has popped up on my screen, I've noticed a distinct absence of information. That's cool, of course, but it is notably different. So, the difference has got me wondering. Then worrying. Then praying. Then questioning myself...

Observation #2- I read an online opinion article the other day. The topic was about the suicide of a reality tv star, but more specifically, her social media posts and the lack of warning signs on social media. The author of the article was bemoaning the fact that a person in such emotional or mental distress would post their life as a "lie" online, looking perfectly happy, yet harboring dark, brooding, dying thoughts. The author was angry, judgmental even. I found myself defending the other perspective and haven't been able to shake my defensive mental response...

Observation #3- I have questioned the motives of the public and private nature of my own social media posting. Honestly, as I look back over the eight or so years that I've been publicly online, the privacy settings have been of utmost importance. Do you know that there are people out there that want to HURT you? Seriously, some make a game of causing pain. It's a real hurt too, it's not the kind that gets kissed away by your mother at the end of the day. Some of them want to take your kids, or your marriage, or your peace, or your beauty, or your faith, or your life...

Observation #4- Randomly, I got into a discussion with someone about tattoos and salvation this week. (Yes, this ties in, sorta; I'll get back around to it.) He was convinced that if a person has tattoos, he/she can't possibly be "holy" or "saved." Obviously, I disagreed with him, but that blog journal post I'll only write if I absolutely must. This blog has nothing to do with the concept of tattoos, but specifically what my husband's mean to him. He is covered in tattoos that are designed specifically to match his former life's perspective and belief system. Often, he has said that he is thankful for those marks because all he has to do is look at the ink on his hands, arms, legs, neck or body to remember his lifestyle and counter-belief and life narrative before he met Christ, and to recall the cost of his purchase by Jesus' blood and resurrection...

Observation #5- Life has reallllllllllly been difficult for this last year or more. I nearly drowned in tears. I've been afraid. I've been without faith. I've been without hope. I've been alone. I've been angry. I've been rejected. I have rejected. I've been rude. I've been defensive. I've been harassed. I've lashed out. I've been in anguish. I've quit. I've huddled in the dark. I've screamed in the wind. I've begged for mercy.

I have posted so. many. smiles.

These observations- with their thoughts and emotions have marinated for a month or more as I've considered writing it out. They've been pillow talk with my husband after we've kissed the kids goodnight; they've been hashed through with scripture references and possibly a few expletives and giggles and tears with my fake big sister- who is an unfailing, faithful, forever kind of friend.

What are people supposed to do anyway, post an audio recording of an unsolvable argument with their spouse? Oooooh, how about photos of their teenager's worst mistake? What about the gruesome details of the very life slipping away from a parent? Should we really air the false accusations of former in-laws, or ex-husbands, or maybe tongue lashings from the new wife who doesn't know a single truthful thing about us? Maybe we should include strangers' overheard murmurings about us from church on Sunday? How about the parental abuse or neglect of bonus children that I love like my own? How about clients, patients, students or peer parents and coworkers- should their accusations, opinions, insensitivities, or injustices towards us be something we daily make public?

Should our status update include the mourning cries of a small child who is realizing that life isn't fair and that even parents lie? What would be the social media protocol in those cases? Do we photograph our worst selfie days? How about an audio post of our unspoken thoughts? What, seriously, would Jesus post on His Facebook or Twitter or Instagram or Snapchat or TikTok in these situations?

The truth is, it's human nature to put everything we've got going for us out in front- to make it our cover photo or status update. Likewise, it's human nature to sweep under the rug or shove in a closet the things that would cause another to grimace or shun or outright slam us to our knees. We are all grasping and shoving and pushing and posing and dying and screaming silently to be known and hidden all at once. We are all simultaneously condemning each other while begging for mercy for ourselves. Somehow, we are all believing a facade about each other and comparing our full story to the partial story of another. Let's just remember that we all have joy and struggle. We all have laughter and tears. We all have victory and defeat. We all need prayer, praise, and encouragement.

I'm sad because I see that all life is hard. My life is hard. My life has been ugly. Yet, my life is not my own. My sin and mess cost the same as my husband's tattoo-scarred life, which cost the same as the thief and murderer next to Christ on the cross- therefore my story is no longer mine. I no longer own the rights to it, or the ability shove the details into a closet somewhere. That terrifies me, but it also frees me.

I am joyful because I see that life is redeemable. My life is worth overcoming the "hard." My life has beauty in the messiness. My life is not my own and every time I am given an opportunity to share a piece of the uncomfortable ugliness of my story with someone, I see tangibly that there is purpose in the past and present pain. Every snapshot of a smile means there is VICTORY in that moment. There is a Comforter. There is a Protector. There is a Peacemaker. There is a Lover. There is a Father. There is a Savior. There is Reconciliation. There is Freedom. There is Hope. I have so much to be thankful for! If you don't mind, I'm going to keep posting smiles. The rest of that nonsense I'll just take to my knees in prayer, so the world wide web doesn't have to sort it out for me.

Self
Nancy Bowser

Daddy

March 13th 2016

I didn't sleep much tonight. The word "heart" relentlessly permeated my wild and restless dreams. They've been saying his heart is starting to fail. Maybe it's the medications or possibly another tumor pressing on vital nerves. Maybe it's whatever is causing all his other muscles to atrophy. A visit with his oncologist on Monday may provide a solution, but it's just as likely not to.

He was a disciplinarian. The kind of dad you'd fear coming home, if you did Mom wrong during the day. He was organized and meticulously well-kept, always clean-shaven, and polished. Whether it was his Naval career or his upbringing to credit, he had high expectations and little patience for foolishness or disrespect. He was seemingly immovable in his perspective, and a lecture was ever ready for the kid that needed to be taught. We worked hard for his approval in all things, and he would give it. However, we were never overly lavished with his praise and his compliments were hard earned. I grew up feeling protected, but often wrestled with not feeling particularly cherished by him as I observed other little girls' relationships with their fathers, or maybe that was just something I picked up on in the movies...

He always wore a cowboy hat. *"White is the color the good guys wear,"* he always told us. He was a Louis L'amore fan and an avid reader. As a family, I think we watched every Western and John Wayne movie ever made. Dad's first pair of shoes as a toddler were cowboy boots; as has been every pair since, excepting only his government issued footwear during his Navy time. Aside from his aftershave, my favorite fragrance lingering on Dad is forest-fire smoke. From his college days all the way through last summer, my dad travelled the U.S., fighting the nation's wildfires. Today, one of his deepest griefs is the loss of his physical strength that forced the hanging up of his fire pack.

Dad has always been an intensely productive man. He grew up in an era and in a culture that demanded he be outside working if the sun was up. He told me recently that he struggled with college, not because his studies were particularly difficult, but because he didn't feel right reading books or sitting around indoors while it was still daylight out. His own father had high expectations of him and required that he look for physically laborious projects around their farm to work on in the hours between sunrise and sunset; the work was never done.

As a married man with two, then three, then ten mouths to feed, my dad's work ethic and desire to produce a quality lifestyle for us paid off. Integrity mattered throughout his career, so often he took the longer road just to ensure quality. Because of his provision, our mom was able to be home with us for most of our upbringing. She supplemented his income by baking pies for a local restaurant out of our kitchen and later, by driving our school bus route. Dad's financial policy required that he never owe anyone money, including Visa. If he didn't earn it, we did without. Although our secondhand government-retired green station wagon was embarrassing to me as a teenager; he had paid cash for it along with every other vehicle we ever owned. I honestly cannot tell you what I lacked, if anything, growing up.

Dad worked long, strenuous days. Many nights he came home to pray with us, kiss us, send us to bed, then eat his own dinner and return to the office. As we got older, our parents both made it a priority to be at our science fairs, band and choir concerts, drama meets, and sporting events. Dad even taught our hunter's safety class to remain involved in our activities. As a parent now myself, I can fully appreciate the exhausting work and schedule sacrifices they made for us.

Aside from fires, I cannot recall Dad ever working for pay on a Sunday- his understanding of the day set aside for the Biblical Sabbath. Every week, anyone who cared to notice, could expect to see him sitting, worn Bible in hand, at the end of our pew at a non-denominational or inter-denominational church. While his arm was certainly long enough to reach the fidgeting far end of the pew, all it took was a look from Dad to straighten our fidget and silence our whispers. Dad has always taken his relationship with Jesus seriously, although during my 18 years at home I never remember hearing why, or how, he came to have one. I never wondered, so I never asked. Dad's approach to teaching us on spiritual topics generally was less relational in nature and more practical. It made sense to me that there were rules for my protection and his character was proof enough that running upstream in a counter-Biblical culture was possible.

For Dad, weekends at our house were for cutting, splitting, hauling firewood, shoveling snow, mowing lawns, hauling trash to the landfill, paying bills, preparing taxes, cleaning and treating the leather on his boots, and going for drives around one of his beloved forests. In our younger years I vividly remember him setting aside weekend days for canoe trips, camping trips, horse pack trips, road trips, hunting trips, or simply trips to the cafe for a cup of coffee and slice of pie. These were the times I felt most connected to Dad. While at home he tended to be burdened, tired, and stressed, away from home he was funny, relaxed, open, and confident. He told stories from his past, taught lessons on flora and fauna, and tapped his fingers to any number of old country or marching band songs.

I have never heard a word of gossip cross my father's lips. As an adult I have come to the harsh realization that not all adults are adulting the way my father defined adulthood. I now am aware of multiple injustices and horribly stressful situations Dad was put in by other grown men-professionally as well as personally. He endured criticism from "friends" and family regarding his family size and choices as well as for his staunch determination to live in every way with integrity. We never knew any of these situations as he was enduring them; Dad always took the high road in front of us, his children.

As a young adult I counted on my father for advice regarding cars, finances, education, jobs and other practical decisions. It never occurred to me to rely on him for matters of relationship or emotional risk. After my separation from my husband of 14 years, I assumed I knew what Dad would think and say. I had watched my parents wrestle through tough times and come out stronger than ever as a couple. I knew his expectation that marriage is a vow and vows are non-negotiable, unbreakable. I believed that *"God hates divorce"* and so did Dad. I was certain I would lose my dad in some way because of the fact that I was losing my husband.

In the early spring of 2010, the separation already had happened, divorce on the way. Dad asked for a breakfast meeting with me on one of my visits. I approached the cafe with defensiveness already welling up in me. I presumed I would have to hash it out with him and, as we were being seated, I was already mourning the double rejection of the men I loved. He hadn't even spoken yet.

The waitress poured our coffee. This is a scene that has played out countless times in countless cafes over the course of the decades. In fact, the morning of my wedding, Dad and I stole an hour from the early morning for one of these coffee dates. We also had dates on one of the mornings before I left home, the week of my daughter's birth, and a myriad of important and average days throughout my adolescence.

After the waitress left our table that morning, I managed the courage to look into dad's eyes. They were soft. In fact, for the second time in my life, I saw that they held tears. He started talking. He said that he had lost sleep wrestling over, around, and through my situation. He told me of deeply invested prayers and emotions for me and of the seeking of wisdom on my behalf. He viewed me, my separation and impending divorce differently than I had assumed. I had never seen this dad. I had never seen this heart for me. With five words, *"little girl, I support you,"* our relationship was changed forever and the invisible boundaries between us were melted away.

It has been said that earthly fathers tend to represent our Heavenly Father, at least subconsciously. We tend to view God or our belief in the absence of God based on who our fathers were or were not. I don't know and I can't speak for everyone, but I can say that after self-examination, this is true for me. In the weeks and months following that breakfast date, I discovered that I had come to expect God himself to be a little demanding, relationally distant, holding high expectations and conditional affection. I felt that same invisible boundary between me and God. Somehow that one cup of coffee and a single conversation began to alter my perspective on everything "Abba" for me...

The following six years have been transformational for me regarding spiritual things. By the time our family got the news of Dad's Stage IV cancer three years ago, I had already grappled and grasped the truth that God is good and that I am accepted and deeply loved by him.

I cannot fully explain the changes that I have witnessed in my father since that horror of a diagnosis day, October 31, 2012. Oh, his heart... He is gentle, open- wider than I have ever seen. He is humble, yet with more resilient strength. He is deeper. He is more intentionally articulate. He loves. He is patient. He is relaxed. He is funny, able to make light of his physical limitations. He is approachable, even to the messiest of emotionally out-bursting daughters... Nearly every phone call winds down with the words *"Collene, can I pray with you?"* Nearly every text declares his love for me; nearly every response to my search for his advice is covered in scripture and the promises of God for me. Every time we see each other he reminds me that, at 38, I am still his "little girl."

They say his heart is failing, but I disagree.

"My heart and flesh may fail, but God is the strength of my heart and my portion forever." (Psalm 73:26)

Abba
Collene James
Larry G. Sears- Happy Jack, AZ

A Father's Breath Away

Curtains drawn
Night has won
Chased the sun away

Dark prevails
Shadows hail
My soul cries out in fear

Song of Love
Comes breaking through
With certain Truth and Peace

"Child, do not doubt-
I am here-
I've always and forever been
A Father's breath away"

Jesus comes
Light has won
Hope restored this day

I will not fear
Never will stray
More than a Father's breath away

Arms wide
Where I'll abide
Safe, secure

A Father's breath away

This Song of Love
Will always and forever be
A Father's breath away

Nancy Bowser

Flee
Collene James

The Grief Season

April 25th 2016

Seasonal Allergy is the name of my silly little blog journal for a reason. I hate the constantly changing seasons of life. In fact, ever since the day I became a mom, I have been aware of the internal sound of "whizzing" as the calendar sheds its pages. With each calendar season changing and a billion pictures that prove that another year has altered my first baby, turned toddler, turned awkward-toothed pre-teen, turned young adult, turned MAN, I have always deeply craved a circling of my wagons and had the desire to hold everyone I love close. I neeeeeeeed things to stop, to BE STILL.

Today I took the day off from the salon. Internally I feel the practical pull to use my one day alone wisely. I know I should be re-filling the refrigerator and the snack cupboards, processing mountains of laundry, dusting, mopping, sorting stacks of mail, doing the bathroom mucking... or at the very least, teaching someone else around here how to do those things correctly. I've been gone from this house for too many days, and we've all seemed to slip into a "camping out" mode. Internally I also feel the emotional reality that I have absolutely nothing to offer. I don't believe I can muster the emotional energy it would take to get out of my car in the rain, wander through the aisles and make choices, then to stand in line at the grocery store, Costco, or heaven-forbid, Walmart. Sadly, I'm out of milk, eggs, bread, all meats for lunches and dinners, vegetables, contact solution, cotton balls; even my toothbrush is in poor shape- those are just the things I can think of off the top of my head. I haven't polled the rest of the family, it's absolutely possible that they've completely given up on brushing their teeth and washing their faces, and I. DON'T. CARE.

This morning the dog and I are sitting together in the still-dark living room, avoiding making the rest of the shopping and to-do lists. While he sleeps next to me, I'm envious of his cozy rest. How am I going to purge a grief that I can't even really feel? I am aware of Grief's presence- it has put nearly tangible weights on my heart, my mind and even my body, yet I am numb to its pain.

I am irritable. I want everyone home and near me, but I don't want to hear a single sound. I want to hear about their day- their perspectives, but I cannot concentrate on their words or needs. I want my hand held, yet I feel suffocated by being touched by anyone and everyone. I want my children,

270

their smiles and joy, but I'm annoyed that they are completely unaware of my numbness and desperate emotional depletion. I want to talk about him, but I'm tired of the sound of my own voice. I want to remember him, and the final 9 important days I have yet to blog about, but I cannot force my mind to think on it anymore. I want life to carry on, but I cannot stand that life has moved on.

I want to be able to discuss all of the things like bike racing and politics and the summer plans my family has been contemplating for weeks, but I hate trivial conversations and cannot even handle overhearing the bickering at the sink as the kids load the dishes, much less the bickering of politicians and canned antagonism on the stupid TV. I want to be a friend, but I wrestle with simply not caring. I don't like this version of me. I assume I'm not always going to be this way, but then maybe I will- I only know that I was changed forever when Dad left us for good on April 7th, 2016.

I'm pretty sure my life today, on the outside, looks normal. I look like I'm coping well and that we are all back in our routine of work and home and kids' activities. I shower and dress well, I put on my make-up and pick out a smile and an attitude suitable for each and every day. Except, I want to scream and cry and rage, but can't find the energy or tone for that particular voice.

I envy my mother's tears. My sister's sobs look almost cozy. I've reviewed those final pictures a time or two, yet...

I am numb.

I am exhausted.

I feel like a frozen roast, waiting on the counter to thaw, slowly bleeding, unusable, cold.

I am alone, yet I am surrounded. I'm starting to understand what little I know now about the grieving rituals of the Old Testament. Smart people, they were, I think...

I can imagine a good aloneness.

In my daydream I see me sitting on a beach. Waves of grief are rhythmically washing over me. There is a pattern to them; each make sense and soothe, even while the salt and sand hurt my open wound. I crave those waves and the stillness in between them. I crave the expectation and the ability to make room emotionally for the power of the next one as I anticipate it washing over me. There is a cleansing in the power of those waves that my imagination tells me I need...

My emotional reality is not the right kind of aloneness...

What I'm experiencing is more like a bustling sidewalk. There are low, strong tsunami waves washing in from every direction, clipping me at my ankles as I hurry along. There's no predicting the next one, no anticipation and no routine to any of them. There's no time for embracing them in any kind of productive or useful way, they are simply another annoyance for me to cope with and behave myself through. My feet are wet and cold; I'm slipping and slopping and keep stumbling along, still hurrying. Maybe I'm getting somewhere, but the ankle-deep water doesn't let me measure distance. I don't have time to fall, so I keep myself righted and try to keep "it" all together. There's no rhyme or reason to any of the madness; nothing feels productive, not the grief, not the busyness, not the water swishing through the streets of my imagination. I keep seeing mud and debris being brought in by the surges, but nothing is being removed or resolved by these ridiculous waves of grief.

"Make sure you take care of yourself."

It's the advice I keep hearing over and over. Although I've said it a bazillion times to other people, I can't help but wonder: What the heck does that even mean? How is that supposed to that look for a person in my situation? I'd love to check-out for a week, or two, or fifteen... But that doesn't do anything except prolong my responsibility and ruin my relationships and destroy my business and obliterate my finances and abandon my children in their needs. None of those options fulfill the advice to take care of me, really. In this season of grief, mixed with the season of motherhood, and the season of great responsibility to my family and career, how do I find that emotional beach? How long would it be sufficient for me to sit there if I ever do find it, and how do I express my beach needs to the people who don't understand that I haven't really "moved on" to anywhere? I'm not now, nor will I ever be, "over it."

The Calm Before Our Storm
Collene James
Port Orchard, WA
(Taken the night I got the call to go help my dad for the final nine days of his life.)

273

April 16, 2016- We buried my daddy today, but he's been gone for a million years already. I haven't found the right words for describing this last two weeks... I only have pictures. Maybe it's morbid or offensive, but it's all I have for now...

Burial Day
Collene James
Trego, MT

A Widow's Cry
Collene James
Trego, MT

"Learn to do good; Seek justice, Rebuke the oppressor; Defend the fatherless, Plead for the widow." (Isaiah 1:17)

Weep

I will not weep over that which has been razed,
or suffer sorrow for leveled idols once praised;
for out of the ashes of lost desire - smoked -
flashes of glory will rise - set fire, once stoked.

My sacrifice provoked armies of black.
Counter-attack, my frenzied brain clamped - ensnared;
my benumbed heart encamped in an endless nightmare,
nowhere to hide or to cower!
Empower me, Lord, where is your right arm?
Disarm my foes, release me neath hellish thumbs, hounding;
silence war drums - beating, pounding.
Sunshine slinked away like a petrified prowler;
soul sunk into spikes in the trap of the fowler.
Darkness exhaled like a breath of stale air;
hope impaled on a pike of despair.
Sank to the depths, in the ground, vile - all alone;
bound to the stile of perdition's throne.

My God! My God! I cannot see through the shroud;
a dark cloud overwhelms my senses!
My enemy dispenses stark retribution;
accusations color his dark elocution.
Where is my righteousness imputed?!
Why does my Savior let these lies lie undisputed?!

Up in the air - rises the scepter of wrath;
its path leading straight for my skull -
senses dull, I brace myself for the blow,
I know that there will be no abdication.

A sensation swells in the air above,
like love mingled with blind fury.
A winged warrior descends and suspends in the air;
look there! - a host - a heavenly jury!

A light blinds my eyes,
the cries of my foe fill my ears;
fears of death all scatter like roaches;

276

my Savior approaches!
His enemy's face, 'neath raised mace, falls
like defectors falling from heaven.
His heart, unleavened, sinks to hooves, cloven;
his fate interwoven with sovereign will!

Be still, my heart, for these dank dominions,
'neath holy pinions, cannot pierce;
for fierce is the sword of my savior; my Lord,
my God he is mighty to save!

The beast, he roars as I'm pulled from his hand;
like sand, my soul slips through his fingers.
He lingers too long, lulled by the song
of the throng of white seraphs that sway.
Demanding tariffs of blood that he cannot pay,
he looks away, and to his utter alarm -
a right arm grasps my fraise; the left, lifts my head,
with a word we raise from the place of the dead.

On solid ground, my head turns,
my soul burns with remorse
that its source of delight
was rooted in what was not right,
or true, or pure, or lovely.
That my eyes had been too blind to see
His beauty - His sufficiency.
On bended knee, I wash his feet
with tears from my eyes, flowing;
knowing that my mind - deranged,
has been now, forever changed.

I will not weep over that which has been razed,
or suffer sorrow for leveled idols once praised;
for out of the ashes of lost desire - smoked -
flashes of glory will rise - set fire, once stoked.

Vicki Joy Anderson

It's Raining

Shhh.
It's raining.
It's raining and I ask you –
does He cry.

A storm.
Is that Him,
our Creator,
does He mourn.

Made in His image.

We have tear drops
and yet
there are raindrops.

Was the garden wet with mist
that night,
the night they were barred from Eden.

In righteous anger the earth was flooded
but after,
were there 40 days 40 nights of grieving.

He is perfect and just and beautiful,
in that perfection
does He pain.

Justice was done,
Gomorrah and Sodom fell.
in the quiet,
did showers cool the brimstone.

It was finished.

The Ghost was given.
Was Golgotha turned to mud that day.
Did water stream down in ribbons.

Was He weeping.

He calls His remnant.

Does the air rain in yearning.
In the dawn, is the dew
Him aching.

Shhh.
It's raining
and I ask –
does He cry.

Ashley Fugleberg

Lament

We were the only two people in the room.
Oh, so dark, inside my heart;
haze creates a spooky gloom.

As I watched my mother die, I lost my head.
Blessed and bold ascension,
so I speak for the dead.

Lips concealing the secrets of the joy.
Blur where the rest of the world is -
where moth and rust destroy.

See these bleeding hands that you left to dry?
A fallen rose is dead,
ranting, "Too soon to die."

Remember this is but a part of life.
Summer of winters merging,
did meet in glorious strife.

Inferno and thunder are burning the sky.
But I still can't kill the pain;
sadness lives after we die.

Vicki Joy Anderson

Uh-Oh Dad's Coming Back

October 28th 2016

Tonight, I went to bed in the way I normally do. I turned the channel on our T.V. from my husband's show (something political) to something comedically nonsensical. It has become an unofficial agreement that "us" time does not include debates, pundits, spins, or childishness in suits.

Step two of the going-to-bed process requires me to set the alarm and check/respond to messages on my phone, including the online ones. Yes, I know the arguments against such screen time so close to trying to sleep. Whatever, it's not the point.

Online message-checking inevitably leads to article-reading. Tonight, for example, I browsed past about a dozen presidential race articles- the titles of which already had my blood pressure rising, to a local news story about an officer involved shooting. That link led to an article about the justice (read lack thereof) for a local child rapist who was convicted recently and now is facing his so-called sentencing. I skipped the second article in my feed of the day about a set of parents who inflicted abuse on their toddler, breaking his ribs and one of his legs. They are finally having their day in court...

Looking for something less icky, I tried swimming for safer bed-time-reading waters. I found a missionary lady's blog link. She's usually funny and light. Nope, not this one- not funny or light. Reading her article and then the opinion-piece articles that published it, all of which brought me to a related Matt Walsh blog link. I read all of this with open-hearted and intellectual interest, trying to reconcile the seemingly opposed views from alleged members of the same spiritual family. I recalled the wisdom of Jesus, who responded to these types of direct and complicated questions with broad answers, aimed at the heart of the questioner, who only meant to trap him legally or religiously in a response.

Then, unfortunately, I read on. I nearly drowned in the waters of a billion shouting opinions and accusations, while I dodged missiles that were aimed by Christians, at Christians, in the comment sections of each link. And now I can't sleep. My heart hurts- screams out in agony.

Initially, as I shut everything off and closed my eyes, I visualized one of the noisy eight-kids-still-at-home, everyone feeling needy, days of my childhood. Often, I was the lucky one who was assigned to be the free babysitter. It didn't always go well, I'll admit.

"QUIIIIIIIIIIIIIIIIIIETTTTTT!!!!" I would scream at the end of the day, trying to be heard over the noise- the blaming and the defending, the crying, and the mocking. I just needed to hear nothingness; to feel some sense of calm and a presence of peace. Tonight, I remembered what it meant to hear my father's cowboy-boot footsteps as he came up the walk at the end of one of those days. I had a healthy fear of what we'd all have to answer to once the door opened. I also felt a sense of relief because as the biggest sister, I always felt helpless to resolve all that need or the error that lay in front of me. Only now do I realize that never really was my job as the big sister babysitter anyway; it was Dad's.

Chances are on a chaotic day like that, we had all been naughty to varying degrees. Some of us were always antagonists because personality dictated it. A few of us were stubborn enough to learn every single, dang lesson the hard way. Now and then a few of us triiiiiiiied to be self-disciplined, but lost our focus because of immaturity or distraction. We were hungry, tired, unheard, selfish, fearful; we had hurt feelings, we were annoyed and overwhelmed and needy.

My father usually got it all sorted out before dinner was served. Of course, the method of correction was as varied as the crime; age mattered, cognitive ability mattered, heart attitude mattered, the number of infractions mattered...

So tonight, I lay there trying to darken the blue-screen imprints behind my eyes and dull from my mind the sound of the shouting words I had read. I mentally embraced the oddly nostalgic flashbacks of those chaotic battles from my youth as well as the sometimes-bitter-sometimes-sweet fatherly parenting I was blessed to receive. I whispered for Jesus to come. I searched for thoughts of my Savior to help me drag my distracted mind back to a real hope and continued to whisper into the dark:

"SSSSSHHHHHHHhhhhhhhhhhhhhhhhhhhhhhhhhhhhhhhhh..."

Can't you hear them? The footsteps of our Father as He walks up to the door on His return? Tonight, I'm feeling that same big sister sense of dread as I view online proof that we have all been naughty since He left.

Some of us are antagonists and liars and pot stirrers because we like to see people squirm. Some of us just scream to be heard by someone, anyone.

Some of us are arrogant and proud and always think we know the answer in every dang situation. Some of us know we are unseen and that we don't have answers or feel that we don't deserve them anyway. Some of us are quick to be defensive; some of us lead with offense. Some of us fear being forgotten or unloved. Some of us want to ignore the suffering of others because it's just plain inconvenient. Some of us haven't gotten our way... or justice... we haven't gotten justice. Some of us love the letter of the law, but not the spirit of the law. We loathe the lawbreaker, altogether forgetting that we are one too.

In the mess, we've taken on a role we weren't assigned- to bring attention to a problem as we perceive it to be, with no understanding of the other viewpoints, the other hearts, the other abilities, the other ages, the other experiences, the other broken-nesses. We have been desperate or immature. We have lacked self-discipline and some of us just plain insist that we learn best in the deep pain of the mistakes.

I have gay friends, lesbian friends, straight friends, bi friends, friends who have had abortions, friends who have picketed abortions, police-officer friends, minority friends, transgender friends, cross-dressing friends, city friends, country friends, addicted friends, recovering friends, theologically educated friends, theologically uneducated friends, friends who have been or are currently being abused, friends who have never been abused and couldn't possibly understand why someone would stay. I have divorced friends, widowed friends, married friends, forever single friends, incarcerated friends, correctional officer friends, parole officer friends, republican friends, democrat friends, pastor friends, atheist friends, angry friends, passive friends, rich friends, poor friends, gossipy friends, and tight-lipped friends...

...and every single one of us has something we will answer to for how we conducted ourselves while the Father was gone. How can Jesus be pleased with a single one of the agendas that our voices have been promoting, when we have promoted them with anger or when we have been quick to speak and slow to listen? What about when they have been detached from any personal relationship and have merely been used as weapons to be lobbed across world-wide-webbed-waters at faceless, fleshless enemies, who will only listen to respond, but not to hear? Did He personally and directly bring us under this spotlight for the promotion of those cold agendas through His truth-with-the-deepest-of-loves perspective by the shedding of His own Son's blood? This, precious family, is not how we were taught by Him to make disciples...

I'm guessing the majority of us would have to say our trigger fingers aren't that well guided most days. Lord help us, we're launching attacks out of our own injuries and that is a dangerous and misguided and unwinnable kind of war. Also, it occurs to me that it's not our job to resolve or correct all of that need or error that lies in front of us anyway; it's His.

All of us need some Fatherly correction and all of us need Him to look us in the eye and tell us of His LOVE and family expectations. We need to be reminded that *"no"* is sometimes protection and *"don't"* is sometimes *"don't hurt yourself."* We need Him to pick us up from our pit, wipe our tears and sort out our mess. We need our thirst and our hunger quenched. We need to be heard. We need to be humbled or maybe just carried. We need help to put away the missiles and to clean out the shrapnel wounds and then for Him hold us while we cry. We need to rest in His embrace until we fully trust and respect this perfect God.

Oh, and a house divided against itself cannot stand. Jesus, we're going to need a lot of help working this out with each other too.

"If a house is divided against itself, that house cannot stand." (Mark 3:25)

"The weapons we fight with are not the weapons of the world. On the contrary, they have divine power to demolish strongholds. We demolish arguments and every pretension that sets itself up against the knowledge of God, and we take captive every thought to make it obedient to Christ." (2 Corinthians 10:4-5)

SPRING

BY COLLENE JAMES

Spring
Collene James

Prospering
Collene James
Gallatin County, MT

"For as the rain comes down, and the snow from heaven, and do not return there, but water the earth, and make it bring forth and bud, that it may give seed to the sower, and bread to the eater. So shall My word be that goes forth from My mouth; It shall not return to Me void, but it shall accomplish what I please, and it shall prosper in the thing for which I sent it." (Isaiah 55:10-11)

Father

It was a big fire engine, shiny and red.
With a banner, "Happy 4th" it said.
A little girl holds her father's hand.
"Lift me up daddy I can't see when I stand.
Lift me up like you do.
Please daddy please I want to see too."

He picked her up, that very moment.
She saw the whole parade, will never forget it.
They went home that night, and he tucked her in.
"I love you baby girl forever, amen."

A few years down the road, it's wedding day.
A nervous boy waits for him to give her away.
Halfway down the aisle the high heel breaks.
Down goes the bride, on her wedding day.

She looks at her dad, misty eyes and sad.
"Lift me up daddy if you still can.
I'll never get up on my own, I can't stand."
He picked her up, that very moment.
Embarrassed and a mess, but she'll never forget it.

Years went by and people got older.
The phone rang her daddy was getting colder.
She rushed to the hospital to say goodbye.
Before she went in, she started to cry.

Down on her knees she started to pray.
Dear Father, don't take him today.
If you do oh if you must,
Then be Your will, in You I trust.

Her father passed- just minutes went by.
She fell to the ground and started to cry.
Then as if a Heavenly Ghost came down from above,

The Father the mighty Father lifted her up.

Matthew Bailey

Purging the Collection & Stepping Off

February 8ᵗʰ 2018

I've been thinking a lot lately about what is required of us as people; a childhood favorite chorus of mine comes from **Micah 6:8**, which says:

"He has told you, O man, what is good; and what the Lord requires of you but to do justice, to love mercy and to walk humbly with your God."

These words have been posted in various places throughout most of the homes I've decorated. Yet only this last month have I taken the time to dwell on each of the three "rules" of that verse and let them meander through my methods to the deeper "heart" place.

I'm a rule follower, which is both a blessing and a curse. (The concepts of "blessing" and "cursing" are a simultaneous theme, actually, but that's for a different blog journal post.) Being a rule follower requires me to have at least one rule-maker. However, just like shoes, coffee mugs and jewelry, I've found I am a collector of rule-makers. Did you know that all good collectors border on hoarding? If I'm honest, I've been a rule-maker hoarder.

Oh, I only collect the best, so don't worry. I don't collect your average gas station attendant's rules, or fellow rest area utilizer's rules. I discount the average fellow shopper's rules and depending on personality, even some of the other people's rules who live on my own neighborhood block.

I like to collect the rule-makers the average church produces. Or maybe the educated business owners I call friends. Parents and older godly mentors are favorites of mine as well. I like the rules of people who have "been down the same road" I'm on; I like to give a special seat in my heart to their voices. Local and national lawmaker's rules are a given, because court is expensive and scary and traffic tickets mean fewer shoes... I've collected some siblings' rules, a handful of pastors' and teachers', and a couple of husbands' who fit the bill of rule-makers. These are all intelligent, gifted, and dogmatic in their area of expertise kind of people. All are "Type A" and confident that they know what is best. I also look to professionals such as medical doctors, therapists, and attorneys...

These make up the Collection and are the rule-makers that I prefer. It's pragmatic, after all, to let people who claim to "know," set the rules for my own personal conduct and thought patterns. Right? Right.

Or maybe, just maybe, it's utter foolishness.

Bear with me, I'm coming back to that after I tell you about this:

As usual, there's a roaming word in the quiet places of my thoughts. This is often how the God of heaven chooses to communicate with me. For a few months the word, again, has been "fear." This time, however, fear isn't "scared," but rather attaches to "of man" or "of God" in alternating thoughts.

I've heard these phrases in the fellowship halls, in the doorways and stairways of and from my seat in the pews or at the Sunday School tables in the churches I've attended for my whole life. Apparently, I've never actually paid much attention to the definitions, or more specifically, the ramifications, of those two phrases.

Side note: how many of these churchy phrases have slipped into my life, unnoticed, untested, misunderstood by me? Ugh, I shudder to think about it.

Another subtle phrase I've tried wrestling into silence during this season is "self-sufficient."

(See *Jeremiah 17:5* to see how this also simultaneously weaves the aforementioned blessing/cursing thoughts, in case you're curious: ***"Thus says the Lord: 'Cursed is the man who trusts in man and makes flesh his strength, whose heart turns away from the Lord.'"***)

You see, as I was dusting my Collection this winter, I also found me on the shelf, very much near the top.

To recap, the idea that this Collection and method of operation is utter foolishness, God has shown me these woven themes for these two or three months:

I (mostly) trust me. I trust you- well, at least the ones of you I personally vetted and placed in the Collection, which is also to say *"I trust me to choose those of you who will care more about me than I do...* I SAY I trust God. But, when He tells me to do something that is declared unadvisable by the other rule-makers, I have a long history of disobedience.

I "fear" the approval or disapproval of my self-collected mob of professionals, religious people, elders, BFFs, peers, and critics, MUCH stronger than I "fear" the God I claim to follow.

Oh, and this is not-so-fun to see: when my collection of rule-makers disagrees, I trust myself slightly more than I trust the Lord. But did you know that my Collection doesn't EVER all agree, and it never actually has? At the end of the day, the loudest, most insistent (read abusive), or most agreed upon voice gets my obedience. In the case of a tie, I do what's preferable to me and lobby HARD, at utter exhaustion, to convince the Collection of the "rightness" of my choice. All of this has been happening at a sub-conscience level for FORTY YEARS. And this method already had a name, long before I engaged in it:

PRIDE (Which, for those of you younger than fourth grade, is the opposite of "walking humbly" with God as Micah charges.)

Guys! I'm tired.

In December, as God began to reveal this truth to my spirit, I had a choice. I could hush Him (again) or I could finally reject the instinct of my flesh and just obey:

Doing justice is easy, until it's my turn to receive it. Loving mercy ("kindness" as some translations say) is a given, until it's required of me to be kind or merciful to the personally cruel or the hateful. Walking humbly... nope, that's not easy no matter how you cut it. Do you know how WEAK it feels to choose to speak, out loud, to someone who is very capable and respectable (and probably has pride of their own), a complete confession or admission of major, or minor, personal failure?

But, because the mercies of the Lord are new every morning, I've had choice all along, to obey or to hush Him; to fear Him, or to consult one of the Collection opinions...

Roughly six weeks have passed since I made the choice, face down on my hardwood floor, to dismantle the Collection and place only One Opinion, only One Rule-Maker at the front of every choice, every thought, every step... It certainly hasn't gone flawlessly for me, and the cost of obedience has been immense. I have had many of my out loud confessions outright ignored or rebutted or spun into a lie. Oh, how the enemy hates TRUTH and will fight to quench it! Forgiveness has frequently been denied towards me, and yet a funny thing is happening! I just don't care what happens next. In fact, I'm a little excited to see how it plays out, because this is no longer a "transaction" relationship to obedience- a "giving to get" or a "doing to have." Rather, this is a cleansing process of obedience before that Lord that is bringing complete healing that is for only me and will not be stolen, cheapened, or stopped by anyone else's choice.

I didn't come this far through that war to give back gained ground now. Truth is FREEDOM and admission of my weakness and failure is BUILDING STRENGTH and now this is becoming easier! Ohhhhhh, and the people I collected and "feared," some of those are TICKED to not be a part of my Collection anymore! I'm sad about that, but I'm not sad for me. The opposite is true too, some of them are so relieved to have the weight of their words towards me lightened because of my lower expectations. What a blessing those friends have become!

Today, I'm reminded of Peter, sitting in a boat with his BFFs and professionals from all walks of his life... Dr Luke would NEVER medically approve of Peter's move to step out ONTO the water. No psychologist, oceanographer, professional seaman, good friend, or human with an ounce of wisdom of any kind would support his ridiculous choice to obey the One calling him out... If I had been there, I would have probably been in the very least, critical, annoyed, and frustrated at his choice...

In Peter's case, obedience motivated by fear of just One proved miraculous and THAT is what I'm counting on for my own Walk of Humility out on the waters of obedience; and even if none go with me, or approve of my going, I will still step off the boat.

"Blessed is the man who trusts in the Lord, whose trust is the Lord." (Jeremiah 17:7)

Faith Walk, Where the Sidewalk Ends
Collene James
Lake Erie, OH

Seeds Waiting on Ruach
Collene James

293

School's In Session

May 20ᵗʰ 2018

Hi friends! Sorry for the six-ish months' absence. I had hoped to spend more time writing this year, but my real-life-educational opportunities have taken me away from the phone, television, and computer and into my Bible in a brand-new way.

One of the exciting and terrifying things about coming to understand this business of following and knowing the God of the Bible, and to develop real intimacy with Christ, is that He gets to choose what He teaches first- and to what extent He tests the lessons. Additionally, the future purpose of the individual lessons doesn't always take shape during the training. I have finally been given the green light to share with you all a teensy window into my process- not because you need it, but because I do.

Last fall I was encouraged by a friend to read the Bible, in its entirety, chronologically.* Since the whole deal isn't put together that way, my friend wrote out the chronology of it and told me to take my time, write notes and questions and, above all, don't give up when things get hard. So, I started. Then I did- give up that is.

I wasn't disciplined enough to go at my own pace and get anywhere fast, so I researched a printable "map" to help me navigate my endeavor and started again, January 1, 2018. This time, following the "rules" of a daily reading plan, I will get to the last sentence on the last day of this year. Now I'm a solid five months in and there are at least 12 inescapable themes emerging in my "syllabus." Oh, and there've been tests. Because most of the themes intertwine and I'm not sure which came first, I've listed the "easier" half first, and the more difficult ones last. Here's the first half of my top 12:

1. Righteousness
2. Stronghold (Shelter, Defender, Dwelling)
3. Blessings and Curses
4. Fear
5. Cry
6. Corporate Repentance

Because these one dozen concepts as individual ideas have depth enough for a book of their own, I'll give you a very brief overview of the first six tonight and finish my processing of the others later. Meander with me, will you?!

Righteousness
No, not "right"- "righteousness." I've always been intuitive and somewhat insightful. My first husband told me (well after our divorce was final and we were both remarried, mind you) that one of the most frustrating things about me was this:

"Everything you say is true Collene. You were basically always right about what you saw in me, but the problem is you didn't need to be the one to say it. Sometimes I just needed to figure it out for myself."

What a valuable statement, right?! When he said it, it was balm to my soul because it resonates as accurate with me. I had no need to fight it or defend it. Quite frankly, he knows me better than anyone and I trusted his words and the way he delivered them. Ugh, had he had the courage to tell me 21 years ago how might this particular life-lesson have been less painful?

Proverbs 27:6 tells us ***"Faithful are the wounds of a friend."*** In my 41st year of life I have determined that my most trusted and valued friends wound me (gently) with truth. As a side note, because of the not-so-gentle wounding I've already received for four decades, I do still react poorly to truth without love or to false accusations, however I'm digressing and that's for another time.

The Lord has impressed upon me these lessons from His interactions with His people in both the Old and New Testaments, as well as today: While He is and was always "right," as in "correct" or "accurate," His Righteousness title requires a supernatural response that sometimes causes Him to be silent and still and at other times causes Him to boldly speak up or act. "Righteousness" is deeper than "right." It's a conviction on a moral level that does not require explanation and is its own defense, that requires no further argument, and is based solely on the Creator's standard of morality. I'm still getting the act of being righteous wrong a lot of days, but SEEING it makes all the difference. I'll move on with the transparency that I am possibly a little behind the class on this one.

Stronghold (Shelter, Defender, Dwelling)
This family of words is mashed together although the words aren't completely interchangeable at a glance. Stronghold is a word we don't use often anymore except in religious circles or on battlefields. Back in the day of David, Moses, Job, and the Apostles, they knew it like we know the word

"bunker" today. It's a secure place, or a prison perhaps depending on context.

When scripture uses it, it sometimes refers to a spiritual struggle with demonic connotations- a negative for sure. Often it refers to a sin a person just can't stop no matter how hard they will themselves to- they are stuck securely in a spiritual, and often emotional, prison.

The Psalms often use it in exactly the opposite way by referring to it as a secure place of peace. Because most of us war internally, and not actually on a physical battlefield, I'd like to submit to you that the word "stronghold" can be interchangeable with the phrase "house of thought." Where do my thoughts dwell? What defends my thinking? Where do I run for shelter mentally when I'm afraid? Am I placing myself securely in prison or in peace?

Friends! I can truly say that for the first time in 41 years, my "stronghold" thoughts bring me peace! *Isaiah 26:3* says, *"You will keep (her) in perfect peace whose mind is fixed on you, because (she) trusts in you."* Seriously, my heart has tested this verse a hundred ways a day in this session of school I'm in, and it is FACT.

Blessings and Curses
I told you before this could become its own blog journal entry, and it still might. I have more to dig into concerning the topic, BUT it's very clear to me that words have power. *"The tongue holds the power of life and death and those who love it will eat its fruit." (Proverbs 18:21)*

The obvious power can be seen in the example of verbally motivating or de-motivating of a child or athlete. Clearly how we speak TO a person matters in our relationship with them. What I'm seeing and experiencing is deeper. Come in with me, the water is fine...

What we speak ABOUT a person matters in our relationship with them too- even if they never hear or know about our chosen words... Are you with me? This concept is related closely to the previous "house of thought" concept.

The point is: I HEAR what I say about others. I am changed by the words I think and speak, quite literally. Not only that, but my hearers are changed by my words, even if they don't believe them. This works both in the positive and in the negative!

The entire canon of scripture incessantly talks about blessings and curses, by parents over their children, by leaders over their nations, by teachers over their disciples... This matters deeply to Abba and has the power to change families, communities, futures, and an entire world. Testing the concept has had mixed results, mostly because it requires training a "thought muscle" that has been used very little before now.

Fear

Here's another positive/negative word in scripture. We are told to *"fear God, not man"* and to *"not be afraid"* or *"fear not."* I've told you already about my man-fearing issues and all of us have varying degrees of fearful things we encounter in life.

For me 2018 Fear School started with the fearing God part of the equation. If I worry ONLY about how He views me, and trust His perspective of my sin, guess what? I get changed permanently in the deepest parts of me. In the process of allowing, no- BEGGING- God to know me, expose me and heal me, I have begun to develop a reverence for Him that was not taught to me in a healthy way before. I no longer feel the need to jump through anyone's hoops to be "enough" in churchy circles, or social circles, or relationships of any kind. Those people can't see inside me anyway, but God can. Getting exposed before Him isn't nearly as scary as I once believed it would be. In the process of fearing Him, His position, authority, power, and opinion, I have found that He's exceedingly protective and is a master provider! He's also generously teaching me how to access His strength for myself. I now fear NOT being exposed before Him first and above all.

Because of the kind of fear I mentioned above, other kinds of fears are being addressed too. Financial fear? Whatever. Snakes? Meh. Broken relationships? They come and go, but HE is forever. Hungry? Lonely? Insecurity? War? Disapproval? Insufficiency? Addictions? Death? It's all capable of being addressed in the fearing of HIM.

Cry

I played with a few words here, but quite frankly "pray" and "ask" seem a little too neat and tidy for what the lesson really looked like. This was more akin to a brutal gym class than a boring lecture hall. Perhaps I should have made it the phrase "cry out" because "weep" is not what I'm getting at here.

The book of Job was one of the earliest chronological lesson books I read. He does a good job describing the sentiment I'm going for. There's almost a violence, an urgency, a desperation to his outcry.

Then there's Israel... this bunch of dummies disobeyed and got themselves in a pickle more times in a month than most climbing toddlers. Aaaaaand then they cried out, aaaaaand the Lord heard, aaaaaand then He rescued them from their self-made predicament. Over and over and over. Charming, right? Except I HATE those kind of perpetual screw-up stories. I just want the lesson learned and graduation to occur, at least in my own life. You all can do what you want, I guess.

The whole desert wandering thing really annoys me these days, BUT this year's read-through of it highlighted the same quality of the good Heavenly Father that David sang about over and over a few hundred years later. It's also the concept that Hagar relied upon back when Abraham and Sarah had their stupid idea to get her pregnant and then later kick her out of the house into a wilderness with a child and not enough food or water.

The idea is this: In the day of trouble, in that very day, IF we cry out to Him, He HEARS. He also SEES. He definitely KNOWS.

He then moves to deliver, protect, sustain, provide for... He answers every single cry. He counts every single turn in the tossing and collects every single tear. (**Psalm 50:15** and **56:8** are a good place to start your own proof text research.)

Friends, I tested it. It's true. His answers are occasionally *"shhhhhhh, wait Sweetie, I'm aware"*... and then, like Job, my trust is renewed regardless that in some ways I still am sitting in the dirt, in the same anguishing predicament. Then there are days that BAM! I cried out in the morning and the answer was waiting for me after work. His timing is no longer a daily trust issue and for that I am incredibly in awe.

Corporate Repentance

You know how when you were in school, and you had a substitute, there was always one or two kids that ruined the rest of the week with the real teacher by being disrespectful or disobedient? Or, if you played sports and one or two of your team-mates weren't "all there" for practice, so the coach made everyone run the rest of the session? My parents occasionally took away the privileges for all of us if they couldn't find out who the one was that broke the window, or told the lie, or whatever. Yeah. As a rule-follower those corporate punishment days used to seriously make me sick to my stomach- and still sometimes do.

As I re-read the story of The Exodus and noted Moses's behavior as the ultimate God-fearing rule follower, it bothered me that he was constantly having to answer to Almighty God for the entire group of 600,000 rule-breaking campers he had been charged to bring along with him. Oh, and not only did he have to answer, beg, and plead on their behalf, but he ALSO got slapped with the extra 39 years of circling in a sandbox as a consequence for acting out in his frustration. Ugh! Why?

Then God started showing me the POWER that comes with agreeing with Him for the group's benefit. I started to notice that Moses was also changed by the interactions with his Father on their behalf. His heart was invested, he became a lover of the people, not just a babysitter. It happened again with David after Saul had made unnecessary enemies with some of Israel's neighbors. It happened with Joseph with his disobedient and hateful siblings. It happened with Hosea and his whoring wife... It happens over and over- culminating with Jesus's irrational yet merciful trip to the cross to corporately repent and accept the consequences on my behalf. We are promised it will happen for us regarding our nation, family, marriage... if only we will love like that.

So, I may not be the one that put the fire in the substitute teacher's trash can, but I can be the one that makes it right. And maaaayyyyybe when the real teacher gets back, we won't be writing extra "good behavior" papers for days...

Okay, on that note, I'm going to bed. May the Lord bless you and keep you and cause his face to shine upon you!

"The Chronological Bible Reading Plan" is a booklet that we have put together; it is available at www.Amazon.com

Heaven Meets Earth
Collene James
Clear Lake, IA

Into the Storm
Collene James

Second Semester: SERE School

May 21ˢᵗ 2018

I woke up yesterday thinking about my brothers. More specifically, I was thinking about some of their military training courses. With two Naval officers and an enlisted Marine for brothers, I've heard a few stories about what it takes to discipline a body and mind for battle. One of those such opportunities was gifted to a couple of them in the form of SERE School.

Survival, Evasion, Resistance, Escape School is designed to equip our military for complex "worst case" scenarios and is especially vital for leaders who will deploy into enemy territory. This is different than Marine or Navy boot camp, Officer Candidate School, War College, or Tactical Training Schools, and yet works in tandem with the other equipping military service members are provided.

The spiritual implications that are emerging as I recall these worst-case scenario battle prepping concepts, are profound. OFTEN over the last 6-9 months I realize there are floating thoughts in my head such as *"God is building His Army"* and *"the angels of the Lord are warring angels."* There has been a very real sense of the urgency of understanding "battle" as in **"the battle belongs to the Lord," "we do not war against flesh and blood,"** and *"don't neglect to take up your armor Collene, they are trying to devour you."*

I'll leave those thoughts there for now because I think you get my point. The Lord has a military-like, specific purpose in the testing of me and that fact has become a very real source of comfort. *2 Samuel 22* is almost a complete summary of my top 12 concepts, but for this morning's purpose I'll direct you to verses 35-36 which say **"He trains my hands for war so that my arms can bend a bow of bronze. You have given me the shield of Your salvation and Your gentleness made me great."** Then in verse 40 David writes **"for You equipped me with strength for the battle; You made those who rise against me sink under me."**

I HATE conflict. I hate war. I hate debates and I am often uncomfortable with disagreement. However, do you know who LOVES war, conflict, bloodshed and especially death? My enemies do. So, I can play in what I'd like to believe is a field of daisies and avoid noticing the brutal truth that it is in reality a battlefield; If I choose not to look up and see the truth, I will be destroyed... OR I can armor up and war successfully every time doing it the King's way. As a brief side note, one of my favorite war stories is

Gideon's "attack" on Midian in **Judges 7** using only trumpets and empty jars. The sound of the jars breaking and the trumpets blaring terrified the enemy who turned on each other and defeated themselves. This is the kind of war a girl could wear her heels to!

Doing it the King's way is irrational OFTEN to our flesh mind's understanding but is ALWAYS successful. What a kindness of the Lord to force me into SERE school this year, and not a moment too late! I'm keeping the daisies I've picked though, because, well, I like daisies and dancing in pretty dresses and I'm positive warrior princesses still get to enjoy the "still waters" and "green pastures" of **Psalm 23** after the battle.

As a reminder, we were in the middle of the top 12 theme words or phrases that have characterized the last five months of a spiritual SERE school. I still owe you the final six:

1. Walk
2. Forgiveness
3. Humility
4. Faithfulness
5. Mercy
6. Steadfast Love

Walk
There's not anything altogether profound in this concept. However, there are days- or full seasons- of every life in which sitting next to the road and quitting the fight seems like a better option than trudging through the mud, rain, wind and hail- or even to the slow crawl in the scorching sun. Maybe day-to-day life has become "uphill both ways" and there is no way to reconcile it. Quite frankly, just to let you know, the side of the road in some sections has steep drop-offs too, so sitting isn't comfortable either. There's no city up ahead and no fellow travelers to satisfactorily keep you company around the clock. There's only you. And God, of course, but He usually seems silent and distant when He's administering a test. This is the kind of season that fits the "Day of Trouble" concept I referenced in the "Cry" section the other day.

I read out of duty through Leviticus; I found some encouragement and an interest in details for sure. Then there was Numbers... and real life around me was experiencing a hurricane. *"Walk"* was the whisper I heard. In the days of Numbers after my "assigned" reading for the day, I skipped ahead and then backwards in my reading to what had comforted me before.

Here's where "religion" falls off and "relationship" takes shape regarding a person and his or her Maker.

I couldn't care how many *"men equipped for war belonged to what tribe"*... and I needed peace and hope STAT. I found verses like ***Genesis 13:17*** which says ***"Arise, walk through the length and the breadth of the land, for I will give it to you."*** This obviously is a specific promise to Abram, but it bounced off the page like it was personal to me when I saw it. I also saw and hid in my heart verses that told me how to walk: in the truth, in integrity, in faith- not by what I see, but by what I know... I was reminded about the lesson I blogged about last which requires me to walk impossibly "on water," against human advice and wisdom and with my eyes fixed on the Fixer... I was reminded where to find shelter and told not to be my own defender... I found energy to keep moving. I found nearness to the Lord in his silence. We walked. We are still walking...

While I'm still on the road of the same circumstances, it seems a whole lot wider because of the promises I'm discovering and the nearness of the Lord that I'm experiencing. I do believe there is a city of rest up ahead. I'll probably order the steak when I get there.

Forgiveness

We all know something about forgiveness. It's a nice word we were taught when our little brother took our toy. Like my mom, yours probably also made him say, *"I'm sorry"* and then made you say, *"I forgive you."* The case for forgiveness I am finding in the stuff I am reading is not the lip service version that leaves deep resentment building in the basement of our heart and mind.

What I'm seeing is MUCH more profound, impossible to do alone, and is a literal requirement as proof of salvation. ***Matthew 6:15 says "but if you do not forgive others for their sins, your Father will not forgive you of yours."*** and ***1 John 4:20*** reminds us ***"whoever claims to love God but hates his brother or sister is a liar..."*** Those are blunt reminders that ***"to whom much is given, much will be required"*** and that we were ***"bought with a price and for a purpose"***- forgiveness being one of the keys to unlocking that requirement and purpose.

We can all get over someone taking our toy or calling us a stupid word. We can even fathom setting aside conflict inside ourselves to build relationship with someone who passed us over for promotion, or quite possibly allowed a lie to interrupt our trust. Humans can do all of that alone, without supernatural intervention. Some choose to; some do not.

I'm reading about people who were faced with situations that required a real intervention by God Himself who promises over and over that He will have vengeance and execute perfect justice if we back off, hush, and let Him. The thing about the Bible that seems to really tick some people off is the record of all the terrible disfunction. That's my favorite part! God doesn't hide our mess for us. He exposes it, deals with us in it, and heals it and restores us- if we're willing. As I've read some of the most commonly told Sunday School stories, I've tried to place myself in the shoes of the B, C, D-list characters. I already mentioned Hagar's unplanned-by-her pregnancy with Abraham and subsequent rejection, last time. And yet, that poor woman did not a get reputation for bitterness, but rather was specifically protected and blessed by God for her obedience and trust.

I wish I had time to re-tell all the profound cases of forgiveness and the tragic cases of un-forgiveness that have challenged my spirit these months. There's Absalom who had a very good case for anger when his sister was raped by their half-brother and then was nationally disgraced. His justified anger brewed and boiled for years and then morphed into rage. As a result, he became angry at nearly everyone around him, always finding a way to justify his bitterness. He decided his father should have done more to punish his brother, so he took the matter into his own hands and murdered his brother himself. Since un-forgiveness is not solved by revenge, his ire needed a new target. The obvious choice to him was his father the king. Absalom skipped town to avoid facing murder charges and marinated in madness as he plotted his continued revenge. He worked diligently plotting and scheming for years to turn people in the kingdom against his own father, their king. You really should read it for yourself, but ultimately Absalom's un-forgiveness resulted in his own violent and completely unnecessary death and added to the loss-of-yet-another-son grief for his father. Forgiveness would have changed everything.

There was also Joseph's little sibling rivalry in which he wasn't just thrown into the school locker between classes. His brothers soaked him in well-water for a while before deciding to sell him as a slave to some strangers passing through on their way out of the country. They kept the money and said, not just that he was dead, but that he had been devoured by a wild animal. They went so far as to kill an animal and cover his coat in blood to sell their lie.

Imagine the trauma of that as a parent, just for a minute. Imagine the fear and feelings of betrayal young Joseph felt. Think of the wickedness it takes to devise and carry out such a scheme. Think of the hatred they had for

304

their brother in the first place, and why? Because they were jealous and unforgiving- not because of something he did- but because of their father's affection for him.

Wow.

Is it any wonder why he was a favorite and they were not? Now, remind yourself that the story doesn't just end happily ever after in a few weeks or months. The entire life story of Joseph is one of hardship and endurance- and a masterful covering of protection because of his obedience to forgive and trust God's plan. In fact, because of Joseph's obedience to forgive, even and especially without his brothers' repentance or even a vague *"I'm sorry,"* God used him to be reunited with his father and to save his family as well as the entire country from a famine years later. All of that was made possible from having been blessed by God, rising up to second in command over the entire country of Egypt- his country of slavery, nonetheless.

Here I would like to insert the word "exalt" as a micro-theme which I will put on pause as it segues nicely into number 4...

Humility

This concept is easy to understand academically and hard to live as a lifestyle. We are born with human reflexes of pride, defensiveness, self-protection, promotion, and interest. The idea of humility is to lay down my right to justify, explain, defend, ask why, go first, have the best, the biggest, the nicest... It literally means to have a low view of your own importance in comparison to another's. It's not wimpy or insecure, but rather gives a picture of strength intentionally deferred to another because of their best interest. Essential at its core is the recognition that I am not a god, but that I am at the ultimate mercy of The God. He gives and takes away and that needs to be okay if I am to be humble.

My favorite Old Testament example of humility can be found in various situations in the life of King David. He wasn't a perfect guy for sure, but he was the king of a gazillion people and had an impressive war-time resume. Oh, and he was hand-picked by God himself through a prophet to be king when he was just a pre-teen kid working the family farm. Additionally, as a kid, he was chosen by the people who worked for King Saul to play music at the palace. The guy was handsome, talented, chosen, intelligent and all around successful. And yet, he deferred his strengths frequently to seek the heart of God on matters you and I would have just thought through and pulled the trigger on. He even chose humility to minister to his people from a cave when they lacked hope, all while his own life was in danger, appeared to be falling apart and while he still held the title of king.

So, ***"humble yourself in the sight of the Lord and He will exalt you"*** became a heart anthem of my own as I read of the proof for Joseph, David and Job. *"Get low to get through,"* are the whispering words of advice on this obstacle course. If you want to be noticed, get low and stay low until God exalts you; THAT is a lasting exaltation and requires the most minimal effort.

Faithfulness

I'm having a hard time really articulating how incredibly threaded together these concepts are- especially the top three. When I went to Turkey in 2016, I was blessed to have an opportunity to watch a woman hand-weave one of the country's famous and expensive exports, a Turkish silk rug. The time consuming, physically demanding, knotting strands of silk together to form an entire floor piece is intense- and I haven't even begun to describe what it takes to get the silk to begin the project in the first place!

If each of those teeny-tiny, thin, strong, silk knots represents a page in the syllabus I'm studying, you'll understand the complexity and the beauty of my process. I don't have time to make a rug here so I imagine a few of these concepts will get their own blogs in the future.

In nearly every chapter of my Bible I have found the word "faithfulness." It used to be one of those religious bumper sticker words that would cause me to roll my eyes. It's almost an archaic idea in our modern culture. We aren't really faithful to anything; absolutely everything is disposable. There's always a new, more convenient option or method- out with the old, in with the new. In the name of "progress" we don't commit to anything or anyone anymore. Careers, styles, spouses, technology, ideals, locations, churches... we are not a faithful people, and we even mock faithfulness as though it were a "stuck" mentality, and an unhealthy way of thinking or behaving. Until, that is, we need someone to be faithful to us...

This is true in the realm of business and the workplace as well as in marriage and family relationships. We need our bosses to NOT replace us with a computer. We need them to be faithful to appreciate our instincts and skills. We need them to faithfully pay us, and to faithfully consider us in their decision making. Recently I was listening to a near-retirement aged woman lament about the unfaithfulness of her boss. The entire company found out on a Friday that they no longer had jobs- not because the boss notified them, mind you, but because the bank showed up and repossessed all the company assets while they were working that day. The boss was nowhere to be found. Unfaithfulness is terrifying.

It's also heartbreaking. We all know of stories about parents who are unfaithful to their children in protection or provision. Maybe you were that child... We are keenly aware that faithfulness to marriage vows is at an all-time low statistically worldwide; but heartbreaking statistics don't compare to the gut punch of finding out your spouse has cheated on you, or rented a place of their own, or filed the final paperwork to dissolve your love forever. People simply do not view covenants and contracts as unbreakable anymore in any context. Finding loopholes is big business and entire companies are set up and maintained reliant on our unfaithful nature.

God is FAITHFUL.

Israel was, and still is the family of God. (I'm not talking about the 1948 political nation state, rather the Biblical family that God named Israel.) They were the epitome of unfaithfulness. I know I bring up Israel and the wandering after the Exodus a lot in this blog journal. I don't apologize. The Lord, in His wisdom, chose that family to represent Him, His character, His attributes and His plan so should it be a surprise that through their story, I should find solace in mine? I even named my dog Moses to remind me in case I should forget...

This past weekend was the Hebrew holiday Shavout. Because I'm starting to understand that obedience to the words of the Lord is the key that unlocks the door of the stronghold of safety in the battle, I have become very interested in the feasts and holidays set up by God. There are seven and they are all important to Him. Shavout, or Pentacost, is one of those. In my research I discovered it is the celebration of the marriage contract and the giving of the Covenant Law to the entire nation of Israel at the foot of Mount Sinai. In other words, it was the first covenant, the original wedding anniversary, that the Bridegroom wants to celebrate with His Bride, every year...

CONSISTENTLY, throughout history God has been the faithful groom- in thoughts, words and actions. Consistently His bride has been chasing the newest, most progressive, most convenient, shiniest, tastiest, most self-promoting method, ideology, god, or habits of the day- all the while wanting the benefits of the marriage without the responsibility of it.

You see the heartbreak here? The faithfulness of the Groom is incredibly motivating to me as a bride. I have a deep desire to offer Him my faithfulness in return. All that other stuff has an expiration date anyway...

Mercy

Mercy as it pertains to the Lord is most certainly not a new concept to me. It's what I've been banking on for decades. It's not that I didn't see it before, but I didn't experience its cost before this year:

The Lord's expectation for us as disciples of His Son is NOT that we simply hang out with a pretty great God for the rest of our lives. His expectation as His adopted sons and daughters is that we BECOME the attributes of Jesus in order that we show others what He looks like- so that they in turn desire to be saved and then also become like Him.... You see the pattern here? It's not enough to receive it, we are supposed to give it, so others can receive it and give it... and on and on.

So that's fun when people are nice and their past is- well, not present.

The online dictionary definition of mercy is this: *"Compassion or forgiveness shown towards someone whom it is within one's power to punish or harm."*

Now do you see the threads knotting a bit here? "Compassion" is also on my list of words, and you've already briefly seen my thoughts about "Forgiveness." I'd like to focus on the part about *"...within one's power to punish or harm."*

The idea of mercy is not only in a *"not giving someone what they deserve"* context, but also contains the power, right, or authority to do so. It would be like a federal prosecutor choosing to lessen or drop the charges of a crime, setting a prisoner free to live a life of their choosing- with no strings attached. It's the parent overlooking the lie to bestow a gift on the undeserving child instead. It's the wife who has proof of abuse, or the husband who has proof of infidelity, who chooses to remain kind and committed rather than to retaliate, prosecute, or discard. It's the child who was too small to defend himself while he was young, but now has the height and strength to teach his abusive parent "a lesson" of their own yet chooses to be a loving caretaker instead in their final years. It's the employee who has information that could get a coworker fired but chooses to instead befriend and encourage him.

My favorite scriptural example is found at the end of the story of Job. He had been deeply tested in his faith and endurance. I think most of us know the story. If not, do go read it today! After Job's friends had spent the greater part of the story harassing Job and trying to get him to admit to a sin they assumed and deeply believed he had committed, God showed up and put them in their place.

308

He's more than a little irritated at their treatment of Job and the careless and false way they used truths about God's character to speak lies about Job's situation. Job had remained truthful, alone, and in excruciating pain and horrible confusion. After dealing with the friends, God commends Job for graduating the testing and justly gives him the power to decide the friends' demise. Job chooses to ask the Lord *"NOT to deal with them according to their folly"* but to deal mercifully with them. Scripture then says, *"and the Lord restored the fortunes of Job when he had prayed for his friends and the Lord gave Job twice as much as he had before." (See Job 42)*

Mercy is irrational, not required by law, and usually appears to be foolishness to others standing around watching the mess. So, how does one NOT become a victim of an abuser of God's system? Well, I'm seeing that mercy is not for everyone. *Exodus 33:19* and *Romans 9:15* make it clear: *"... I will have mercy upon whom I will have mercy and I will show compassion to whom I will show compassion."* Other places in scripture assure us that there is a lack of mercy for some.

"For judgement is without mercy to the one who has shown no mercy. Mercy triumphs over judgement." (James 2:13)

"Blessed are the merciful, for they shall receive mercy." (Matthew 5:7)

"With the merciful You show yourself merciful; with the blameless man You show Yourself blameless; with the purified You deal purely, and with the crooked You make yourself seem tortuous. You save humble people; but Your eyes are on the haughty to bring them down." (2 Samuel 22:26-27)

It's not a free-for-all, which is a comforting thought. God gets to sort out the ultimate judgement. However, since most of us could benefit from a bit of mercy there's a LOT of opportunity to practice with each other until that day. Meanwhile, we ARE called to walk (remember that word?) in step with the Spirit's leading. Not prosecuting abuse, for example, could be based on foolishness or fear. Prosecution may be the very thing the Lord set up to protect us and heal us. "His way" is not the exact same for every situation, although His principles are. It's vital to be operating outside of our own understanding and to be well connected in relationship to the Father through His Spirit.

His ways are higher and more courageous than ours. They remove mountains of impossibility and **"it's not by might or by power, but by My Spirit, says the Lord."**

Steadfast Love

Initially the pervasive word was simply "steadfast," but that quickly melded together in my studies with the word "love." Because of the insane number of times I've read it, heard it, and thought it in the last five months, this is easily the number one concept the Lord is teaching me in this school. Both words have power as a stand-alone concept, but I'm learning that together they are simply supernatural in application. To put it another way, it is a human impossibility to live in "steadfast love."

I'll tell you why, but first I should define them for you:

Steadfast- *"resolutely or dutifully firm and unwavering."*

Love- *"a great interest or pleasure in or, to put it another way, to seek the highest good of another."*

Obviously, "love" is much more complex of a word in English than "steadfast" but clearly, we are not talking about the love of pizza here, but rather, people. This is relational; God the Father and Creator is relational. His expectation for His followers is that we would be relational, as He is, and NOT just with those we are most comfortable loving. Again, we aren't talking about transaction- a giving to get, we are talking about the kind of relationship that took a perfect man to the cross, intentionally, out of his deep affection for me- WHILE I was still His antagonistic enemy, cursing His very existence and mocking His righteousness.

So, you see where I'm going here, right? It's easy to love our children, or our parents (for some of us), our best friends who laugh at our jokes and eat our cooking. It's easy to "love" in the brief interactions with the cashier at the grocery store, or the kids that hang out with our kids. We easily love the football team or the neighbors- whether they shovel the snow for us all winter or not. Some of us can even love our in-laws and their in-laws without even stretching a single muscle. Love itself is not hard.

Steadfast Love, now that is graduate school kind of effort. "Resolutely" and "unwavering" give the idea that there's a bit of resistance to, or against, that kind of relating. It gives the idea that it withstands the storms, unscathed. This is more than a "my spouse had a bad day and acted a bit cold towards me" kind of a storm...

The only way to really understand this love is to go to places in scripture that had almost become innocuous to me before January. The obvious place would be *1 Corinthians 13* to get an understanding of what God means when he says the word "love," because Webster keeps changing his mind and God never will.

Clearly the entire (short) chapter of *1 Corinthians 13* as it is written is important and valuable for further understanding, but for the sake of time I am going to bounce into the list of Love's credentials and benefits found in the chapter and develop them for you a bit:

It *is patient*; it is not impatient.

It *is kind*; it is not mean.

It *is not envious or boastful*, but it does celebrate other's success.

It's *not arrogant or rude*; but is humble and respectful.

It *does not insist on its own way*; it does defer to other's ways.

It's *not irritable or resentful;* it is peaceful and forgiving.

It *does not rejoice in wrongdoing*; but does rejoice in the truth.

It *bears everything*; it does not crumble under the weight of hardship.

It *believes everything*, it does not doubt or call into question the truth.

It *hopes in everything*; it does not ever lose hope.

It *endures everything*; it does not quit.

It's *eternal*; it does not expire.

It's *the greatest of all* of the attributes- above even faith and hope.

It is the key to attaining, and the vehicle of sharing, everything of prophecy, knowledge, mysteries, truth, and sacrifice.

So, this starts to hurt when I line myself up to this list. Let me just show you by taking the most natural love relationship, the love of a mother for her children as an example. If you're a parent you'll hear me, but even if you aren't, you see this in nature and in your community every day. There's no question the natural human love of a mother is the strongest and most pure form of love available to a human. *Isaiah 49:15* says of mothers, *"Can a mother forget the child at her breast and have no compassion on the child she has borne? Even if that were possible, I would not forget you."*

Now that I've established the impossibility of a mother to NOT love her child, I line myself as a mom up to the standard:

Have I ever lost patience, or insisted upon my own way with them? Have I ever lost hope or called into question the truth about them? How about irritability? Or resentment towards them? Well, you catch my drift without perusing the rest of the list. I haven't even loved the children of my own womb perfectly. There's a limit to the storm-proofing of my steadfastness even in the most natural of relationships. SO, how do I emulate the kind of love that wins the war and keeps me safe on the battlefield?

And so, I'm learning that the question above directs the silk of Truth to loop back and knot into forgiveness, and then back into humility, picking up mercy and faithfulness as it weaves back into corporate repentance and carefully re-loops into righteousness and all the others; then He carefully ties them all together in me. This tapestry culminates in the woven display of the bloody and terrible day on the cross when my enemy, Jesus, cried out in His day of trouble, ***"Father, FORGIVE HER, she knows not what she is doing..."***

Today I find myself one day closer to being prepared for war.

Grown
Collene James

Son Shines Through
Collene James
Marble, CO

Crazy

Am I crazy? Or is this reality?

How I hope that the nightmares that continue to haunt my days are only dreams, even if they originate from the torment of demons.

How I hope that the distant voices speaking words that seem to come from some long-buried grave within my mind are only the product of my imagination.

How I hope the smells that suddenly assault my nostrils and disappear as quickly are derived from an unseen, yet present source and not from a memory in the past.

How I hope that the morbid and obscene thoughts, snapshots, and video clips that invade my mind at random times are only horrifically fanciful thoughts and not reality.

Am I crazy insane?

The fear of remembering, the fear of pain, torture and discipline, the fear of being drugged, the fear of demonic beings in the spiritual realm, the fear of being out of control and controlled by others, the fear of being institutionalized and isolated. None can compare to the fear of realization that all is not a dream or imagination, and that none are derived from a present source or from another's story, nor are they a scene from a movie, but from reality. The reality of my past.

I don't want to admit it, but I'm afraid reality is:

That the voices concealed in a long-forgotten compartment of my mind are coming to life while their words rise up from the depths of my soul and into my consciousness.

That the smells are not of this present world, but are memories from the darkest of places in the past that are choosing to assault my body with their stench of destruction.

That the unwelcome pictures in my mind are actually memories of reality, struggling to make themselves at home in the conscious part of my mind, overwhelming my emotions, and undoing all that I have come to believe about my life and who I am.

That the demons are very angry that programming and mind-control have begun to break down and that they are being exposed.

If you wonder what it is like to be the survivor of SRA, ritual abuse, MK Ultra, this is what I have found it to be like.

There are times when I have wondered if insanity would be better than reality, but I know this is a lie. Insanity means that I would not be in control of my mind, and my mind is exactly what I've been fighting to regain!

Yet, when I ask if I am crazy, it is a plea for you to agree that I am, for if I am crazy and simply suffering from a sick mind, then none of this other stuff can be true. I don't want to be insane, and I reject and renounce insanity for I don't want to speak a curse upon myself. But how can all this be true?

I beg You, God, that none of it would be reality. Deliver me! Please prove to me that it isn't true or real. Jesus prayed in the Garden of Gethsemane, "Father, if it be Your will, remove this cup from Me." I echo this prayer now Father. If it be Your will, remove this cup from me.

Jesus surrendered. I choose to surrender. I know Your Word, Your promises, Your Salvation (Yeshua), Your hope, healing and freedom. And I thank You that in the middle of all of this, that You deal in truth. I am in You, and You are in me. I have died to myself and *my life in hidden in Christ with God. (Colossians 3:3)* Truth must reign. And so Lord Jesus, I surrender all this to You. I surrender all of my mind to You. If this is reality, then You will help me to overcome And I ask that if this is real, then Lord, please confirm it so that I do not have to question my sanity and reality any longer, so that I can move on, and so that You can use my life such as it is. You have saved me for a purpose. Maybe I can help others with what I know. With what I see and hear. With what I feel.

What I cannot understand is why You, God would bring all this to my mind if it is not real. And if You have, then there is a purpose beyond myself. There must be! I also know that Satan and demons can influence my thoughts and perceptions. They can create false memories and stir up emotions. Therefore, I *cast down imaginations and anything that would exalt itself above the knowledge of God, and I take every thought captive to the obedience of Christ. (2 Corinthians 10:5)*

Examine me, know my thoughts, and see if there is any wicked way in me. Lead me Father, in Your way. (Psalm 139:23-24)

I believe what Your Spirit spoke to me some time ago. You clearly said, *"Go rescue the children."* And yet, I feel helpless to do so. The burden of my heart is that if this is reality for me, then it is surely reality for others. I have found Your love, hope, healing and freedom. But many, most have not. What God, do You want from me? What can I do?

I hear the tortured cry of the innocents inside my mind. Please Lord, hear their cry.

I see the hopelessness on their faces buried within my memories. Please Lord, come help!

I remember the pain and suffering and torment and death that they are experiencing right now. Please Yeshua, come save.

I know You can.
I know You have.
I know You do.
Will You?

I will wait.
I will pray.
I will watch.
I will obey.

Nancy Bowser

Best Season Ahead

June 10ᵗʰ 2018

This morning I was reading my scheduled section of this Bible-in-a-year-chronologically deal I'm doing when the word "prudent" jumped out at me somewhere in the middle of one of the Proverbs. Immediately the phrase "reasonable and prudent" popped back into the foreground of my memory.

Somewhere around my 20th birthday, my home state of Montana tried a new thing in which the voters and law makers changed the interstate speed limit to "Reasonable and Prudent" during the daylight hours. I probably would have never admitted it out loud then, but I wasn't completely a fan of the new law. That year I did a lot of I-90 driving back and forth between my city and the town my high school aged brother was living in with a host family for the entire school year. Several times a month I made the 5-hour round trip to give him (and me) some sense of family after ours had moved a couple of thousand miles away. As I drive those roads today, I occasionally have a clear memory of those trips and especially the nervous insecurity I felt driving my version of "reasonable and prudent," while those around me drove a very different version.

This morning's thought process had me look up the online definition of the word, because although it makes sense to me contextually, occasionally an accurate definition sharpens the focus of the context of a verse or a law. Here's what I learned:

pru·dent
ˈpro͞odnt/SubmitSubmit
adjective
acting with or showing care and thought for the future

I was always a cautious little girl, prudent, a rule keeper, a coloring pre-K artist whose mediums were always perfected well within the lines and with the appropriate hues. I like the security that comes with knowing the rules, following them, and being protected as a result. I've never liked taking risks and could be accused of bordering on being overly cautious at times. I constantly thought ahead, over-thought really, and *"showed care for the future."*

I've always wanted to learn my lessons, your lessons, and history's lessons to escape as much pain as humanly possible. In the middle of my 41st year I've discovered it's just plain too late to live my life scar-free. Yesterday, it was pointed out to me that sometimes wanting to forgo the pain and the

317

process is simply my pride assuming I can get there another way. Ouch! The pointer-outer of that is right and a true friend who gently spoke that truth into my heart...

So, this weekend's little "prudent" concepts looped into the concepts that have emerged since I last blogged, and admittedly had me in tears much of the day. Here's why:

The week after I last wrote, my second-born graduated from high school. That night I had an out-of-context-to-the-week dream, not brought on by the week's events or the ingredients of my meal prior to falling asleep. I've told you before throughout my life there have been certain dreams that are different than most. There's a "knowing" in certain dreams that I've began to trust are an actual message from my Abba, God. While it has sometimes been years, or even decades between them, I'm in a season of the "knowing" dreams for the last several months. Often, lately, the nocturnal situations I've been privy to aren't super encouraging to my human perspective or understanding, however I've experienced enough of these situations throughout my life to see amazing miraculous ends to the sometimes-devastating stories the dreams start to tell. As a result, I was not discouraged by that dream or the others like it I've recently had.

Maybe the most profound experience that night wasn't what I dreamed as much as how I woke up and what I woke up to. I woke up to my own voice praying over the situation in the dream. Next to me my phone had been playing a video and although I had been asleep for over an hour, I woke up praying along with the person in the video. That's cool and all, but not miraculous. What followed, was. As I tried to return to sleep, the Lord gave me a very specific and profound understanding of what my life will look like in the near future. I'm positive as I type this that I'm not communicating any of this effectively, but that's okay. It's a documentation to mark a place in time for me more than it's a story for your entertainment anyway.

Three days later I had four separate prior-scheduled meetings with old friends I don't get to see regularly, not all of whom know each other. All of them unknowingly spoke into my life in exactly the way only God could orchestrate regarding the "know" He had just given me days before. I'm intentionally being ambiguous, for now, but I am certain portions of my next adventure will be recorded here.

Anywhooo, the tears this afternoon were a cocktail resulting from the vivid understanding of the direction I'm heading, which will be a complete leaving of the cautiously prideful little girl I've been. The recipe you ask?

Oh, it's just one dose of grief, stirred with a dash of fear, blended with two bunches of excitement, then poured over the ice of "wait."

Wait: I've never been comfortable with that word. I've always operated under the assumption that if we know what's supposed to happen next and we aren't making it happen, we are in disobedience at the very least- or even being downright risky and foolish. Except today's battle plan of "wait" is so good for me, because I have NO idea how to proceed to this "Promise Land" vision- for the first time ever. You should understand that I am exceedingly aware that my "knowing how to proceed" in prior circumstances is exactly where I got most of my scars, but I've been a slow learner despite all my afore-mentioned prudence. I'm also keenly aware that once I get there, I will not survive without armor and a sword. The intel I've seen doesn't exactly have the words "paradise" next to the word "adventure" on the brochure.

Excitement: Because I have a purpose! My entire life has shaped me for this, from my earliest memories to yesterday's conversations. Nothing was wasted, no scar, no class, no experience, no relationship was without reason.

Fear: Because I told you, I'm not comfortable outside of the lines, off-roading, without a net, in the desert wandering... "What ifs" are my enemy and there's a list of them. I'm not joking about the armor and sword. I'm really doing my best to *"fear not"* and to *"take every thought captive"* and to remember we were not *"given a spirit of fear but of power and of love and a sound mind." (2 Timothy 1:7)*

Grief: Because I had just started to get used to the season I was in. I liked it. I was comfortable in it. It's over. But "good" is the enemy of "best" according to Oswald Chambers and that season was good, but it wasn't the best.

So, tomorrow I have an opportunity in front of me. I'm a bit anxious, but I'm taking the first step knowing that will ultimately lead to the next and the one after that, and yet another... I don't have to even know the best way or even the compass direction that ultimately leads to the fulfillment of the vision, but I do trust the best life is ahead and one step isn't that far to travel for tomorrow.

As a side note: I'm starting to see that the "Promised Land," eventually geographically called Israel, wasn't actually Heaven- or even a paradise really. Also, it's a notable concept that the desert wanderers had all they needed by way of the pillar of clouds and fire and eventually, the Ark of the Covenant- the very presence of Jehovah- protector and provider.

I'll take my time, as long as He is there too, taking His time with me...

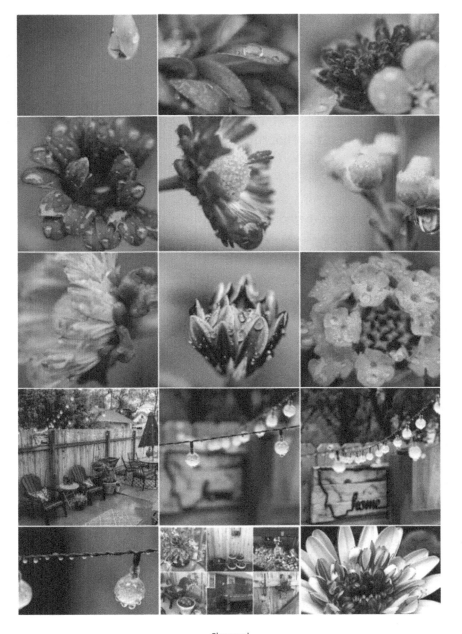

Cleansed
Collene James

Second Spring

Sometimes life goes too fast.
Sometimes we blink and that moment we had
is gone.
Sometimes that is as it should be
and other times, other times, it isn't.
That moment lost was taken –
it was taken and
we're told it can't come back:
that stolen years are gone
and that missed youth is just that –
missing.
That memories leave and
life's fire fizzles out.
That youth's tender shoot shrivels
by the hand of summer's blazing sun,
it dries out in autumn's death and
blows away in winter's breath.
Sometimes we're told to give up:
to let go what is gone,
to accept
the missing things
and maybe – probably –
some of them we need to.
But other times,
other times,
special times,
we have One who hears us.
We have One who speaks for us and over us:
One who declares life
and what was dead is now not.
And we watch that tender root
emerge there and there and there –
everywhere life breaks the ground and rain,
a living rain, pours out and
we're made new once again,
years given back.
And we stand, hands full,
holding
what once was lost but now is not:
a double portion,
a second spring.

Psalm 92
Ashley Fugleberg

The Birth of the Blessing Season

September 11th 2018

For several days I've been working on three separate posts here. I've been sipping from spiritual firehoses again and I've been trying to shape something readable as a benchmark of this season of my life. However, the gentle Spirit of God has held the reins a little tighter than normal and has not allowed me to publish my essays about how He has walked me through meandering thoughts and lessons on "seasons," "suffering," "overflowing love," "being peace," "being immovable," "standing firm," "humility," and the "joy that comes in the morning."

It's a little daunting to keep sitting at my computer early in the morning, after late night, after mid-afternoon to figure out what exactly I'm supposed to be getting out of all of this. What is the one simplified prize I could declare to you (us)?

I woke up Saturday, September 8th, with a heaviness I couldn't understand. I had been to divorce court first thing Friday morning and had been elated to announce that my divorce had been delayed until mid-to-late October, because my husband and his attorney had no-showed. The appropriate signed paperwork had never been filed by their side in response to my petition to separate rather than dissolve our marriage. Because my husband was not required to be there, the court (run by a VERY sweet-to-me Standing Master) had found it all so confusing and was inclined to grant my separation. She held off, pending hearing further from them.

I know I haven't spent any time on my public blog journal discussing my current marriage, the issues, the separations, and the ultimate paperwork filing. All of that was out of obedience to the *"let it die with compassion,"* *"I will be your defender,"* and *"when you are reviled, answer without a word"* directives I received from the Spirit of God. I still sit in a place of silence, only able to see what He has shown me that He is and has been protecting me from. I have still not been given the green light for me to express all the heartache, victory, advocating against witchcraft and thought-life-warfare, so I'll move on.

Also occurring Saturday, was my involvement with a fundraiser 5K for a non-profit human trafficking safe-house that has become a personally precious ministry to me. I was joined by a handful of old friends and a hundred-and-something new ones. I had every reason to be joyful, and I was... except for that nagging heaviness under the surface of my heartbeat.

By Sunday I was actually kneeling and falling on my face in prayer throughout the day. The spiritual pain was starting to come in waves. It was the same burdened, almost cramping feeling that comes with labor pain- but in my chest. Sunday night to Monday morning I was out of bed every few hours to feel the cold floor on my forehead. I didn't even have words to pray, only silent agony. I'm not usually silent- except when I'm in labor. (I know it's weird, but this isn't the movies and it's just the truth for me when I'm in that kind of pain.)

By mid-day I was in the straight-up "transition phase." I may be under-explaining the physical (although, clearly not medical, for all you sweet nurse friends of mine) heart cramps and near breathlessness. By this time, there was at least something tangible happening to explain some of the distress- in the form of an online, heartbreaking exchange with a loved one and a few dozen lookie-lous. Still, my maturity and intellect could absorb and explain the harshness of those words and choices made by a younger, less experienced soul and it was clear within a few hours that this was not the source of the pain.

Monday night I received a phone call, for the first time ever, from a new friend. Her voice has been familiar for months because I have been watching her online, teaching God's Word in fascinating ways almost weekly since the beginning of this whole ordeal. We met randomly, awkwardly even, a couple of weeks ago in a state more than 1,500 miles from either of our homes. She wasn't even there to teach... Maybe someday I'll tell you about those details, but tonight the phone call is all that matters to this story.

As soon as I picked up the phone, my new friend began to speak and health, teaching, love, scripture, and discernment poured off her lips and flowed over my life. She then prayed by-far the most scripturally "in tune" prayer over me that I had ever heard. We both were in tears.

Prior to that call, I had not ever had the opportunity to tell her a single sentence of my life details. Not my testimony, facts about my family of origin, my current family situation, or what I'm most passionate about in life. She didn't know I had lost my father to cancer, or how I make my living. However, the woman breathed life over every detail of my suffering before knowing a single fact.

After 1 hour and 41 minutes we both needed to wrap up the conversation; she suddenly remembered why she had called! THAT, my friends, is obedience to the Spirit's leading. I want to be like her when I grow up!

This morning I again had the birth-pain feeling, but my emotions were not so intensely involved. I felt like the "water" had broken in the early hours of the morning and now the heart-contractions were producing something. Sorry fellas, it's the only way I know how to describe it. As usual, I had joyful chats, grief filled hugs, and lighthearted exchanges with my clients. By the time I got home this evening I was in a peaceful place, like I imagine an epidural would feel, still pressure, no pain.

I got my mail. There was a package from a beautiful friend I haven't met in person but have enjoyed hours of phone conversations and text exchanges with. She sent me books, a real-life handwritten letter, and a couple of photocopied entries out of a daily devotional.

There were a few bills.

There was a document from the county courthouse.

"Oh good," I thought as I noticed the address, *"they set the trial date."* I answered a friend's call at the same time. She has been at the hospital with her husband for a couple of days. I opened the envelope as I listened to the update about him.

There wasn't a date. I spoke to answer my friend while I simultaneously read out loud the cover page title: *"DECREE OF DISSOLUTION OF MARRIAGE"*

"I'm divorced," I told her quietly- bracing for emotions that never came.

And then, the relief of pain that comes with giving birth. I cannot explain it, but over and over I heard in my spirit ***"When (it) had died, David got up, washed his face, ate, and worshiped God."***

I know I'm not directly quoting your personal favorite English translation of the story of the death of David and Bathsheba's son in ***2 Samuel 12***. I am also quite aware that my context is not about having a dead baby after seven days of pleading for restoration of health, but rather the death of a marriage and a family of eight after seven months, five days of separation, fasting, prayer and wise (and even some unwise) counsel... David knew that his son would die; yet he also knew he was supposed to ask for him to live. He fasted, wept, prayed, fasted, prayed, cried out, wept, fasted... agonized and distressed, he pleaded for life not to leave the precious thing he loved- the very thing he had been given by God himself.

A few months ago, when I was reading that, I could relate to that part, in every way. I could NOT relate in any way to his calm, accepting reaction to the loss... Until today.

I haven't been able to escape the incredible JOY that replaced the heartache and "labor" pains of this weekend. There is such relief in the answer, not the answer from an angry hardened human, but from my tender and loving, merciful Abba! This is His good and perfect will for me in this season. It is not what I prayed for specifically, and it is not the end of the testimony for me. It is, however, the essence of seasonal change that I have blogged my "allergies" to for years here. I am starting to believe that the Healer heals allergies...

You know what? I am okay; excited even! I know my Father is on the Throne, because NOTHING passes through my life without His approval. Not the gifts, not the pain, not the injustice, not the oppression, not the blessings. He gave, and He took away. Blessed be the holy character and powerful Name of the Lord God Almighty, the One who knows me and who keeps me and who protects and defends me. My provider, my shelter, my stronghold... and now, my deliverer.

Please don't take my reaction as anything other than resolute faith that God will still do what He said He will do. He has spoken; He will do it. While He is doing that, I am free to dance in the rain showers.

Without the nonsense of my preaching about these verses that have been marinating for weeks in my heart like I've attempted to do, I'll simply post them for what they are and let you see for yourself what I'm excited about...

"Ask, and it will be given to you; seek, and you will find; knock and it will be opened to you.

For everyone who asks receives, and to the one who seeks finds, and to the one who knocks it will be opened.

Or which one of you, if his son asks him for bread will give him a stone? Or if he asks for a fish, will give him a serpent?

If you then, who are evil, know how to give good gifts to your children, how much more will you Father who is in heaven give good things to those who ask Him!" (Matthew 7:7-11)

"I will make with them a covenant of peace and banish wild beasts from the land, so that they may dwell securely in the wilderness and sleep in the woods.

And I will make them and the places all around my hill a blessing, and I will send down the showers in their season; and they shall be showers of blessing.

And the trees of the field shall yield their fruit, and the earth shall yield its increase, and they shall be secure in their land. And they shall know that I am the LORD, when I break the bars of their yoke, and deliver them from the hand of those who enslaved them." (Ezekiel 34:25-27)

And ESPECIALLY:

"The Spirit of the Lord GOD is upon Me, because the LORD has anointed Me to bring good news to the poor;

He has sent me to bind up the broken-hearted, to proclaim liberty to the captives, and the opening of prison to those who are bound; to proclaim the year of the LORD's favor, and the day of vengeance of our God;

to comfort all who mourn; to grant to those who mourn in Zion to give them a beautiful headdress instead of ashes, the oil of gladness instead of mourning, the garment of praise instead of a faint spirit; that they may be called oaks of righteousness, the planting of the LORD that He may be glorified.

They shall build up the ancient ruins; they shall raise up the former devastations; they shall repair the ruined cities, the deviations of many generations." (Isaiah 61:1-4)

God's Heart.
Do we feel it?

God's Mind.
Do we think with it?

God's Eyes.
Do we see through them?

God's Ears.
Do we listen with them?

God's Mouth.
Do we speak with it?

God's Body.
Do we use it?

God's Heart.
Do we feel it?

Do we want to?

Nancy Bowser

Please Protect Me Father,

One and Only God.
I don't want to be a dark thing,
a dark thing,
a pawn
used by the enemy.
I don't want to let go
of everything
I know,
of everything that is True,
as soon as I'm presented
with a false gift, a lying dainty,
a lying dainty.
And frankly,
everywhere isn't here,
in this secret place, in the now
with You.
Please protect me Father,
don't let me forget:
I don't want to be a dark thing.

Ashley Fugleberg

Blend In, They Said- Be Set Apart, He Said
Collene James

Pieces of the Whole
Andrea Fugleberg

If We Are the Body

September 14th 2018

This morning my time in the "secret place" of prayer and journaling and Bible reading was so rich! I sat down to type this and as I was about to hit the "publish" button my phone rang. It was my new friend that I told you about the other day, whose teaching voice has been familiar to me for months. Until two weeks ago she didn't know I existed, but because of the power of her discernment during that last call I instantly knew this was my "wait" sign from Abba regarding the publishing of the blog.

After a goofy joke, she launched into her message for me. She had two things to say. Those two things filled an additional five pages in my hand-written, college ruled, full sized notebook journal. It also took 1 hour and 58 minutes to convey- using three different languages to develop it. It blows me away how much what she had to tell me, matched much of what I had already written here, in my Bible, and in my journal this morning. If I didn't already know she simply has complete connection with the Lord and is obedient to say the "weird" things to a perfect stranger when He moves her to, I'd be a bit creeped out.

Following that phone call, I needed to run a few errands with one of my kids and then prepare to attend a funeral. I knew I didn't have time to revise this blog while those thoughts were still fresh, and I worried I would forget what I needed to remember. No worries there; it turns out the lessons are woven tightly through my life experiences these days and the funeral solidified the message.

What my new friend had to say pointed out that the initial blog attempt was not wrong, but was woefully undeveloped. I plan to do my best to fix it now; you may need to get comfy while I recall what happened last December:

After hearing the personal testimony of healing, restoration, and an established-by-God purpose of a husband-and-wife ministry couple I had just met, I prayed a life altering prayer in the center of my living room floor. Their own testimony of faith and God-sized love for each other included sharing a prayer they committed to, using the example of one of King David's prayers. They challenged me to do the same; so, this is what I boldly asked for on December 17, 2017:

"Father, reveal the hidden sins in me and in us, both those that we have committed against You and those that have been committed against us that

still hold us each in bondage; then help my husband and I to understand love the way you do it. Draw us both closer to You in intimacy as individuals and then unite us together in deeper intimacy in marriage. Establish in us the ministry You called us together to do. Show us individually that nothing else matters outside of what You've purposed us to be."

The next day, just over 24 hours later, seemingly the opposite played out in that same living room. In tears I asked the Lord the "whats" and the "whys" of the event and I felt the Spirit breathe the answer over me:

"I'm answering your prayer, Collene."

Thus began my own solo journey to the Throne of the King, who has graciously offered to know me and to be known by me.

I haven't thought about that word "intimacy" much over these nine months, minus four days since I prayed that prayer. "Steadfast Love" is the closest my thoughts and studies have gotten to the word, but that particular concept is potentially one-sided; God loves me steadfastly even when I ignore Him. He loves me with the same steadfastness when I cling to Him...

While there has been an expectation of my understanding, then following after my Teacher in modeling steadfastness, this morning it occurred to me that "steadfastness" isn't enough. Because it is merely one of the "love characteristics" of the Father, to be satisfied with a potentially one-sided love would be a major travesty to any developing relationship.

Now that I've come to recognize the pattern of the Father's teaching and subsequent changing of me by using repetition of words or phrases, I took note when the word "intimacy" came up nearly every day at my salon and in conversations with friends this week. I was never the one that said it first, and each time I heard it the Holy Spirit reminded me of my December prayer.

People usually equate the word immediately with sex. Often it is used to "appropriately" or discreetly reference the act for those of a certain age group or personality type. However, it doesn't take much thought to realize there is a whole lot of sex that isn't intimate, and a whole lot of intimacy that has nothing to do with sex. Intimacy requires two to participate and is a graduate level class. He has always been present in every true love story ever told.

So, my thoughts rolled over the word and then retrieved the word "love," this time without the "steadfast" attachment. If we claim salvation and forgiveness from our sins in and because of Christ, there is no getting around the Biblical concept of exchanging of our brokenness and filthy "rags" of behavior for His wholeness and new behavior. We are to trade our desires for His and scripture is very clear: Of all the things we put on, put off, choose, choose not, LOVE is the number one priority action. There are verses about loving God first (easy to do, emotionally at least, when you understand His character and know Him the way He wants to be known) and others next. That's it. It's simple, right?

Right. Except when... there's a long list of kinds of people that are nearly impossible to love based on the surface behaviors and historical choices coupled with a poor grasp on what God actually means when He uses the word. I've already developed on the blog what the actual definition of love is as it pertains to the one-sided, steadfast, choice of God and requirement of the true followers of the Messiah as found in *1 Corinthians 13*. Let's go deeper and get a better grasp, shall we?

The related thoughts pertaining to love as a verb, rather than an emotional high or a currency to transact relational "business," brought back to mind the concept of the "body of Christ." It is no secret to those of us who have sat under any amount of Bible teaching, that there is a maddening-to-some bumper-sticker phrase- *"we are the body of Christ"*- that is wildly under-developed in terms of practical, useful, definition. Most of us understand "feet" and "hands" as the "go" and "do" of ministry, but very few of us know how, when, where, and for whom...

Because I'm a visual learner I started picturing a body with only a bunch of hands and feet. Ridiculous. So, I imagined the knees, the mouth, the shoulders, the spine of Christ. Maybe those are the pray-ers, the teachers, the burden bearers, the lobbyists... then I imagined the ears and the familiar "voice" in my spirit confirmed: *"DING DING DING, that's IT Collene! I'm asking you to be My ears right now!"*

I began to remember the times in my relationships that the most "closeness" was developed. For me, BY FAR- because I'm a natural talker- I feel most loved when I'm listened to. When I feel heard, I feel trust begin to build... The more trust, the more talking, the more open, the more vulnerable...

Ugh, that's the word I've wrestled with for years. It's a word that was used in a gentle chiding conversation with a friend a few days ago in context of my potential emotional fragility. "Vulnerable" in that regard is where the enemy of my heart wants me. When I've trusted and it has been used against me, I've determined to flex the restraint muscles on my jaw and hush my heart and hide my needs and solve my own fears and put on my stomping boots and get through "it" alone. I've chosen over the years to cut myself off from the so-called "body of Christ," at least in its Americanized traditional sense. Some of the body's mouths bite, rather than teach and some of the hands hit rather than "do."

I realized somewhat recently that IF God is going to answer the "establish the ministry" portion of my prayer, vulnerability is a must in order for the "body" to work together appropriately. This morning's phone call expanded that understanding. If I'm going to have the "understand and experience intimacy" portion of the prayer answered, I'm going to have to get WIDE open. Okay. I want that, but I'm scared. I'm tired of the firing squad, frankly.

My new friend heard my angst and changed the word, giving me a synonym: Transparent.

I like that better, it sounds stronger. "Vulnerable" tastes like "weak" on my tongue. Any girl that's been kicked around, or neglected, or left unprotected, or had her boundaries crossed, needs never to feel weak. She must provide for herself and never ask for help. However, "transparent" gives me a very strong option of opening the curtains into my soul. I get to choose to show you my injuries and my fears, my gifts, and my darkness.

Then my friend uttered the very same prayer of King David that the December couple had encouraged me with: ***"Search me God and know my heart, test me and know my anxious thoughts. See if there is any offensive way in me and lead me in the way everlasting." (Psalm 139:23-24)***

This kind of prayer reveals the crooked ways in a person. Perfect love helps to straighten the ways that are bent. Then my friend said this:

"Intimacy requires vulnerability, transparency, to be searchable by the one who loves and who you love. It is the kind of thing that leads to conflict and even wars. There is crookedness in all of us and the weak run from being seen. It takes a very strong person to stand the test of inspection by God. Only strong people get to have the gift of intimacy."

My heart and every cell in my body wants to give and receive that kind of love!

And then, I told you I went to a funeral... A brand-new teenager was lost to her own hopelessness- a victim of a sneaky serpent lie. The message was given: *"A Hope That Does Not Disappoint."* The speaker had a school full of 7th graders' full attention as he described the "hopeless" agenda of our enemy in this current culture. A plea was made to this generation to be in relationship with Jesus, the One who bore the shame and took the pain for them and you and me... and then to be in real relationship with each other- to bring hope back to the culture and the generation...

And as I sat there absorbing the words and the pain, "intimacy" again screams in my head.

I'm frustrated because there's a Suicide Prevention Awareness 5k fundraiser this weekend in this city and while I'm sure there will be many "feet" in attendance, I can't help but know in my gut that it's not sufficient to save the next of our sons or daughters, or mothers or fathers, from the lie. Money doesn't give hope. Lectures don't bring hope. Posters and banners and screen-printed t-shirts DO. NOT. BRING. HOPE.

What if the body of Christ chose to take Paul's words seriously in *2 Corinthians 12* and started to actively *"boast in (their) weakness"* and trusting that, like he said, Christ would be the sufficiency and strength- even in the midst of the *"insults, hardships, persecutions and calamities"* brought by the firing squads? I wonder if that would make me approachable, relatable, my testimony usable?

Perfect love that destroys fear, overflowing from the spirit and soul of a real Christ follower in a real intimate relationship, using transparency and steadfastness, is the only vehicle in which HOPE is delivered to a wounded soul.

This is the answer to the "establish the ministry" part of the prayer.

If you join me in choosing this weakness boasting and then go out with me and be an ear, or a set of eyes on top of a shoulder, connected with a hand, I think the parts of us could start to function like a real body. Maybe then these children wouldn't die, and they wouldn't be left wide open to traffickers, or ritual abusers, or addictions, or homelessness, or scary unplanned pregnancies to be faced alone- and maybe their moms and dads and grandparents could sip out of that same cup of HOPE, and we together could change the world...

Still, if none goes with me, I will follow.

Ruminate

Archfiends descend
wearing mask of Friend.
Teeth stain black beneath eyes that
      eclipse and dilate;
goblins gormandize,
      lick their lips, clean their hate.
Cerebral throbbing, my brain is caught:
thief aboard robbing my train of thought.
Mind sears – fiery lies prying – no use trying to tarry on
when hope rots and demons feed on woebegone thoughts like carrion.

Accuse! Insult!
Full frontal assault.
Incisors pierce and bite;
      I wallow, I cower;
with fierce appetite,
      they swallow – devour!
My every hope and dream, suppressed –
they ingurgitate and digest;
they binge and purge and feed on me – cogitating gluttony –
every thought they find, they mock; and make my mind their catafalque.

Vicki Joy Anderson

Bickering and Backbiting
Collene James
Yukon Territory, Canada

Split
Andrea Fugleberg

The Devil Lies

What's a goofy smile? He wandered through the halls of a school he never would complete.

He didn't seem to care about anything at all, just a blank picture in his mind when he slept.

But the devil is a liar, he has a big ole grin, he laughs at those who turn and walk away.

Walk away, walk away in the end.

Have you heard about the devil in his heart?
Deep in the pain of his veins?
Have you seen the fear in the tears of his eyes?

The Devil lies…. The Devil lies.

A few years after high school, I read the local paper, his goofy smile and profile from the side,

He was heading to prison, leaving a baby behind and a woman with a broken home,

She cried…oh yes, she cried.

Have you heard about the devil in his heart?
Deep in the pain of his veins?
Have you seen the fear in the tears of his eyes?

The Devil lies…. The Devil lies.

Then came the day, he took his own life,
He didn't feel the world should have to see him again.

He believed it was better, to end it all together,
After all he didn't really matter,

Have you heard about the devil in his heart?
Deep in the pain of his veins?
Have you seen the fear in the tears of his eyes?

The Devil lies…. The Devil lies.
But the devil lies…he lies…he lies….in his heart..

Matthew Bailey

Cover Me Softly

(Psalm 34:17, 18, 22; Isaiah 42:3-4; Isaiah 6:1-3)

```
F        Bb2/C   F              Bb2      Bb
```
Cover me softly, Cover me gently;
```
F        Bb       Gm              C
```
Cover me with Your Love from above.
```
F        Bb2/C   F              Bb
```
Fill up my spirit, With Your Spirit;
```
F            Bb       Gm              C
```
Pour out the cleansing Blood of Your Son.

```
C           Dm       Bb           F
```
Father of Mercy, Spirit of Comfort,
```
C           Dm           Bb              C
```
Son of God rain down On these dry bones.
```
              F              Bb
```
(Breathe life into my spirit)

```
F            Bb2/C   F              Bb2    Bb
```
The Lord is near to   the broken hearted
```
F              Bb   Gm       C
```
The crushed in spirit He will save.
```
F            Bb2/C F          Bb2    Bb
```
He will not break A bruised reed
```
F            Bb       Gm              C
```
A smoldering wick He- He will not quench.

```
F              Bb2/C     F                  Bb2 Bb
```
Consume all my darkness, Free me from evil
```
F              Bb       Gm              C
```
Draw my heart close and restore my soul.
```
F              Bb2/C   F          Bb2    Bb
```
Take my heart captive into Your presence;
```
F            Bb       Gm              C
```
Display Your power, Your majesty.

A Song of Nancy Bowser

I Want To Live

The demons cry, "Destroy!"
The battle has begun.
I fight for life,
They fight for death.
Will victory be won?

I want to live.

War is raging deep within;
Battle cries are heard.
Am I winning?
Am I loosing?
This fight seems so absurd!

I want to live.

Deception has enveloped me.
Life is fading fast,
When I slowly realize
These devilish tricks come
From my horrid past.

I want to live.

I see the truth now,
But I cannot feel it.
The choice is mine.
What shall I do?
Embrace it!

I CHOOSE TO LIVE!

I choose to live by Jesus' truth
Though this war seems never ending.
Jesus is the Truth,
The mightiest warrior ever,
And the reason I am winning.

Nancy Bowser

Innocence Lost

(With ending from You Are the One)

```
      Dm        C                 Am      Dm
The age of innocence has passed away.
Dm          C           Dm
Hear the funeral bells tolling.
Dm                 Am
The children cry, the children die.
Dm            Am      Dm
Will God's people pray?


Dm
Innocence lost.
      Am                        Dm
The world is full of hurting people.
Dm
Innocence lost.
      Am                        Dm
The nation's lashing out in anger.
Dm
Innocence lost.
      Am              Dm
Our children cry for help.


Dm        C                 Am      Dm
The age of innocence has passed away.
Dm          C           Dm
Hear the funeral bells tolling.
Dm                 Am
The children cry, the children die.
Dm            Am      Dm
Will God's people pray?


Dm
Deception has enveloped us
Arms are open wide.
Desire's been awakened
And purity, it hides.

Gm
Destruction's running rampant
Dm
And no one seems to mind.
```

Gm
God's people sit in apathy;
Dm
How can we be so blind?

Dm
Where is the hope?
Where is the love?
Where is the courage to be set apart?

Dm   **Dm/C   G**
Shower, oh heavens, from up above,
                Dm   G   **Dm**   **G**
And let the skies rain down righteousness.
Dm   **Dm/C   G**
Let the earth open and salvation come forth,
         Dm   **G   Dm**
And righteousness.

                    Dm   **A**
You are our God; We are Your people.
                  A   **Dm**
We seek Your face; and humbly we do pray.

A Song of Nancy Bowser

Lost in Thought
Collene James
Bath, England U.K.

343

Prayer of Promises, Hope and Praise

Lord, You are my Rock and my Fortress.

I choose to believe Your promise,
That if I wait for You, You will renew my strength,
And that I will mount up with wings like eagles.

You bless those whose strength is in You.
As I go through the Valley of Weeping,
Tears of sorrow and suffering mix with the blessings of Heaven,
Transforming desolation into beauty,
And despair to hope.

I will hope continually and will praise You yet more and more.
My mouth will tell of Your righteous acts.
With Your mighty deeds I will come;
I will praise Your righteousness, Yours alone.

Your power and Your righteousness,
O God, reach the high heavens.
For Yours is the Kingdom, and the Power, and the Glory forever.
Amen.

*(Prayer adapted from **Psalm 71:3, 14-19; Isaiah 40:31; Psalm 84:5-7; Isaiah 61:3; Matthew 6:13)***

Nancy Bowser

Crowned
Collene James

Contributor Epilogues

Collene James

I am a master questioner. The how and why questions seem to never cease...

When I began writing the *"Seasonal Allergy"* blog publicly in 2011, I had no intention of ever writing a book about my healing process, much less two. In fact, I was hopeful that very few people would be able to see my internal mess. The public blog journal was intended simply to be used to keep me accountable to complete what I had started. For a long time, it was how I processed the "adventure" of life and the spiritual and emotional "allergies" I tended to have to life's changing seasons.

As the process of writing and then photographing, brought forth real healing, I found that I needed the public accountability less and less to maintain forward motion and growth. Prior to compiling these journal writings and photo journal pieces, I had not re-read any of my earlier writings in years. I was surprised to find that my blog entries were almost exactly 7 years- from the Fall of 2011 to the Fall of 2018. I know beyond all doubt that the woman that started these writings is not the woman that finished them, is not the woman I am now. I have learned to embrace and enjoy each of the seasons of change as I am altered, grown, and more deeply rooted in Him to bear His fruit in His time.

Since putting away the journal keyboard, I have strongly felt the call to "reconcile others to the Messiah as I was reconciled." *(2 Corinthians 5:17-20)* I have spent the years between the Fall of 2018 and the Spring of 2023, now almost reflexively, trusting the Word of God and His promises, in ways that were once foreign, even maddeningly bumper-sticker-simplified by well-meaning people when I began this healing journey. I've learned that He can be trusted, however some of "them" and what they say He says, cannot. The oversimplification of His Word deserves to be challenged and proven, for you, in your own relationship with Him.

The drastic changes in my physical life reflect the drastic changes in my spiritual life. While very few of my life-long friends understand why I walked away from my "normal" life for one of this kind of full-time ministry, and most don't understand or want to know the realities of "the trenches" I step into, the friends I have consistently around me all encourage me in Truth and spur me on to do even deeper work. There is a tangible Peace that permeates the vast majority of my inner thought life. I am married again, this time to a partner. He is a strong, yet gentle leader, quick to prayer, slow to anger- who takes seriously the call to minister the Truth of God's Word as his primary focus. This new life is hard in a satisfying way, and while I would not have chosen it then, I would never not choose it now. God can be trusted with a life...

Nancy's and my first book together, *"The Lie Effect: Overcoming Soul Abduction"* is the culmination of the Truth that I, and the overcomers I now work with, have found to be powerful for healing. It is my sincere hope that with it, *"An Overcomer's Journal"* will clearly display examples of the Spirit's application of those concepts in a way that can help connect your spirit to His...and that you can truly begin to worship Him in Spirit and in Truth through the creative, intelligent, precious sets of gifts He has given you.

Nancy Bowser

When I began my healing journey, I started writing my prayers out to God. I told Him what I was experiencing, I asked Him for guidance, and recorded scriptures that spoke to my heart. This helped me to process all the crazy thoughts, emotions, and pictures inside my mind. Over time, my journaling included poems, songs, Nancy's Notes that are shared on my blog and then several books.

My biggest journaling project was writing *"The Soul Redeemer"* trilogy. It is my story told in a fictitious manner. When I first began writing it, I thought I was "done" dealing with the past. Little did I know! By the time I started on Book 2, dissociative parts that I had not been aware of, came out and got involved in the writing. They had been deeply buried in spiritual darkness and programming, and the Lord used this venue to give them a safe way to tell their story. I have to say that I am thankful now, but it was not an easy road of discovery and healing. There are many people who have experienced deep wounds but don't know how to gain true hope, healing, and freedom. It is my prayer that the spiritual keys, tools, and weapons for overcoming that I have found, will flow through these books in the power of the Holy Spirit, and that others will be able to apply them to their lives as well.

I would like to share what was going on behind the scenes when several of the poems and songs in this journal were given to me. I offer all glory to God for anything of beauty and value that flows through me.

Innocence Lost was the first song I wrote. My husband was a junior high math teacher at the time, and this song took shape as I became aware of certain tragic situations in the lives of these children. I was also dealing with my own "inner children" as vivid memories were being brought into my consciousness. Death and destruction appeared to be running rampant, and yet it seemed as if God's people were happy to have their heads buried in the sands of ignorance and apathy when they should have been busy praying and obeying. My heart was crying out for help in rescuing these little ones who were being led to the slaughter.

Before I wrote *Stripped of all Defenses*, I was feeling fearful, emotionally, and mentally defenseless and vulnerable. I was not supposed to use my old defense mechanisms of running from reality anymore, but I wasn't sure what else to do. As I cried out to Him for help, the words to this song began pouring into my mind. I started writing, and ten minutes later, it was done. The miracle was that I no longer felt as I had before. I knew in my spirit and soul that I was clothed with Christ's love and righteousness, and I felt protected, safe, and secure. Jesus had set me free, and I didn't need the old defenses any longer. In fact, I didn't want them! I wanted the love and power of my risen Savior, and I made a conscious choice never to go back.

I Want to Live was born during a battle that I was having with severe anorexia and overwhelming suicidal temptations. I didn't really want to die, but some of my dissociated parts were trying to fulfill their duty to their programming, and they were being influenced by demons attached to them that were also trying to accomplish their assignment. At times the battle seemed unbearable, and I grew weary and weak in spirit, soul, and body. As I fell on my face in a final cry of desperation for help, the Holy Spirit suddenly revealed the roots of the problem, the demons involved, and the lies that the effected parts of me were believing. I, the core part who knew God and believed the truth, made the choice to act on the truth even though I couldn't feel the effects of it at that moment. I took authority over my whole body, soul and spirit and began to declare the truth of God's Word. I renounced all lies and commanded the demons to go in Jesus's name. Immediately, the demons left, the thoughts and the compulsions began to subside, and within five minutes, that battle was won.

For *Make Me Like You*, I remember being in a specific ritual when I was four years old. There was also another little girl my age, and we were holding hands, standing in front of a stainless-steel table where babies and others had been sacrificed. The master was saying, "One must die that one can live. Now which one of you is going to die?" Carrie was chosen. I was allowed to live, believing that she had been sacrificed for my life. Her sacrifice was held over my head to cause me to believe that I owed a debt, that my life had to be lived according to the orders of my handler and the demons that had been transferred to me. Oh, what a perversion of God's truth and His plan of redemption!

But now I know the truth. Jesus paid the debt, and His sacrifice has set me free! I am no longer a pawn in the hands of Satan; I am a priest in Yahweh's kingdom. I am no longer enslaved in Satan's service; I am a bondservant of the Most-High God. I am no longer Satan's sullied bride; I am the pure and holy bride of Christ. I have chosen to engage in an ongoing process of dying to self so that I can live for Christ according to His plans and purposes.

The cry of my heart is that I would become like Jesus in nature, character, attitude and action, and it is this desire that motivated Make Me Like You. The only way that this can happen is as I willingly surrender every part of my life to Him. It truly is the most beautiful, fulfilling and exciting life, full of love, hope, joy, peace, and adventure.

Being clothed in God's spiritual garments and armor is just as important for me as wearing my physical clothing. Understanding and effectively using my spiritual weapons is key in the daily battles I face and in my interactions with others. Being inspired by the musical score from the movie Zorro, *You Are the One* is the song that was fashioned inside my mind. I realized that it brought a good balance to Innocence Lost, and so I often pair them together.

Memorizing scripture always comes more easily when it is put to music, and this one particular Psalm had become such an important passage in my life that I wanted to sing it and teach it to children in that way. So Holy Spirit gave me the music to put to His Words and *Psalm 91* was born.

Just a quick story about how God used this chapter in my life:

I had a vivid dream that my husband was standing on a narrow ledge partway down a steep mountainside. He was very frightened, hurt, and crying out for help. It was as if I could feel his terror, and yet I was powerless to do anything because even though I could see him, I didn't know where he was or how to get to him.

The dream continued to haunt me for several months, and so I just kept praying Psalm 91 over him. Then one morning, our boys and Jim went four-wheeling. Jim was far enough ahead that they didn't see him when he hit a rock and went flying down the side of a very steep and rocky mountainside. He tumbled about seventy-five feet before he landed on a soft, pine needle covered ledge. As he lay there dazed, he heard the quad come tumbling after, but it flew over top of him, and continued on for another four hundred feet or so. The boys came upon the place where Jim had gone over and suddenly stopped because the quad's seat was lying in the road! I believe that an angel took that seat off as a marker so that Jim wouldn't be lost as he had been in my dream. The boys quickly found and rescued their dad. Although he was badly bruised, he didn't have any broken bones, and he had not hit his head on any of the many rocks as he fell. In looking at the site later, it was as though angels had prepared that soft ledge just for him to land on as they guided his fall. Praise God for His Word!

Door of Hope came tumbling into my mind when I read **Hosea 2:15**, and it struck a chord with me (pun intended, lol!). *"From there, I will give her vineyards to her, and the Valley of Achor as a door of hope."* Achor means "trouble," and the Valley of Achor is where Achan and his family were stoned for disobeying the Lord and taking booty from Jericho (*Joshua 7*). The consequence of Achan's sin had been their defeat in the battle at Ai, and now, having the wind knocked out of their sails, the people were hopeless and afraid to continue on. Hosea is reminding us that it was in the valley of trouble that Yahweh gave them the keys of repentance, worship and obedience that renewed their hope and confidence.

When we find ourselves in trouble, Jesus Christ is the Door of Hope. Knowing Who He is and choosing to praise and worship Him, to turn from sin, believe in Him and to obey His Word, these are our spiritual keys that remove the barriers that keep us from God's love, that lead us to hope, healing and freedom, that make us whole.

Jesus gave *Hold Me in Your Arms* to me in a unique way, and several months after, I came to understand why. In a dream, I saw Jesus standing beside me with a boom box. He turned it on and beautiful music flowed out of it. I could hear every word, and it was as if I knew the song even though I had never heard it before. When Jesus turned it off, I could not remember any of it. He went through this routine several times of playing the music so that I could hear and know it, then He turned it off again. When I woke up, I could not remember the words or tune, but I knew I was supposed to write it down. In faith, I went to the piano and asked the Holy Spirit to bring it to mind. He did, and the song that had come from a heavenly boom box, was birthed on earth.

Two months later, Jim and I were visiting our son and his family. I felt compelled to ask him to play his guitar and sing it with me. I quickly taught it to him, and as we ended the song, I looked over at my daughter-in-law who was struggling with severe depression. I had a distinct impression that this had something to do with her. Soon after, Kim took her life. I realized that Jesus had given me this song to prepare me to face this darkest of night, to overcome the destruction of this fire, and to pass this test by running to Jesus, allowing Him to take me in His arms and hold me tenderly and tight, rather than running from the pain of reality and hiding within the dissociative recesses of my mind.

Yahweh is always good. His faithfulness reaches to the heavens. His compassion and mercy are new every morning. His unfailing love endures forever. Great is the Lord, and greatly will I praise Him! Amen.

Ashley Fugleberg

To the dear reader who finds themself here,

Not all readers will arrive here; for those who do, I believe The Most High has brought you to this place. What you have read (if any) of my poems are those written as a conversation between my Father and I. They are not overly ornate and are very much imperfect. However, they are from deep within the wells of my heart and reveal the musings that happen there. In this book, you can witness my attempt at understanding as I work it out through free verse (a style of poetry).

I read somewhere that Walt Witman is one who can possibly be credited with the creation of free verse; it is also speculated his influence to write in such a manner came from reading the book of Psalms. I can't say for certain whether these statements are true or not (I don't personally know Walt Witman), but I can say that if they are true - I can relate with Walt. Before I was ever exposed to traditional poetry in high school, the book of Psalms spoke to me in a deep way that influenced how I process information. While I love all forms of poetry, I most naturally write in free verse and this, I believe, is due to my early love of Psalms. Psalms, in my opinion, is a beautiful expression of art.

Art has always been the language of my being. It is typically the means by which I pray or am spoken to by my Father. It is almost always the means in which I process the more complex questions of life.

I would like to present you, dear reader, with a question: what is art?

When I refer to the word "art," I am speaking of it in my own personal interpretation: I think of art as something that extends out over any form of expression, understanding, and communication. Art then, in my perspective, includes not only the traditional definition of arts and writing, but also mathematics, the sciences, the culinary world, etc. All of these various mediums of understanding are used by the Most High to communicate to me and me back to Him. I find beauty in these various expressions and therefore choose "art" as their descriptor. All have been used to teach me and influence my perception of reality, of myself, and others; all, I believe, point directly back to the Living Word Made Flesh, the One who Created, Yahweh (YHVH).

If I had been asked as a child, are you a poet? Are you an athlete? I would have said no, what is poetry? No, I came in last during a running race with all the other kids in my kindergarten class. If I had been asked, can you cook? Are you a fighter? I would have said no, I can't read a cookbook and no, I'm not one of those girls who is strong enough to fight. If I was asked, Ashley, are you an artist? I would have said no, my sister is the artist; she draws.

I would not have said the book of Psalms was my favorite scripture. I would not have said I loved to watch athletes perform or a sprinter run at full speed -that I yearned to experience the rightness they communicated in those movements. I wouldn't have admitted that I attempted (and succeeded) in frying two eggs by myself at age of two and a half; I hadn't needed a cookbook. I would not have said the hand-to-hand fight scenes in movies seemed so beautifully balanced and I yearned to experience that balance. I wouldn't have said since birth, sunrises and sunsets moved me beyond what I could express and led me to wonder about the One who Created them. Was He as beautiful as they? I wouldn't have said I was an artist.

I should have.

I can tell you now, I am a poet. I write. I learned how to read and then use a cookbook (sometimes I still don't). I became an athlete and experienced the precision it takes; I can say that a volleyball team functioning in complete unison is what I hoped it would be: that it too, is poetry. I can say that poetry extends to a well-balanced kick and the leverage it takes, the geometry that occurs, is art. There is exquisite beauty in that balance. I can say to you now, yes, I'm an artist. And as others in this book have indicated, art can, and has attributed to so much healing. I can tell you that the Great Healer has used it to heal me - is using it to heal me.

People are described as either those who are right brained or those who are left brained with strengths that are left brained or strengths that are right brained. I don't think I quite believe that anymore. As I have grown closer to the Most High and have continued repenting (leaving behind) sinful (missing the mark/functioning outside of scripture's guidelines) actions and heart musings in my life, my understanding of identity, gifts/strengths, personhood and personality types has changed. I would like to pose my previous question to you again, dear reader, what is art? What is it you are drawn to? What makes you feel alive, or perhaps could possibly make you feel alive? You have been created so uniquely, so marvelously ornate, no one has ever before or ever again will be like you. No one will have the desires and capabilities you have. If there are expressions in this book that move you, perhaps consider venturing out. Attempt something you're curious about or love seeing. Ignore the voice that says "yes, but I'm not a _____" or "I could never_____." Perhaps you can. Perhaps you will. Perhaps you were created to. It will be messy. It will definitely not be perfect, but it just might be healing, and it will probably bring you closer to your Creator.

If Walt Witman was, in fact, influenced by the book of Psalms and chose to begin writing poetry in a completely new (or at least rare) way, what can we be inspired to do through our own relationship with the Most High? Perhaps, dear reader, it is time to start paying attention to what speaks to you and what you yearn to or maybe only wonder about doing. Perhaps it's time to heal.

Vicki Joy Anderson

My first brush with poetry was in 2nd grade. During a rainy day when outdoor recess was cancelled, my teacher, Miss Green, set up activity tables around the classroom. We were supposed to rotate to all the tables, but once I landed at that Haiku table, I was hooked, and spent the entire recess hour writing little ditties about leaves and laughter. Poetry didn't re-enter my headspace again until I was 11-years-old. During a Friday afternoon, pouring over a *Weekly Reader* magazine with my 6th grade class. I was deflated after raising my hand and being mocked by the class for an incorrect answer. I "tuned out" at that point and went deep into my own mind. In the margin of the *Weekly Reader*, in bold capital letters, I scratched out 7 letters, scrawled out in jagged, red ink that looked as though they had been carved into the page by daggers. **R-E-A-L-I-T-Y**. Those seven letters formed the first words of a 7-line *Acrostic*.

> **R**oses are not always "read"
> **E**ven beauty has thorns in its bed
> **A**lways look at every side
> **L**ook in deeper, see the pride
> **I**n your heart you'll find the key—
> **T**ry to change it, you will see,
> **Y**ou cannot change reality.

This became a defining moment in my life, because I realized that expressing my feelings of shame and rejection in words that were *beautiful,* rather than ugly, brought a wave of relief, hope, and healing. Having heard the phrase, *"But you're beautiful on the INSIDE"* a zillion times in my short life, I had come to understand that everyone perceived me as ugly. So, I must be. I was shocked in this moment to discover that there was beauty inside of me—a beauty that was only uncaged by the key of suffering. At this point, I embraced the sovereign purposes behind my sorrow AND a life-long love of writing poetry.

Poetry is among one of the few "escapes" from pain that is not only *not* self-destructive, but also healing. For the next 8 years of jr. high and high school, I absorbed the hurtful words, the bullying, the shame, and the rejection in silence. Only to rush home and grab the only weapon I knew—a pen. There I would pour out all the emotions, painfully aware that these moments of loneliness and heartache were the necessary seeds needed to nurture what would become a beautiful garden where I could walk alone, in safety, with my Savior. Poetry became a sanctuary—a place to hide my face—the one thing I wanted to hide from a world of prying, unsympathetic eyes.

But my poems were not always beautiful. Many of them were full of despair, self-pity, anger, shame, bitterness, fear, failure, and self-hatred. Little did I know at the time that God was using my trauma, shame, and rejection to mold me into a psalmist. After all, wasn't this what David was doing when he poured out all his shame upon his scrolls?

It wasn't until I was much older, however, that I realized the difference between a poet and a psalmist. A poet bleeds on the page and walks away; while a psalmist forces themselves, in the very pinnacle of their pain, to peer forward and meditate on the future grace of a sovereign God. With the exception of **Psalm 88** (not written by David), the psalms always ascend from the pits of despair and rise on the wings of faith to a day that has not yet come—the day of deliverance—thus cajoling the heart to turn its eyes away from its hurt, to gaze instead upon its ultimate Hope—Jesus Christ.

Andrea Fugleberg

I have come to understand that artwork is always a representative of a person's walk. It will always convey what is going on inside the mind, heart desires, and the spirit of an artist. Being mindful of that, I have learned to pay attention to my own emotions, desires, and motives while I work on a piece. I have found that my artwork can be read as a form of "journal entry," depicting my thought life on paper. I believe artwork can be used as a very personal and vulnerable conversation with God. I find that when you can't "word what you feel," drawing, painting, sketching, (as well as other artforms) are extremely effective as a way of conveying to Him what you have been through, believe, struggle with, or need.

Artwork can be particularly healing, especially when the primary focus while you work is given to intentionally choosing to depict only what you want to depict, while choosing to restrain what you do not want to convey. In so doing, it will help you produce healthy creations that bring glory to the Most High as well as to reinforce safe internal perspectives for yourself and others.

Because artwork is very visual and impactful to people emotionally, it can be, and often is, used as a programming tool or a medium for the enemy's kingdom. Done righteously, using the gift given by your Creator, it can also and especially be a powerful tool for the Kingdom of Yahweh. At this point in my faith walk, I take it very seriously when I sit down to produce a piece. I always cover my work from beginning to end in prayer. I recognize that because of the emotional and spiritual power of my illustrations, it's possible to reinforce a deception, even to my own heart and mind.

When I recognize that something I have produced comes from a dark place in my healing process, I now realize it is a starting point in allowing the Messiah into the depth of that emotion, trauma situation or perspective. It can also be a valuable conversation piece to have with myself about what's truly in my own heart and what I need to pray through or be healed from.

Currently in my healing and journey as an artist, I have been honored by Yahweh to have been able to produce and submit various pieces for His Kingdom's purposes as a form of ministry! Aside from the pieces I have contributed to this project, I have had the opportunity to also contribute pieces for Real Dark News, Canary Cry Newstalk, Now You See TV, and Rob Skiba's SEED Project. I am also being led to use the talents He gave me to illustrate a children's book for another author.

I love depicting people in my work, especially as a form of ministry. When I am working on a piece, I intentionally pray about depicting what it is the Father wants me to see. When I draw someone, I need eyes to see what a person is going through from His perspective. I can then allow my art to bring my own emotions to the surface- to grieve along with the subject as I draw their grief lines or to rejoice with a joyous child as I draw their carefree playtime.

Matthew Bailey

I started writing long before I truly found God. I would write stories and poems as an emotional release. Every time I felt I had nowhere to go, when I felt I didn't have a home, when I felt hopeless, I would write. Many times, I wrote about God, to remind myself who He is, who I am, that I do matter and that I am loved. Drawing and writing became very therapeutic. It helped me to focus and learn to express my emotions. After coming into relationship with God through His Word, my writings have become more focused on expressing the joy that Jesus has brought to my life.

Shawn Carter

Folks, my intention for sharing some of these prayers with you, is that you will know that you can talk with God and must not worry about using right words or sounding bad.

What is Prayer? Prayer is talking to God, speaking your thoughts, needs, and cares. It's having a private conversation with the mightiest King and knowing He hears you. You have the ear and attention of the King of Kings, and He is your close friend. Yet, we must remember He is the King. He is not our waitress or server. We serve Him. Yet we can be tender with Him, we can tell Him all our deep things and He will bring healing, power, and grace to us. Prayer, it's talking with God.

We all should be respectful in our talks with God, for sure. Yet, we should also know that we are to be ourselves. Sometimes we are in so much pain that we can only yell out, "I need you God." Don't wear a mask or try to impress God, but do cast yourself, as you are, into His presence.

Sometimes I write down my crude thoughts and just pour them out before the Lord. Sometimes I cry, Sometimes I yell, and sometimes I sit in silence in His presence. The truth is, it's all about talking with God. Be yourself and just talk with Him, even if it means being messy or angry to start with.

Vine and Branch
Collene James
John 15

357

The Lie Effect
Collene James
Rifle Falls- Rifle, CO
(Original cover photo for "The Lie Effect: Overcoming Soul Abduction, A Survivor's Handbook")

Homework Journal

The following section is an invitation to join Collene in some of the soul strengthening exercises she participated in, in order to dig into the internal emotional and spiritual wounds in your own heart and mind. Be blessed, dear reader!

Restoration Promised
Collene James

"So I will restore to you the years that the swarming locust has eaten…"
(Joel 2:25)

Internal Narratives

The following are the most often rotating mental narrations that I think about myself, others around me, and God:

God's Truth

God's Word validates or nullifies my internal narratives in these sections of scripture:

100 Blessings

1.

2.

3.

4.

5.

6.

7.

8.

9.

10.

11.

12.

13.

14.

15.

16.

17.

18.

19.

20.

21.

22.

23.

24.

25.

26.

27.

28.

29.

30.

31.

32.

33.   50.

34.   51.

35.   52.

36.   53.

37.   54.

38.   55.

39.   56.

40.   57.

41.   58.

42.   59.

43.   60.

44.   61.

45.   62.

46.   63.

47.   64.

48.   65.

49.   66.

67.

68.

69.

70.

71.

72.

73.

74.

75.

76.

77.

78.

79.

80.

81.

82.

83.

84.

85.

86.

87.

88.

89.

90.

91.

92.

93.

94.

95.

96.

97.

98.

99.

100.

Silence in Creation Observations

Day 1

Spend at least five minutes each day in solitude, reflecting on creation and journaling your thoughts. Then do something radical- something that reinforces the truth of what you're learning about yourself and about God.

Silence in Creation Observations
Day 2

Silence in Creation Observations
Day 3

Silence in Creation Observations
Day 4

Silence in Creation Observations
Day 5

Silence in Creation Observations
Day 6

Silence in Creation Observations
Day 7

For Memorization

Psalm 23

1 The Lord is my Shepherd;

I shall not want.

2 He makes me to lie down in green pastures;

He leads me beside the still waters.

3 He restores my soul;

He leads me in the paths of righteousness

For His Name's sake.

4 Yea, though I walk through the valley of the shadow of death,

I will fear no evil;

For You are with me;

Your rod and Your staff, they comfort me.

5 You prepare a table before me in the presence of my enemies;

You anoint my head with oil;

My cup runs over.

6 Surely goodness and mercy shall follow me

All the days of my life;

And I will dwell in the house of the Lord

Forever.

4 Love suffers long and is kind; love does not envy; love does not parade itself, is not puffed up;

5 Does not behave rudely, does not seek its own, is not provoked, thinks no evil;

6 Does not rejoice in iniquity, but rejoices in the truth;

7 Bears all things, believes all things, hopes all things, endures all things.

8 Love never fails. But whether there are prophecies, they will fail; whether there are tongues, they will cease; whether there is knowledge, it will vanish away.

Now re-read the verses; this time put the word "God" in the place of "Love"

Write the phrases and aspects of these verses that stick out to you and note how you feel and why:

Dear Yahweh,

The life I most want for myself is...

Art

The End
Collene James

Made in the USA
Coppell, TX
20 March 2023

14492398R00207